Chilton's MOTORCYCLE TROUBLESHOOTING GUIDE

Second Edition

Joseph Pellicciotti, Senior Editor, Motorcycles

CHILTON BOOK COMPANY   Radnor, Pennsylvania

Member

MtC

Motorcycle
Industry
Council

Copyright © 1977, 1973 by Chilton Book Company
Second Edition
All Rights Reserved
Published in Radnor, Pa., by Chilton Book Company
and simultaneously in Ontario, Canada,
by Thomas Nelson & Sons, Ltd.

Manufactured in the United States of America

123456789   6543210987

Library of Congress Cataloging in Publication Data
Chilton Book Company. Automotive Editorial Dept.
   Chilton's motorcycle troubleshooting guide, 2nd edition

   1. Motorcycles—Maintenance and repair.
I. Title.   II. Title. Motorcycle troubleshooting guide,
2nd edition.
TL440.C457   629.28'7'75   77-121
ISBN 0-8019-6586-1
ISBN 0-8019-6587-X pbk.

Contents

Chapter 1   Introduction **1**

Necessary Tools, 1
Approach To Troubleshooting, 5
Engine Operation, 8
Piston Port Two-Stroke Engines, 8

Rotary Valve Two-Stroke Engines, 10
Pushrod Four-Stroke Engines, 11
Overhead Camshaft Four-Stroke Engines, 11

Chapter 2   Tune-Up **15**

Spark Plugs, 16
Compression Test, 18
Ignition Timing, 18

Tune-Up Analysis, 23
Valve Adjustments, 24
Carburetors, 26

Chapter 3   Two-Stroke Troubleshooting **31**

Starting the Engine, 31
Engine Does Not Start, 32
Poor Engine Performance, 35
Hard Starting or Erratic Performance, 35
Engine Dies When Throttle Is Opened, 36
Low-Speed Misfiring, 36
Throttle Opening Related Misfire, 36
Inconsistent Misfire On Acceleration, 37
Engine Misfires Under Load, 37
High Speed Misfiring, 37

Poor Low-Speed Performance, 38
Poor Mid-Range or High-Speed Performance, 38
Poor General Performance, 38
Engine Overheating and Seizure, 38
Engine Vibration, 39
Engine Noises, 39
Oil Injection Systems, 40
Decarbonization, 45
Engine Troubleshooting Charts, 47

Chapter 4   Four-Stroke Troubleshooting **51**

Starting the Engine, 51
Engine Does Not Start, 52
Poor Engine Performance, 60
Hard Starting or Erratic Performance, 60
Engine Dies When Throttle Is Opened, 62
Engine Misfires, 63
Poor General Performance, 64

Engine Vibration, 65
Excessive Oil Consumption, 65
Engine Overheating and Seizure, 66
Engine Noises, 68
Lubrication, 70
Engine Troubleshooting Charts, 72

Chapter 5   The Fuel System **78**

Operational Description, 78
Construction, 80
Operation, 85
Direct-Control Carburetor, 85
Accelerator Pumps, 87
Constant-Velocity Carburetors, 88
Throttle-Plate Carburetors, 88
Carburetor Troubleshooting, 92
Indications of a Rich Mixture, 92
Indications of a Lean Mixture, 92

Air Filters, 93
Fuel Filters and Fuel Feed, 94
Fuel Petcocks, 96
Carburetor Controls, 97
Carburetor Cleaning, 99
Carburetor Flooding, 100
Air Leaks, 101
Carburetor Rebuilding, 101
Effect of Altitude on Carburetion, 102
Carburetor Troubleshooting Charts, 102

Chapter 6   Electrical Systems 104

Operational Descriptions, 106
Magneto Generator, 106
DC Generator, 106
Starter Generator, 106
Alternator, 107
Capacitor Discharge Ignition, 110
Constant Loss Ignition, 112
Battery Ignition, 112
Troubleshooting the Charging System, 113
BSA, 113
Harley-Davidson, 114
Honda, 115
Kawasaki, 117

Suzuki, 118
Triumph, 119
Yamaha, 119
Troubleshooting the Ignition System, 120
Battery and Coil Ignition Models, 120
Troubleshooting the Starting System, 121
Component Testing, 122
Japanese Machines, 122
British Machines, 122
H1 and A Series Kawasakis, 124
H2 Series Kawasakis, 126
Battery, 126
Electrical Troubleshooting Charts, 129

Chapter 7   Clutch and Transmission Troubleshooting 131

Automatic Centrifugal Clutch, 131
Manual Clutch, 132
Constant Mesh Transmissions, 133
Kickstarters, 138
Troubleshooting the Clutch, 140
Rough Lever Action, 140
Clutch Drags, 141
Clutch Slips, 143
Clutch Chatters, 145
Troubleshooting the Gearbox, 146

Gears Grind When Shifting, 148
Shifter Pops Out of Gear, 150
Shifter Does Not Return, 151
Kickstarter Jams, 152
Kickstarter Slips, 153
Final Drive, 154
Lubrication, 154
Adjustment and Inspection, 155
Clutch and Transmission Troubleshooting
    Charts, 157

Chapter 8   Chassis Troubleshooting 161

Tires, 161
Tire Pressures, 161
Tire Inspection, 161
Tire Changing, 163
Wheels, 166
Spokes, 166
Wheel Balancing, 166
Rim Run-Out, 168
Wheel Bearings, 169
Brakes, 171
Drum Brakes, 171
Hydraulic Disc Brakes, 177

Front Forks, 182
Operational Description, 182
Routine Maintenance, 183
Oil Changes, 186
Seal Replacement, 186
Component Inspection, 187
Steering Stem, 190
Steering Damper, 192
Swing Arm, 193
Rear Shock Absorbers, 195
Chassis Troubleshooting Charts, 198

Appendix 204

Conversion—Millimeters to Decimal Inches,
    204
Conversion Table, 205
Tap Drill Sizes, 206
Conversion—Common Fractions (Inches) to
    Decimals and Millimeters, 206

Number and Letter Drill Sizes, 207
Spark Plug Comparison Chart, 208
Comparison of Wrench Sizes, 210
Common Abbreviations, 210
Degree Wheel, 211

1 · Introduction

This book is intended as a general guide towards the understanding of the various systems which comprise the modern motorcycle, and as an aid in locating and rectifying problems which may occur in these systems from time to time.

While developing our theme of "troubleshooting," we have also endeavored to include information on preventive maintenance techniques, careful attention to which may forstall, to a great degree, the majority of mechanical malfunctions.

While troubleshooting techniques do not constitute an exact science by any means, there are certain steps which should be taken first depending on the nature of the problem. For example, if your motorcycle stalls out a mile after you've left the spray carwash, logic would indicate that water has gotten into the works and is the cause of the problem. You would then check the carburetor float bowl(s). If no water is present there, suspect that the water has caused a poor electrical connection.

This example only illustrates that a successful approach to troubleshooting must be based in some measure on your awareness as a rider, and it should proceed in a logical fashion once you have narrowed down the field of possible causes. Merely rushing in without prior planning or analysis is foolhardy, and may cause more problems than it solves. And of course, as the owner and rider of an individual motorcycle, you yourself are in a good position to locate trouble quickly and accurately. Motor-

cycles may not be intelligent beings, but they may certainly have "personalities" of their own, insofar as one machine may have a quirk that others of its kind are free from. So a thorough knowledge of the motorcycle in question is certainly an asset. Additionally, a degree of mechanical common sense knowledge is helpful. For example, if your single-carb "twin" starts firing on one cylinder, you can pretty much eliminate the fuel system as the cause of your trouble. Of, if the entire electrical system suddenly goes dead, you should realize that an electrical connection or fuse has been broken, and that the trouble is probably not in the battery itself. They seldom just die without prior warning of some sort.

So "troubleshooting" is not just an automatic series of steps which will inevitably lead you to the source of a problem, but a process which must begin with a few common sense directions on your part.

Necessary Tools

Your tool requirements will largely depend on the type of work you are willing or able to do yourself, and, of course, on the kind of machine you ride. The toolkits which come with motorcycles vary in quality from "fair" to very good. In general, however, most consist of only a few open-end wrenches and a number of special sockets for such things as axle nuts and spark plugs, and screwdriver bits. Unfortunately, these tools are not always of the highest possible quality.

Most riders will profit from a basic set of high-quality hand tools. Your tools will be metric or SAE, depending on what you ride. For those who intend to do more than the most basic work, the following are recommended:

a. A set of open-end wrenches;

b. A set of twelve-point sockets with ⅜ in. drive ratchet. Get a set which includes a couple of extensions;

c. A selection of Phillips and slot-head screwdrivers;

d. A set of allen keys, if your motorcycle is fitted with this kind of hardware;

e. An impact driver with Phillips and slot-head bits. This tool is almost a necessity when attempting to remove any of the numerous phillips head screws found on most motorcycle engines. These screws are put on very tightly to begin with, and may sometimes seize in the alloy engine cases. Most attempts to remove them without an impact driver will strip the screw heads. The driver should also be used for installing such screws for obvious safety reasons.

f. A pair of good tire irons. To remove or install tires, always use tire irons designed for motorcycle tires. Two irons are usually sufficient. Never use screwdrivers, crowbars, or anything which may pinch the tube or rip the tire carcass. When the proper tire lubricant is used, almost any tire can be removed or fitted with the smallish tire irons sold in any motorcycle shop.

g. A tire pressure gauge. Many different types are available at relatively inexpensive prices. Since the meters in filling stations are not particularly accurate, a tire gauge is a worthwhile investment, in lieu of the safety factors involved.

These tools may be considered as basic necessities. As you progress in your knowledge of the motorcycle, you may be willing to take on increasingly difficult tasks which may require more specialized equipment. As one basic example, note that we have recommended twelve-point sockets for a start. Really heavy-duty sockets of the six-point type are available. These fit directly over the hex bolt or nut giving greater purchase, which is important on slightly rounded nuts or bolts, but will not slip over the fastener as readily as the twelve-point type which may be a disad-

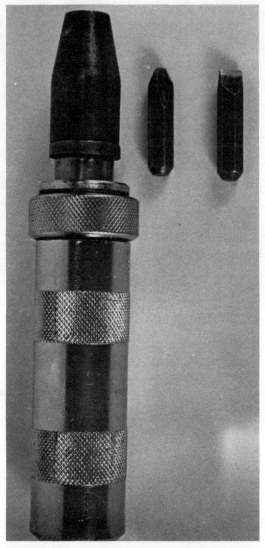

Impact driver with phillips and slot-head bits

vantage when working in tight places. In addition, they are usually a bit more expensive.

A ⅜ in. drive ratchet will be suitable for most work which you will encounter. For heavy-duty jobs, a sturdier ½ in. drive ratchet is better. Of course, you will still be able to use the ⅜ in. sockets provided that you purchase an adapter.

Large adjustable wrenches are useful for items like axle nuts or situations in which the nut or bolt size is larger and a lot of torque is required. However, adjustable wrenches should not be used in place of precision-sized sockets or open-end wrenches, since they can easily round off a nut or bolt head if not used correctly.

When using an adjustable wrench, always position it on the nut or bolt so that the force

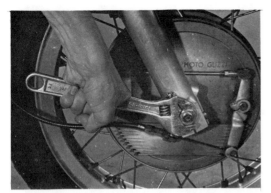

Incorrect use of an adjustable wrench (loosening nut)

Correct use (loosening nut): stress applied to fixed jaw

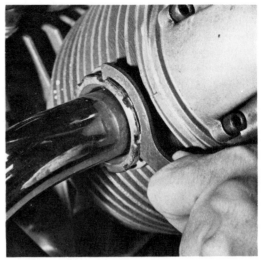

A pin wrench is a necessity when loosening or securing exhaust pipe nuts such as this

will bear against the fixed jaw of the wrench.

You may find that your machine requires one or more "special tools" which will make a job much easier. For example, a very long, thin screwdriver is used to remove the condenser securing screw on late-model Moto Guzzis. Or, a thin-walled socket must be used to get at two of the cylinder head bolts on older Nortons. You will probably learn these tricks and others like them as you do more work on your own machine.

Insofar as factory special tools are concerned, your needs will depend, again, upon the kind of motorcycle you own, and the type of work you intend to do.

A *magneto flywheel puller* is a basic item which any owner of a motorcycle equipped with a flywheel magneto should consider. Removal of the flywheel is usually required to replace the contact breaker points, and sometimes to adjust the ignition timing, both procedures being within the capabilities of the majority of owners. So a device to remove the flywheel, which is usually press-fit onto a tapered portion of the crankshaft, is handy to have.

The motorcycle manufacturers supply these

pullers for their own motorcycles, so this tool will be available at your dealers'.

On some motorcycles, the exhaust pipes are secured at the engine by circular nuts which thread into the cylinder or cylinder head. These nuts are often finned, sometimes not, but always require a *pin wrench* for removal or tightening. A pin wrench which will fit these fasteners is a wise investment.

Another helpful tool, which is becoming increasingly more necessary, is a *"chain breaker"* for use on machines with pressed-on

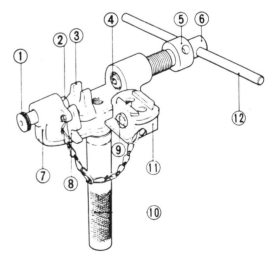

Chain breaker

1. Pin seat knob	7. Body
2. Pin seat	8. Pin seat backing plate
3. Holder	9. Wedge
4. Cotter pin	10. Grip
5. Main bolt	11. Guide
6. Link removal bolt	12. Lever

masterlinks on the final drive chain. The masterlink, with its spring-clipped side plate, is the weakest point of the chain, and to remedy the problem of broken chains on the larger motorcycles, more manufacturers are fitting "endless" chains which require a chain breaker to remove and to install the masterlink.

Other tools, which might be worth the initial investment depending upon how often you use them, include a *plastic mallet*. There are numerous uses for this tool, for example, breaking loose a clutch cover, oil pan, or other alloy casting which stays put even after its screws have been removed. A steel hammer will certainly damage parts like this, and prying it off may damage the gasket mating surface.

A *torque wrench* is a necessity for installing cylinder heads and any other large parts which are secured by a number of bolts. Proper tightening of the fasteners is required due to the stresses involved, and an *even* tightening is required to prevent warpage or distortion and ensure a good seal. Proper torquing of axle nuts and suspension parts is a safety item. On two-strokes, which will require relatively frequent removal of the cylinder head(s) for routine decarbonization, a torque wrench is an essential tool. Distortion of the head due to improperly tightened bolts is a very real danger, and proper installation becomes even more imperative on multi-cylinder motorcycles in which the head is a single casting.

FEELER GAUGES

Feeler gauges are needed for jobs like adjusting valves, setting breaker point gaps, gapping spark plugs and so on.

Blade-type feeler gauges are suitable for valves and points, but spark plugs should be gapped with wire-type gauges, most of which also come with a small lever for bending the side electrode.

Most feeler gauges are stamped with their thickness in both English and metric measure. One type, which is known as a "go-no-go" gauge is very easy to use since each blade has two thicknesses. It is therefore obvious whether the gap being set is within tolerance.

No matter what gap you are setting with a feeler gauge, the proper method is to adjust it so that a blade of the proper size is a light drag when pulled through.

It is important that feeler gauges be properly cared for and kept out of the weather as much as possible. Long exposure will cause

Combination feeler gauge for spark plugs and points

Go-no-go feeler gauge

corrosion to build up on the blade, which will affect the thickness. It may be impossible to remove this corrosion without abrasive methods, which is, of course, not practical since this will also affect blade thickness.

If your tools sits out in a garage, it may be profitable to spray your feeler gauge with a demoisturizing agent from time to time in order to protect the blades. Naturally, make sure you clean off any blade thoroughly before using it.

TEST EQUIPMENT

Continuity lights and *test lights* are very handy to have for any number of tasks. In addition to tracing electrical troubles such as shorts and open circuits, either can be used for static (engine off) ignition timing, for battery-ignition motorcycles.

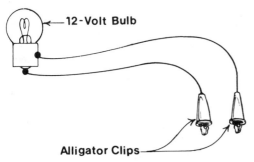

A simple test light. The bulb should be the same voltage as the motorcycle's electrical system (6 or 12V)

A test light need be nothing more than a small bulb of the same voltage as your motorcycle's electrical system (6 or 12V) with two leads attached. Alligator clips are necessary if you intend to time the bike with this light, since your hands will be otherwise occupied during this procedure.

A continuity light can be rigged in a number of ways. Basically, it is a bulb wired in series with a battery. You can use a flashlight battery and bulb providing the bulb is matched to the battery voltage.

With the simpler test light, ignition can be checked on battery-ignition motorcycles by connecting one light lead to ground on the engine case, and the other to the breaker point primary terminal or spring. The motorcycle's ignition must be *on*. When the points open, the bulb will go *on*.

A continuity light used for ignition timing is connected in the same manner as the test light. The difference is that the bike's ignition must be turned *off* when setting the timing. When the points open, the continuity light bulb will go *off*.

On many motorcycles, it is preferable to set the ignition timing *dynamically*, that is, with the engine running. For this job, a strobo-scopic timing light is necessary, and suitable strobes through a wide range of prices can be obtained almost anywhere.

Neither of these methods may work on a large number of magneto-ignition motorcycles, however, due to the characteristics of magneto construction. For many of these machines, the moment of point opening must be checked with an *ohmmeter*. Yamaha dealers sell a sensitive ohmmeter called a "Points Checker" for this very purpose.

In addition, a dial indicator may be needed for your bike. When setting the ignition timing it is necessary to know just where the picton is at the time the points open. On many battery-ignition machines, this is indicated by top dead center and firing marks on the alternator rotor. On some magneto-ignition bikes, however, this is not the case, and a dial gauge is needed.

MISCELLANEOUS

There are a few other items which will make life a little easier when you are working on the bike. A *points file* is used to remove burned marks or flash-over from points surfaces and can also be used to square off spark plug electrodes.

A *wire brush* is useful for cleaning plugs, removing corrosion from bolt threads, etc.

You should also have a selection of emery cloth, sandpaper, and the like, as well as penetrating oil, parts-easing fluid, spray solvents, and thread-locking compound (non-permanent).

Of course, we cannot possibly list *all* of the tools you will ever need, but you may eventually run into the need for most of the ones mentioned above.

Approach to Troubleshooting

Let us examine one logical approach to troubleshooting just as an example. Of course, some of the following may not be applicable to your motorcycle, and this is where your own awareness as a rider comes into play. It may serve, however, to illustrate the kind of steps you might go through.

Say, for instance, that the motorcycle simply will not start one morning. Is this the first time this has happened, or has the bike become increasingly hard to start over a period

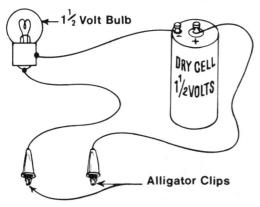

A test light with a self-contained power source

of days or weeks? If the latter, perhaps some mechanical part which must be changed or adjusted periodically is the cause. When was the last time the bike was tuned up? Are the spark plugs old? Have the points been in operation for many miles? Do the valves (four-stroke) need adjustment, or has decarbonization (two-stroke) been carried out at the manufacturer's recommended intervals? These are some common items which may make themselves known through gradual deterioration in performance.

If the machine's failure to start comes on suddenly, however, most of these items can be eliminated as the source of the trouble. In this case, other facets of the motorcycle's system should be examined.

Do the lights work? If not, you can bet that the problem is electrical, and you can begin your investigation in that area.

If you have electrical power of some sort, the first thing to check (since it is the easiest) is the fuel supply. Is there gas in the tank? If so, is there enough to get to the carburetors? Sometimes, even a low supply can make starting difficult. The fuel filters which are fitted to the fuel petcock pipes inside the gas tank on many models tend to clog up starting at the bottom. As the fuel supply drops, it may reach a level at which the gas filter is totally clogged.

Check for fuel at the carburetor(s) by removing the float bowl or float bowl drain plug. Check the gasoline here for water or foreign matter. If the float bowl is not full of gasoline,

Checking for fuel at the float bowl

or has water in the gas, the problem has been isolated. There are a number of things which would cause the fuel flow to be cut off, and they are examined in detail in later parts of this book.

The next thing to check is the ignition system. Is spark occurring at the plugs? Remove a spark plug, connect it to its cap, and ground the body (hex or threads) of the plug against the cylinder head and kick the engine over briskly. You should be able to see the plug

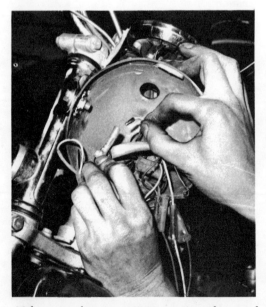

Make sure the snap connectors are clean and tight

Checking for spark at the plug

Checking for spark at the plug lead

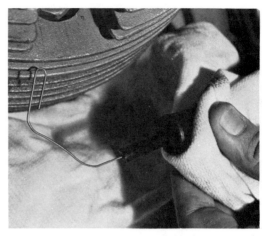

Checking for spark without the plug cap

sparking. If it does not, inspect it more closely. If the plug electrodes are wet or oily, it is possible that you flooded the engine when trying to start it. It is relatively easy to do this, especially if you are using a plug of a "cold" heat range. Are the electrodes blocked or fouled with foreign matter, carbon deposits, or oil? Any of these conditions would cause a lack of spark. Is the plug old or are the electrodes worn or rounded? This type of trouble will come on gradually.

Even if there is spark at the plug, this could be the cause of the problem. More voltage is required to fire a plug in the high-pressure conditions of the combustion chamber than at atmospheric pressure. If the plug is worn out it may show a fairly good spark during the test but still be unable to fire when installed. This is easily solved with a tune-up.

The spark showing at the plug should be fat and blue ideally. A weak, thin, or yellow spark can be caused by a number of things among them an ignition coil which is going bad, worn points, a defective condenser, and so on.

If *no* spark is visible, remove the plug from the cap, and insert a metal object such as a nail or the end of a thin phillips screwdriver into the cap and hold the cap so that the metal object is about ⅛ in. away from the cylinder head. Kick the engine over. If you see a spark jumping from the metal to the head, you can be sure that the trouble was with the spark plug. If not, you will have to work your way back towards the other components in the ignition system.

Remove the spark plug cap. Repeat the test holding the end of the plug lead about ⅛ in. from the head. If spark is now evident, the trouble was in the plug cap. This is not too common, but it can happen with the resistor-type plug caps fitted as standard equipment to the large majority of motorcycle these days. The cap incorporates a resistor of a value of about 5000 ohms to reduce radio interference. Heat and vibration can cause the resistor to break the circuit completely, or to gradually increase in value until the coil cannot overcome it. This will cause spark failure.

If you haven't yet found the cause, next check the breaker points, condenser, and coil. Is current getting to the points? It is easy to tell on battery-ignition machines if you have a test light or continuity tester. Is current from the points getting to the coil? Check electrical connections between the two. On some motorcycles a large number of bayonet connectors are used, and are often shrouded with a plastic cover to keep out dirt and moisture. This is a good idea, but it is quite possible for water to build up inside the shroud and not be able to get out. This may cause a bad connection.

Assuming that you have spark at the plugs, the next thing to check is the compression. Sudden losses of compression are very uncommon, as the more usual reasons for this sort of thing are related to long-range wear of moving parts. If, however, your highly-tuned four-stroke was caught in a mammoth traffic jam the previous day, you could have burned your valves, thereby causing compression leaks.

This, of course, is only a sample of the troubleshooting procedure in its most basic form and is not applicable to all situations. For example, lack of spark with a standard battery-coil ignition system would lead to different areas of investigation than the same problem with a CDI or magneto system. And certainly, as we pointed out, a *sudden* refusal to start

Running a compression check

would be due to somewhat different things than a gradual hard starting problem. It is up to you, the rider, to make the initial determination of possible trouble spots and proceed accordingly.

You should suspect, to give another example, that if a malfunction occurs immediately after you've done some work on the bike, that the trouble is more than likely coming from that area. This can happen even if you are a competent mechanic. For instance, if you have no spark just after a routine checking of the breaker point gap a dirty feeler gauge blade may have contaminated the contact surfaces of the points. Or, removal or installation of the gas tank might have pulled one or more electrical connectors apart. These seem to be common sense items, but you should be conscious of every possibility.

All of this can be considered troubleshooting the engine to get it running, not troubleshooting to cure running faults. Once you have found the general location of the trouble it is usually quite simple to make pinpoint checks or temporarily substitute new or improvised parts to determine exactly where the problem lies. The most important thing to remember is to try to remain rational and approach the troubleshooting procedures logically. If you do this, chances are that you'll find the source of unpleasantness and save yourself time, money and aggravation.

Troubleshooting an engine that is running poorly is often a bit trickier than trying to determine why an engine won't start. You will still be involved with the compression, fuel system, and electrical system of your engine but the problems will be more subtle and harder to detect.

It pays here, if you are making adjustments or are fine tuning, to make one adjustment at a time, thoroughly check the results, and record the findings. Otherwise you will confuse yourself, ruin the results of one adjustment with another, and accomplish nothing.

When trying to diagnose a running fault, remember to check all the parts related to the component you are examining. For example, if you are carefully inspecting a carburetor, don't forget to check the intake tube clamps, the air filter, and the fuel filter to make sure that the carburetor is not being sabotaged in one way or another by those components (too much air, or too little air and fuel). If you are checking for sufficient spark, don't forget to make sure that the plug connector is tightly attached to the wire and that the insulation is not worn or cracked, etc. Look for the little things, and do it systematically and thoroughly.

Engine Operation

PISTON PORT TWO-STROKE ENGINES

Before you try to determine what's wrong with your engine you should know how it works when everything is right. The simplest type is the piston port two-stroke single which only has three main moving parts. The ports are located in the cylinder wall and are opened and closed by the piston's movement. Their functions are:

Intake port—admits fresh fuel mixture from the carburetor into the crankcase.

Transfer ports—provide passages for the mixture between the crankcase and combustion chamber. These are also known as scavenging ports.

Exhaust port—releases burned gases from the combustion chamber into the exhaust pipe.

Basically, this is what happens during a 360° rotation of the crankshaft, beginning with the piston at top dead center (TDC):

Downstroke—the piston descends from the previous cycle and exposes the exhaust port, letting out the expanding burned gases. Simultaneously, the piston's downward movement compresses the fuel mixture from the previous cycle in the airtight crankcase.

As the piston continues to descend, it also exposes the transfer ports. The compressed mixture waiting in the crankcase now rushes through the ports and fills the combustion chamber, while at the same time sweeping any remaining burned gases out the exhaust port.

Upstroke—after reaching its lowest point of travel, the piston begins to ascend and closes off the transfer ports. At the same time, the piston's upward movement creates a partial vacuum in the crankcase.

As the piston continues to ascend, it closes off the exhaust port and begins to compress the mixture in the combustion chamber. Meanwhile, the bottom of the piston exposes the intake port and a fresh fuel mixture is sucked into the crankcase. When the piston approaches top dead center, ignition occurs and the piston once again descends to begin another cycle.

As described, ignition occurs once every 360° or, more appropriately, once every two strokes of the piston (one down and one up). Hence, the term two-stroke engine.

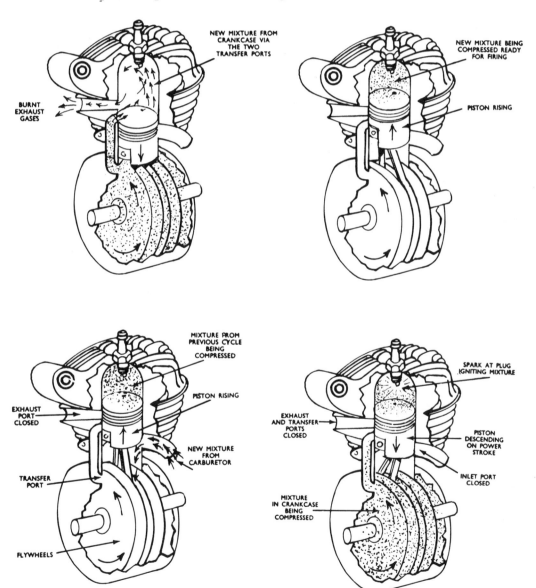

Two-cycle engine operation

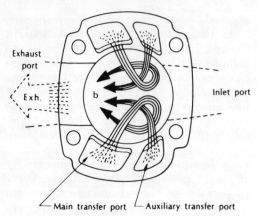

Five-port cylinder exhaust sweep

A recent improvement in piston port design is the five-port cylinder, and the main difference between it and the conventional type lies in the five-port cylinder's more efficient exhaust sweep.

The earlier Schnuerle loop scavenging system has two transfer ports that aim streams of fresh mixture toward the back of the cylinder; this sweeps out most of the remaining exhaust gases, but leaves one area untouched in the middle of the combustion chamber. The five-port system, on the other hand, has two additional auxiliary transfer ports. These extra ports direct a small charge of fresh mixture right at the dead spot and force it out the exhaust port. This complete exhaust sweep creates more space for the incoming mixture, and, as a result, the engine has more low and mid-range power, runs cooler, and consumes less fuel.

The newest development in two-stroke engineering is the seven-port cylinder used in conjunction with a reed valve. The valve consists of a die-cast aluminum block with flexible stainless steel reeds that open and close the intake port. The reeds are actuated by crankcase vacuum and, therefore, admit only the necessary amount

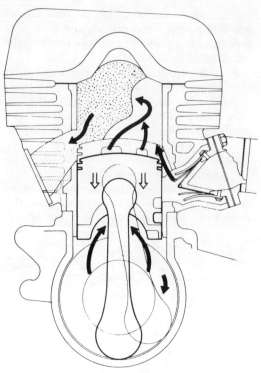

Seven-port cylinder exhaust sweep

of fuel. When combined with the improved scavenging ability of the seven-port cylinder, the valve helps reduce fuel consumption, increase low-end pulling power, and flatten out the horsepower and torque curves.

ROTARY-VALVE TWO-STROKE ENGINES

The rotary-valve two-stroke operates on the same basic principles as the piston-

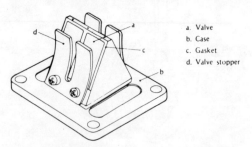

a. Valve
b. Case
c. Gasket
d. Valve stopper

Reed valve components

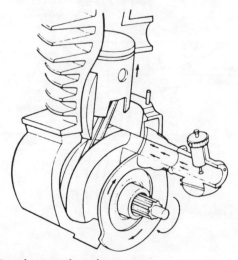

Typical rotary valve induction

port type, but is constructed differently and offers some distinct advantages.

The valve itself is a resin hardened fiber disc with a cutaway section along its circumference. The disc is mounted directly to the end of the crankshaft and is enclosed within a narrow sealed chamber located between the crankcase and the carburetor. As the valve rotates, the cutaway section exposes the port and allows the fresh fuel mixture to be sucked into the crankcase. Then, when the cutaway section ends, the port is sealed by the disc and no more mixture can enter.

What is the advantage? In the piston port system the intake port is located in the cylinder wall along with the transfer and exhaust ports. Therefore, intake timing (when the port opens and closes) is dictated by the piston skirt and limited by the size and position of the other ports. In the rotary-valve type, on the other hand, the intake port is located in the side of the crankcase, and intake timing is determined by the position (on the disc) and duration of the valve cutaway.

This independence from piston control and cylinder design complications allows intake timing to be set, and easily adjusted, for optimum engine breathing. As a result, the engine has greater flexibility and delivers more power throughout a wider range.

PUSHROD FOUR-STROKE ENGINES

The four-stroke engine requires four complete strokes of the piston to complete one power cycle. During the intake stroke the intake valve opens and the fuel mixture is drawn into the cylinder as a result of the sudden vacuum created in the combustion chamber. As the piston moves toward the top of its travel on the compression stroke, both valves are closed and the fuel/air mixture is compressed. When the breaker points are opened by the action of the breaker cam, the spark plug fires and ignites the charge. The resulting combustion forces the piston down in the power stroke. As the piston moves down toward its lowest point of travel, the exhaust valve opens, and as the action of the flywheel sends the piston back up on the exhaust stroke, the remains of the previous charge are forced out past the exhaust valve. Just before the piston reaches the top of its

travel, the intake valve opens and the exhaust flow induces the intake flow which continues while the exhaust valve closes. The process then repeats itself since each of the four cycles has been completed.

The basic valve train of four-stroke engines consists of camshaft driven pushrods which actuate rocker arms, which in turn operate the valves. Usually, the camshaft is gear driven directly by the crankshaft through gears which reduce the rate of rotation to $\frac{1}{2}$ the engine speed. Cams can also be chaindriven off the crank.

OVERHEAD CAMSHAFT FOUR-STROKE ENGINES

Overhead cam engines are those which have the cam mounted above the valves, and is the type favored by Japanese and Italian manufacturers.

The cam or cams ride in the cylinder head supported by plain bearings, usually with inserts, but sometimes as in the case of some

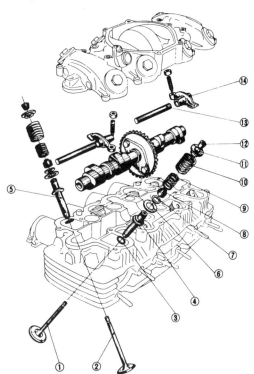

An overhead cam design (shown is a Honda 500)

1. Exhaust valve	8. Valve seal
2. Intake valve	9. Inner valve spring
3. O-ring	10. Outer valve spring
4. Exhaust valve guide	11. Retainer
5. Intake valve guide	12. Split collar
6. Valve spring seat (outer)	13. Rocker arm shaft
7. Valve spring seat (inner)	14. Rocker arm

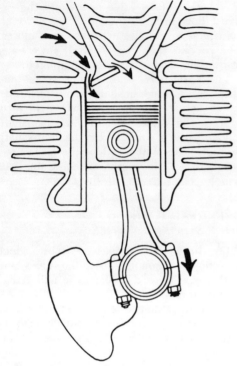

Intake stroke

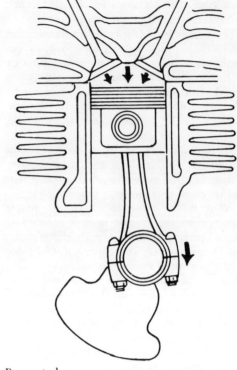

Power stroke

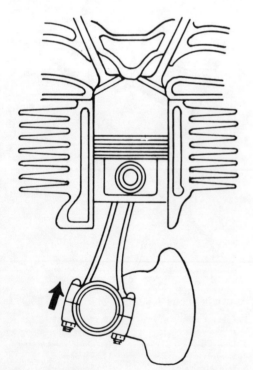

Compression stroke

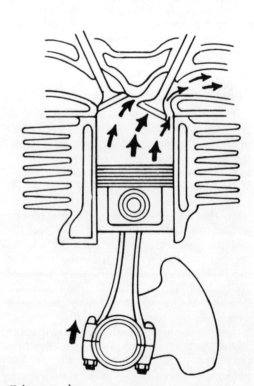

Exhaust stroke

Four-cycle engine operation

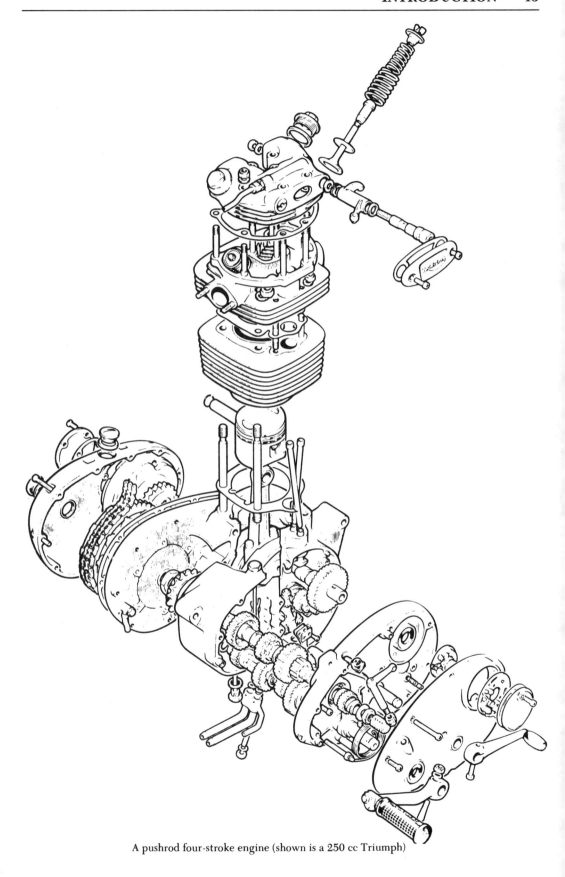

A pushrod four-stroke engine (shown is a 250 cc Triumph)

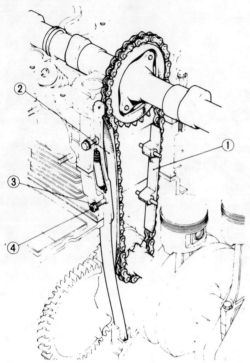

Cam chain tensioner design (shown is a Honda 500)

1. Cam chain guide
2. Cam chain tensioner
3. Lock nut
4. Adjusting screw

Hondas, directly on the alloy head casting itself, or on ball or roller bearings.

The cam(s) may be driven by chain which necessitates the fitting of a chain tensioner somewhere. Both single and duplex chains are used. Other types of cam drives include spur gears (MV Agusta), shaft and bevel gear (Ducati), and reciprocating rods (NSU).

Chain-driven overhead cams predominate since this method is cheaper, quieter, and more compact than other methods, but, as noted, a tensioner is necessary to compensate for stretching of the chain. Tensioners are sometimes fully automatic, relying on oil pressure to function, but more often they are simply mechanical devices which must be set by hand. Usually the tensioner will have a spring-loaded arm which, when released, will push against the chain, and a bolt is then tightened to secure it in this position.

Single overhead cam engines use rocker arms to actuate the valves, while more sophisticated dual overhead cam engines may have the cams located directly above the valve stems, obviating the need for any intermediate device. The chief drawback of this letter method is the difficulty of valve adjustment, which must be done with precisely measured shims, but the advantage is in the higher rpm obtainable, and the longer interval between valve adjustments.

The advantage of an overhead cam design is that the reduced weight of the valve train allows the engine to turn higher rpm. In addition to this, overhead cam engines have much less valve floating problems than pushrod engines where the engine can begin to turn faster than the valves can operate. The only disadvantage of an overhead cam design is that it necessitates a tall engine which raises the center of balance and makes designing a handling frame more difficult.

2 · Tune-Up

In many cases, poor running or hard starting are due to the fact that routine adjustments which should be checked periodically have not been carried out.

A complete tune-up, the procedures for which are described in general terms in the following pages, should in many cases return the troublesome motorcycle to its original operating state, assuming, naturally, that mechanical wear has been kept within reasonable limits.

If a competent tune-up is performed, and the machine still fails to run correctly, then you can begin to check more serious items.

Of course, it should be realized that a tune-up will have little affect on the performance of the machine if there is a defect in some system not related to those with which you will be dealing. A dirty air cleaner, for example, will still prevent enough air from reaching the carburetor regardless how much you fiddle with the carburetor screws.

Tune-up related items, though, are very common sources of trouble. · Replacement items such as spark plugs and breaker points are subject to harsh conditions. Points will become worn just in normal use due to the job they perform. They must make and break electrical connections for spark to occur. They also have a fiber heel which is constantly in contact with the breaker cam, and this will wear.

The points will become unserviceable even faster if they are not properly adjusted, or if the condenser is bad.

Spark plugs can last 15000 miles in some motorcycles under some conditions. They can also become fouled after only 1500 miles in other bikes under other conditions. The number of factors which affect spark plug life are legion. If the fuel/air mixture is too lean or too rich, the plugs may burn or foul. Two-stroke oil pump adjustments will naturally come into play here. If the plug is too hot or too cold for the type of riding you do, this will also have an adverse affect not only on performance, but also on the life span of the plugs.

If you have a two-stroke, even the brand of injection oil you use will have a bearing on the matter.

All these items should be kept in mind when attempting a tune-up. Manufacturers give recommended change intervals for things like points and plugs, but these are really only estimates based on their experience with machines used under "normal" conditions. "Normal" for you, certainly, may be another matter.

What constitutes a "tune-up" will vary according to what you ride. In general, some or all of the following items should be considered:

    a. A compression test;

    b. Spark plug inspection, cleaning, gapping, or replacement;

    c. Breaker point inspection and gapping (if applicable);

    d. Ignition timing;

    e. Cam chain adjustment (if applicable);

    f. Valve adjustment for four-strokes if

called for (Ducati Desmos and Kawasaki 900/1000 and similar valve trains are special cases);

g. Carburetor synchronization, idle speed and mixture adjustments;

h. Carburetor cable adjustments and oil pump adjustments for injected two-strokes;

i. A road test to determine whether settings are correct or should be rechecked.

Some of these procedures are not necessary on certain models. Obviously, you do not have to worry about breaker points on CDI-equipped machines. On most magneto-ignition bikes, changing the point gap is the way ignition timing changes are made, so this will be one procedure, rather than two separate operations.

In other cases, the operation may require special equipment which you do not have, or be extremely complex. Setting valve clearances on a Triumph is easy. Hondas use somewhat smaller clearances, and are therefore a bit more difficult to do with great accuracy. Motorcycles with camshafts which ride directly on the valves have clearances adjusted with shims, and this can be a painstaking operation, and far from the ability of the average owner.

Spark Plugs

1. Spark plug deposits may be cleaned with a wire brush. Remove deposits from the center and side electrodes. Clean out any trapped particles with solvent or air pressure. If a commercial "plug cleaner" (sandblaster) is used, note that oily or oilfouled plugs should

Spark plug gap (1) is adjusted by bending the side electrode (2)

not be cleaned with these devices as the oil will catch and hold the abrasive cleaning particles.

2. Check electrode condition. Replace the plugs if they are worn, rounded or partially melted. "Square off" electrodes with a thin file.

3. Adjust the gap by bending the side electrode. Plugs should be gapped with a wire-type feeler gauge, rather than the blade type, since they are more accurate.

4. If new plugs are being fitted, be sure they are the correct heat range and reach. The latter is especially important. If plug reach is too long, the lower threads will protrude into

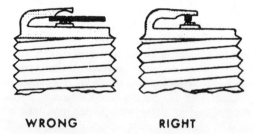

WRONG   RIGHT

The gap of used plugs should be set with a wire-type feeler gauge only

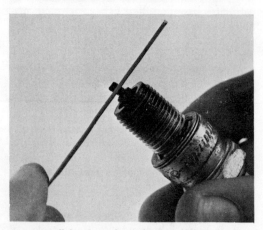

Squaring off the electrodes with a points file

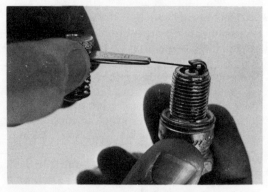

Gapping a plug with a wire-type feeler gauge

Bending the side electrode

Hot type   Medium type   Cold type

Heat range is chiefly a function of the length of the center electrode insulation

the combustion chamber. Even if the piston does not hit the plug when the engine is turned over, these threads will become carbon coated during operation, and it will become impossible to remove the plug.

If a plug with too short a reach is fitted, the plug hole will shield the spark with adverse effects on the combustion process. Additionally, the lower plug hole threads will become carbon covered, making it difficult or impossible to fit the correct reach plug later.

5. Spark plug heat range refers to the plug's ability to dissipate heat, and is dependent upon the amount of insulation around the center electrode.

Spark plugs of a certain heat range are recommended by the various factories after extensive testing, and should therefore be suitable for most riders.

There is, however, some range of choice if performance of the standard plugs is not satisfactory. If the machine is run constantly at high speeds or under heavy loads, a plug one heat range colder than standard may be used. Note that the colder plug may tend to load up during low speed operation, however.

If the machine is run at predominately slow speeds and low loads, a plug one heat range hotter than standard can be used.

CAUTION: *Fittings of plugs more than one*

Standard (left) and projected-type center electrodes

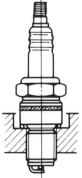 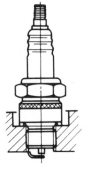 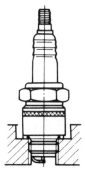

Spark plugs must be the proper reach (center). Plugs with too long a reach (left) may hit the piston or at best be difficult to remove. Those with too short a reach (right) will have an adverse affect on performance

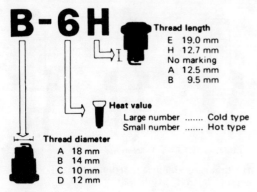

NGK spark plug code interpretation

heat range step in either direction from the recommended plug is not recommended.

6. Before fitting spark plugs, check that the sealing gasket is in good condition. Lightly lubricate the threads with oil or light grease. Use a torque wrench, where possible, to install the plugs. Take care not to overtighten the plugs. Plugs with 14 mm diameter threads should be torqued to about 18 ft lbs. Smaller plugs (10–12 mm) should be tightened to about 12 ft lbs. If it is not possible to use a torque wrench, turning the plugs about ¼ to ½ turn after they are handtight should secure them sufficiently.

Compression Test

1. A compression check should be made before each tune-up, as this will give a general clue to engine condition.

2. The engine should be at operating temperature.

3. Insert the gauge into the spark plug hole. If the gauge is the "hold-in" type, use a quality of oil on the rubber tip to give a good seal.

4. Hold the throttle wide open and kick the engine over briskly. Note the compression reading.

5. Although not all manufacturers provide compression specifications, most four-strokes will average about 160 psi, and most two-strokes about 110 psi.

6. On multi-cylinder machines, the difference between cylinders is important. Cylinders must have compression within 10% of each other. If they vary more than this, suspect some sort of mechanical damage to the low cylinder(s).

7. On four-strokes with low compression, squirt a small quantity of motor oil into the cylinder and check compression again. If it is now higher than the original reading, the piston rings or cylinder are worn. If the second compression reading is not higher than the first, suspect worn, damaged, or improperly adjusted valves.

8. On two-strokes especially, if the compression increases over a series of several tune-ups, the piston crown and combustion chamber are becoming carboned up and should be decarbonized.

Ignition Timing

1. The ignition timing procedure varies according to the type of ignition system fitted (battery-and-coil, magneto, CDI) and according to the number of cylinders, and other factors.

2. In the most basic sense, however, ignition timing is the procedure whereby the spark plug is set to fire at an exact piston position.

3. There are two ways the plug is signaled to fire: by mechanical or electronic means. The "electronic" method refers to Capacitor Discharge Ignition systems. The more common mechanical signal device refers to the familiar contact breaker points found on most motorcycles.

The spark plug fires at the instant the breaker points begin to separate.

4. To check the ignition timing, then, one must know when the points open, and where the piston is at this point.

Piston position can be determined in a number of ways, depending on model. On many motorcycles, timing reference marks are provided on the alternator or magneto rotor. These usually indicate piston Top Dead Center, the plug firing point at fixed advance, and the firing point at full advance.

On other models, however, piston position must be determined by means of a dial gauge or a degree wheel. Since in these cases the ignition timing specification is given in millimeters or inches before top dead center, or in degrees of crankshaft revolution before top dead center, the dial gauge or degree wheel is used to position the piston at the proper spot and to check if the points open at that point.

5. When piston position has been es-

Typical timing marks: "T" for top dead center, "F" for static firing point (no advance); dual marks for full advance firing point

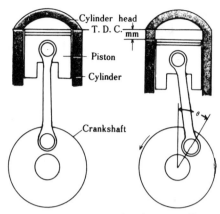

Ignition timing is expressed either in millimeters before top dead center (TDC), or degrees of crankshaft rotation before TDC

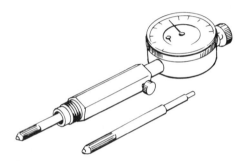

Dial gauge for finding piston position

tablished by one of the above methods, the next step is to determine when the points open. This can be accomplished in several ways.

On magneto-ignition motorcycles, an ohmmeter or "Points Checker" is the simplist method of determining when the points open. One lead of the test imstrument is connected to ground on the engine, and the other to the points primary wire, or primary wire terminal.

When the points begin to open, the meter will register an increase in resistance.

A device known as a "buzz-box" accomplished the same thing, but allows the mechanic to hear when the points open, since it changes the pitch of its signal when this happens.

Battery ignition motorcycles can be timed with a simple test or continuity light, each of which is illustrated in the "Introduction" to this book.

6. On the large majority of four-strokes, and on most two-strokes which are equipped with an electric starter, a timing advance mechanism is incorporated into the breaker cam. As the name implies, this device automatically advances the ignition timing (allow-

ing the spark plug to fire sooner relative to the piston position) as the engine revolutions increase. This is the reason for the two sets of firing marks found on some alternator and magneto rotors mentioned previously. If an ohmmeter, test light, or continuity light is used to check the timing, the engine will not be running and you will be checking the timing at the fixed advance point unless you open the advance mechanism manually. This is "static timing." On some motorcycles, "dynamic timing" is also possible. This is done with the engine running, and it is possible to check the timing both at the fixed advance *and* the fully advanced points. To do this, an automotive-type strobe light is used. Checking the timing at the full advanced position is preferred, since this is more critical to proper engine operation.

7. On most models, the ignition timing is changed by rotating the plate on which the points are mounted, or by moving the points

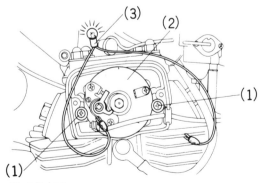

Test light in use

1. Base plate securing screws
2. Base plate
3. Test light

themselves. This allows them to open sooner or later relative to the piston movement. On others, notably two-strokes, ignition timing can only be changed by changing the point gap.

8. Breaker points should be inspected, filed and cleaned if necessary, and gapped before checking the ignition timing.

BREAKER POINT INSPECTION

1. Make visual inspection of the breaker point surfaces. A slight graying of the surfaces is normal.

2. Check for pitting or burned spots on the points.

3. If the surfaces are the normal gray, or if burnt spots are small, the point surfaces may be restored by running a thin, flat points file through them. This file should be designed specifically for contact breaker points, and the points should be open when using the file.

4. A too vigorous use of the file may render the points unusable. Do not remove any more material than is necessary to eliminate pitting or other irregularities.

5. After filing, clean off the points with a solvent. Finish up by allowing the points to close on a piece of business card, and then pulling it out. Continue doing this until the points no longer leave a mark on the card.

6. It is also possible to restore points by working them on an oilstone, which of course will require their removal from the machine. In this case care must be taken to avoid removing too much metal.

7. If pitting or burning is severe, the points should be replaced rather than filed.

NOTE: *New points may have a preservative coating on them to retard oxidation. This must be removed with a solvent before the points are installed.*

When closed, points should be flat, as shown

Points incorrectly aligned

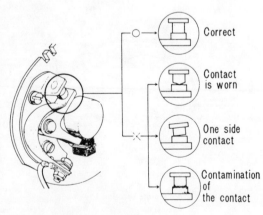

Point condition

Unserviceable points. Note deeply pitted area, cracked contact, and the fact that the pitted area is off center indicating misalignment

Extremely dirty points must be cleaned. Excess breaker cam lubricant is often the cause

These points show normal wear and require only cleaning to remain in use

Filing points

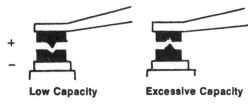

Low Capacity **Excessive Capacity**

Mounds and pits on contact breaker surfaces caused by a defective condenser

The condenser(s) should be replaced as well.

8. When closed, points should lie flat against one another. If they do not, it is possible that one of them is unevenly worn or that one or the other is bent out of alignment. In this case, replace the points.

9. On battery-ignition motorcycles, an ohmmeter can be used to give a further clue to point condition. When closed, the resistance across the points should be zero. If resistance is somewhat higher than this value, the points should be replaced.

10. If the ignition timing is being set by a static method, note that the reaction of the test light or meter should be immediate when the points open. A noticeable hesitation in the meter or light is often due to worn or dirty points.

11. Check the condition of the heel which bears on the breaker cam (if it is visible). Replace the points if the heel is excessively worn.

12. Make sure that point wire(s) are properly arranged. The moving point must be electrically insulated from the engine which is accomplished in most cases by means of insulating washers. These must be properly installed. Check the positions of any such insulators whenever points are replaced. Be sure that the points primary wire is correctly routed through any rubber grommets, and that the wire has no frayed or cut insulation. Be sure that fitting the points cover (where applicable) will not pinch the wire(s) or touch the points themselves. On some machines, clearance between such covers and the points is very small, and it may be possible that the cover will touch the primary wire terminal if installation is not correct. This will ground out the points resulting in a no-spark condition.

NOTE: *Points must be regapped after filing.*

BREAKER POINT LUBRICATION

1. It is necessary to lubricate the point breaker cam occasionally to minimize wear to

Checking point gap

the breaker point heel, which will eventually cause retarded ignition timing.

2. Most motorcycles have one or two felt wicks so mounted that they gradually apply lubricant to the cam. A small amount of high melting-point grease should be applied to the felt, and the felt arranged to that it bears lightly on the breaker cam.

3. On a few motorcycles, like Moto Guzzi, the felt does not contact the breaker cam directly, but sits in the breaker cam shaft. Lubricators of this type should get a few drops of oil.

4. If the felt wick is missing, a small quantity of grease should be applied to the cam itself. Care must be taken in either case, however, not to overlubricate, or the points may be fouled.

5. A drop of oil, or other lubricant such as molybdenum disulphide, can also be applied to the moving point pivot.

TIMING TROUBLESHOOTING

If trouble is encountered during the ignition timing procedure, check the following possibilities:

1. If the points have been replaced, check that the contact surfaces are cleaned. Some points are coated with a preservative to prevent oxidation which must be removed with solvent when the points are put into service.

2. If new points have been installed, check

that all insulating washers, grommets, etc., are correctly installed. On battery-ignition systems the moving points must be electrically insulated from the engine (ground) when the points are open. On magneto ignition motorcycles there will be some continuity here in any case.

3. If there is a no-spark condition after the points have been gapped, the feeler gauge blade probably deposited some foreign matter on the contact surfaces. Clean them and try again. Such a condition may also cause sparking at the points when the engine is running, but this may also be caused by a bad condenser.

4. If it is not possible to set the gap wide enough, the breaker points heel is worn.

5. If it is not possible to set the timing correctly, a severely worn breaker point heel may be the cause. Alternately, a sticking or otherwise defective timing advance mechanism may be the trouble.

6. Using the dynamic method of ignition timing allows the operation of the timing advance mechanism to be checked. On many machines, the mechanism is fitted behind the breaker point mounting plate and is easily accessible after this plate is removed. On those magneto machines which use this mechanism, it is probably incorporated into the back of the flywheel.

Timing advance mechanisms consist of spring-controlled weights which are pivoted at one end. As engine speed increases, the centrifugal force exerted on the weights gradually overcomes the spring tension, and the weights swing out from their pivot point, carrying the cam along with them.

As shown in the illustration, turning the breaker cam in the advance direction will swing the weights out. When released the cam should return to its original position.

Sticking or frozen advance mechanisms

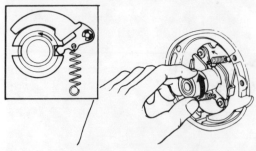

Check for free movement of the spark advance mechanism. When turned counterclockwise, it must return to its original position.

must be replaced. It may be possible to free them with penetrating oil. The most common problem is loss of spring tension which occurs after extended mileage and which allows the advance to come on too soon.

Tune-Up Analysis

1. Spark plug deposits should be light tan to dark brown in color if all systems are correct. Obviously, on multi-cylinder machines all plugs should show the same color.

2. While there are many factors which de-termine what color the plugs will be, the following can serve as a rough guideline to possible problems:

a. If the plug is oily or oil-fouled, it may be due to a badly adjusted oil pump cable (two-stroke), worn rings, valve guides, or valve seals (four-stroke).

b. If the plug is carbon-fouled (dry, black, fluffy deposits), the plug may be too cold for riding habits, the carburetor mixture may be too rich, or the machine may have been subjected to extended periods of idling.

c. If the plug is white or yellowish, or glazed, or if the electrodes are rounded, the engine may be overheating. The plug may

Normal spark plugs will be light tan to chocolate-brown in color

Oil (or wet)-fouled spark plug

A cold-fouled or carbon-fouled plug

Plug overheated: note rounded electrodes. Replacement is necessary

Core-bridged; suspect major engine damage

Splash-fouled; caused by installation of new plugs after long-delayed tune-up. These plugs can be cleaned off and refitted

be too hot for conditions, the carburetor mixture too lean, the ignition timing incorrect, etc.

3. "Rich" refers to an excess of gasoline in the mixture going into the engine, while "lean" means an excess of air. Assuming that the intake, exhaust, or engine have not been modified in any way, it is likely that an imbalanced mixture is being caused by a mechanical fault. Such problems as an incorrect float level in the carburetor, a leaking carburetor manifold, dirty air cleaner, leaking valves, or blown head gasket can cause rich or lean mixtures.

Since the standard carburetor settings work well in the majority of cases, changing jet sizes or the like is not recommended until all other possible causes have been checked.

Some symptoms of a rich mixture are:

a. Visible exhaust emissions without oil comsumption (four-stroke);

b. Dry, black deposits on spark plug;

c. Engine runs better when the air cleaner is removed;

d. Engine runs worse when hot;

e. Performance is sluggish.

Lean mixtures are often indicated by:

a. Engine refuses to idle smoothly, or rpm fluctuates at steady throttle openings;

b. Engine runs hot;

c. Spark plug is white or yellow in color (assuming heat range is correct);

d. Engine runs better when choke is engaged;

e. Engine runs better at slightly less than full throttle than it does when wide open;

f. Engine runs worse when the air cleaner is removed.

If the fault is in the carburetor, it is possible that the imbalanced mixture will only show up at one part of the throttle range. This can be understood by referring to the "Fuel Systems" chapter where a discussion of carburetor operation is undertaken. Included is a carburetor troubleshooting chart which may facilitate isolation of the problem.

Valve Adjustments

For valve adjustment procedures for four-stroke engines, refer to the owner's manual or shop manual.

In all cases, valves must be adjusted on a cold engine.

Most motorcycles use a simple screw fitting on the end of the rocker arm to make this adjustment, although there are exceptions. Some machines, like the 350 Honda, have the rocker arms mounted on eccentric shafts, and these shafts are rotated to provide more or less clearance, the clearance being measured between the valve stem and the rocker arm. Some others use shims between the cam lobes and the valve stems to adjust the clearance, and in these instances you will need a micrometer and a selection of shims of the proper thickness.

Checking valve clearance

On machines on which clearance can be adjusted with feeler gauge blades, note that the blade should be a slip fit in a correctly adjusted valve.

Great care must be taken when adjusting the valves. While some small error is permitted on the loose side (which will result in noisy valves), setting the clearances too tight will often burn the valves after few miles.

Before attempting to check or adjust the valve clearance, always check first that the valve is indeed fully closed. You should be able to feel a little play in the rocker arm if it can be reached.

For single-cylinder machines, position the piston so that it is at Top Dead Center on the *compression* stroke. This will allow all valves

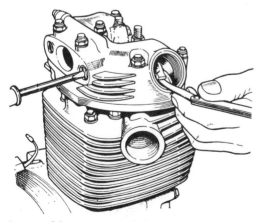

Some models use eccentric shafts to adjust clearance

Adjust valves when the piston is at top dead center on the compression stroke

to be adjusted, since all will be closed. Piston position marks can be found on the alternator or generator rotor, and "T" will indicate top dead center when it is aligned with the stationary timing mark. Note, however, that this is no guarantee that the piston is on the compression stroke: it may be on the *exhaust* stroke. Therefore, check for clearance at the valves before going further. If one valve seems to be open, rotate the engine 360° until the "T" mark is again aligned with the timing mark and recheck for play.

For twins, the procedure is essentially the same. If rotor marks are there, they will probably be differentiated "T" and "LT", the first being TDC for the right cylinder, the second for the left cylinder.

If the twin has a 360° crankshaft (meaning that the pistons rise and fall together), there may be only one set of marks. What can be done in this case is to turn the engine over until the right (or left) intake or exhaust valve is opened by the rocker arm, then you can be sure that the corresponding valve for the other cylinder is closed, and can be adjusted. Continue to turn the engine over in like manner until all valves have been checked.

Three- and four-cylinder engines are somewhat more complicated and information regarding them should be available in your owner's manual.

Carburetors

Carburetor tune-up procedure will largely depend upon the type of engine, the type and number of carburetors, what kind of carburetor controls are fitted, and ancillary systems, if fitted, such as oil pumps and the like which operate in conjunction with the carburetor.

Carburetor adjustments must always be made when the engine is at operating temperature.

PRE-ADJUSTMENT CHECKS

Before attempting to make carburetor adjustments, all of the following points should be checked:

1. Carburetor alignment. On flexible-mounted units, ensure that the carburetor(s) are vertically oriented, and not tilted to one side or the other. This may effect fuel level and high-speed operation.

2. Cable condition. Check throttle operation, ensuring that the cable(s) are not kinked or binding, and that they and the twist-grip are well-lubricated. If the gas tank has been removed and reinstalled, check that it has not trapped or pinched the throttle cables, or that the cables have not been forced to make sharp bends anywhere along their route.

3. Ancillary systems. Carburetor adjustments should be made last after all other systems have been attended to in order to prevent misleading symptoms. Check that the air cleaner is serviceable, the spark plugs are in good condition, valves (four-stroke) are correctly adjusted, and the ignition timing at least approximately correct. Also ensure that the gasoline is reasonably fresh, of the correct octane, and that foreign material, such as water or dirt, has been purged from the fuel system. Check fuel filters, if applicable. Refer to the "Fuel System" chapter for detailed information.

CABLE ADJUSTMENT

1. On most motorcycles, provision is made for adjusting the throttle cable to compensate for stretching. The adjuster is usually found at or near the twist-grip. This device should be adjusted so that the twist-grip has a small amount of noticeable free-play when turned. In general, this free-play should amount to about 10–15° of grip rotation before the slides begin to lift.

2. On oil-injection two-strokes, the oil pump cable adjustment must be checked any time the throttle cable is adjusted.

3. After adjustment, turn the forks slowly from side to side with the engine idling. Idle speed must not change or the cable is too tightly adjusted or too short. Check routing.

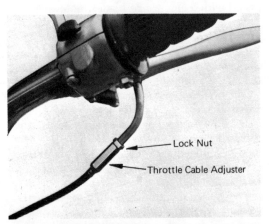

Lock Nut

Throttle Cable Adjuster

The cable adjuster should be used to give about 10–15° of grip rotational free-play

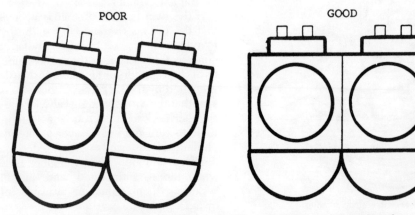

POOR   GOOD

If flexibly-mounted carburetors are fitted, ensure they are vertically aligned

IDLE SPEED AND MIXTURE

Idle speeds which are recommended by the manufacturer should be adhered to in most cases. The idle running of a motorcycle engine is usually the most unsatisfactory carburetor range. There are many reasons for this. For one, the quantities of fuel and air which are going into the engine are relatively small, and are controlled by equally smallish passages. These are more likely to become clogged with dirt or varnish than the much larger jets, and the mixture will then be upset. Further, the relative quantities of gas and air are more critical at idle, a situation which is compounded by the fact that one or the other can be adjusted by means of a knob or screw on the outside of the carburetor, and can easily be adjusted incorrectly.

Finally, since the engine is turning slowly, and is not under load, any irregularities in the mixture flow cause an erratic idle which may be irritating.

On most motorcycles, a satisfactory idle can be obtained by carefully setting the carburetors, ignition, and plugs to the recommended specifications. As noted, above, idle speed should be set to the recommended specification. An idle speed which is too low may cause trouble by making smooth transition to the slow or mid-range circuit impossible. On some motorcycles, too low an idle may cause damage to bearings and other moving parts due to the great lapse between power pulses.

On the other hand, too high an idle speed may cause the rpm to hang up for a moment or so when the throttle is closed. It may also make engaging the gears noisy or difficult, or result in excessive brake lining wear by negating the effects of engine braking.

Because of the low engine speeds involved, minor misadjustments or slightly defective components will be much more noticeable at idle.

The idle mixture is determined largely by the *pilot air screw* which controls the amount of air mixing with the idle circuit jets, or the *pilot fuel screw* which controls the amount of gasoline passing into the circuit.

Carburetors may be equipped with one or the other of these screws. While exceptions exist, on most carburetors the location of the screw will indicate whether it is an air screw or a fuel screw. Generally, pilot *air* screws are located on the intake side of the carburetor, while most pilot fuel screws are located be-

Direct-control carburetor. The pilot air screw (left) and throttle stop screw (center)

tween the throttle slide and the engine manifold. Most "CV" carburetors use pilot fuel screws.

It is only important to know whether you have an "air screw" or a "fuel screw" if you intend to make mixture changes based on plug readings or road tests. Turning an *air* screw *in* will give a richer mixture, while turning it *out* will lean the mixture out. For pilot *fuel* screws, exactly the opposite is true.

Regardless of type, pilot screw settings are given by the manufacturer, and should be

CV carburetor. The throttle lever screw (arrow) adjusts idle speed while the pilot fuel screw (near manifold clamp) controls idle mixture

adhered to, at least to within certain limits. The pilot screw settings are expressed in *turns out from the seated position.* The pilot screw's tip is tapered and is mated to an air or fuel passage. To make the adjustment, the screw is turned in gently until you can feel that it is *lightly* seated, then backed out the given number of turns. For example, if your specification for the pilot screw setting is "2½," you will back the screw out this number of times.

When turning these screws in, it is best to be very careful, as it is possible to ruin the tapered portion of the screw if it is turned down too tightly.

When performing a tune-up, always turn the pilot screws out to the given specification, then make any necessary adjustments. It should not be necessary to vary the screw setting more than ½ turn from the given setting unless changes have been made to the intake, engine, or exhaust systems. If it is not possible to obtain satisfactory performance with the settings as specified, suspect clogged carburetor passages or air leaks, etc.

Due to the large number of differing throttle linkage and carburetor assemblies used today, no general procedure will be able to provide all of the information necessary to properly adjust the carburetors on most motorcycles.

A few of the easier procedures are given below, but on most multi-cylinder machines, idle speed and mixture are controlled by complex linkages and are accomplished in many cases in conjunction with throttle slide synchronization, a procedure which requires a vacuum gauge. Therefore, detailed procedures for tuning these machines should be found in an appropriate shop manual.

Singles

1. Single-cylinder machines, whether two- or four-stroke are easily adjusted in the following manner.
2. After setting the pilot screw to the given specification, allow the engine to warm up, then use the throttle-stop (or idle speed) screw so that the engine turns over at the specified rpm.
3. Smooth out the idle, if necessary, by making careful adjustments to the pilot screw, but do not turn the pilot screw more than ½ turn in either direction from the recommended specification.
4. If satisfactory performance cannot be obtained using the given specifications, check for clogged carburetor passages, air leaks, plug

condition and gap, timing, damaged components, etc.

Twins

For single-carburetor models, refer to "Singles," above. For dual carburetor machines, the procedure is as follows:

1. Adjust the pilot screws for both carburetors to the recommended specification.
2. To ensure that one cylinder is not "leading" the other it is necessary to equalize the idle speed.
3. With the engine at operating temperature, disconnect one plug lead and turn the idle speed screw on the running cylinder in until the engine will run on one cylinder. Adjust the running cylinder's idle so that it is as low as possible, then try to get it as smooth as is feasible using the pilot screw.

Do not turn the pilot screw more than ½ turn in either direction from the recommended setting.

4. Connect the disconnected plug lead. Rev the engine a few times to clean off the spark plugs, then disconnect the plug lead for the cylinder which has already been adjusted.
5. Repeat Step 3 for the other cylinder.
6. Connect both leads. Idle speed will be very high. Back out each carburetor's idle speed screw in small, equal increments until the desired idle speed is arrived at.

NOTE: *On twins using a single ignition coil, disconnecting one lead will kill both cylinders. To get the engine to run on one cylinder it will be necessary to allow the disconnected lead to ground its spark against the cylinder head.*

7. Synchronize the throttle plates (CV) or slides.

On CV carburetors this can be done by

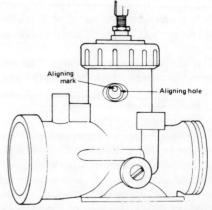

Some carburetors have slide alignment marks to facilitate synchronization

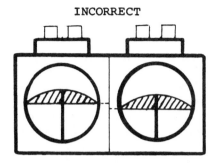

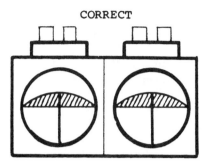

On multi-cylinder machines throttle slides must be synchronized

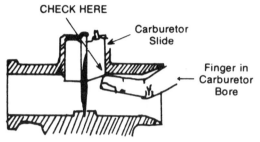

Check for carburetor synchronization by ensuring that both slides clear the carburetor bores at the same time

opening the throttle slightly and checking that both throttle arms begin to move at the same time.

On direct-control carburetors, remove the air cleaner(s) and check that both slides begin to move at the same time.

On some late-model twins, the throttle slides are fitted with a punch mark which can be aligned with inspection holes on the carburetor bodies for synchronization.

An alternate method is possible on some machines. Turn the throttles open until one of the slides just clears the carburetor bore. Check by feeling the top edge of the bore with your finger. The other slide must be in exactly the same position.

Slide synchronization is adjusted on most units by means of the cable adjusted atop each carburetor, or at the side on CV units.

Carburetors can also be synchronized with vacuum gauges if appropriate fittings are there.

Triples

Most late-model triples utilize throttle pulleys and linkages and you should refer to the shop manual for precise adjustment procedures. For others with separate cables to each carburetor, the procedures are very similar to that described above for twins. Many models have punch marks on the throttle slides which

are to be aligned with inspection holes on the carb bodies to effect synchronization.

ROAD TEST

NOTE: *Before carrying out any of the following tests, new spark plugs of the factory-recommended heat range should be fitted. Before making any alterations to the carburetor jetting based on the tests below, be sure that the carburetor does not have any air leaks, or that the engine is not carbon-choked, or running with worn rings, bad valves or seals, etc. Deceptive readings will be obtained in these cases, and if the unbalanced mixture is being caused by mechanical malfunction such as a leaking carburetor float needle, wrong float level, punctured float, blocked or obstructed fuel lines or gas tank vent.*

The following test is for the main jet.

1. Warm up the engine and accelerate through at least the first three gears at full throttle. When the engine is pulling high rpm, shut off the throttle, pull in the clutch, and kill the ignition, all as simultaneously as possible.

2. Remove the plugs and note the color. The plugs should be light tan to dark brown in color if the carburetor settings are correct.

3. If the plugs are black and wet with gas or oil, the mixture is too rich, and smaller size main jets should be installed. If the plugs are white, the mixture is too lean and larger main jets should be fitted. Main jets are sized accordingly: the larger the number on the jet, the more fuel it will pass in a given time, and the richer the mixture will be.

NOTE: *Never change main jet sizes more than one increment at a time; each time new jets are fitted, repeat the test until the plugs show the proper color. All plugs must show the same reading. The use of caution is advised when fitting smaller main jets. Too*

MAIN JET

Larger number : Richer mixture
Smaller number : Leaner mixture

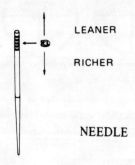

LEANER

RICHER

NEEDLE

PILOT AIR ADJUSTING SCREW

LEANER   RICHER

Carburetor metering components. If the unit has a pilot fuel screw, reverse the direction of those arrows to lean or enrichen the idle mixture

lean a mixture will cause overheating and probable piston seizure.

4. Once main jet size is determined to be correct, mid-range operation should be checked. Mid-range mixture is controlled by the needle jet and the needle. Repeat the test above, but do not use more than half-throttle when testing. Adjust the mixture by moving the needle clip up or down.

NOTE: *After considerable mileage, the needle and needle jet will become worn. This will cause a rich mid-range condition. If this occurs, replace both the jet and the needle.*

5. Mixture at idle and just above idle is controlled by the pilot screw. This adjustment is covered above.

CAUTION: *The effect that other badly adjusted or worn engine components can have on spark plug color cannot be overemphasized. Since main jets and other carburetor settings are determined by the factory after extensive testing, it is wise to suspect that things other than the jet sizes are causing misleading plug readings.*

Throttle Opening	Mixture too Rich	Mixture too Lean
0–⅛	Turn pilot air screw out, pilot fuel screw in	Turn pilot air screw in, pilot fuel screw out
⅛–¼	Enlarge throttle slide cutout	Reduce throttle slide cutout
¼–¾	Lower the jet needle	Raise the jet needle
¾–full	Use smaller no. main jet	Use larger no. main jet

3 · Two-Stroke Troubleshooting

Starting the Engine

Normally, an engine will not decide, overnight and of its own accord, not to start the next morning. Unless a machine has been recently worked on or has been in storage for some time, a flat refusal to fire up will have usually been preceded by hard starting and a noticeable loss of performance. If this is the case, and you want to get the bike running without a hassle, run through the following starting procedure, regardless of the technique you normally use.

Most modern two-strokes do not use a choke, as such, to aid cold weather starting. Instead, a mixture enrichening device is utilized, and it is very important, with a cold engine, to keep the throttle completely closed while operating the starter. Try starting your engine using this method:

1. Turn on the fuel tap.
2. Switch on the ignition and apply full "choke."
3. Kick the engine over briskly four or five times (or operate the electric starter for five full seconds.).

If your engine has not started and you have been at it for some time, take a minute to remove the spark plug(s). With the plugs out, kick the engine through a few times with the ignition off and the throttle closed to clear the combustion chambers. The plugs should then be dried and cleaned as thoroughly as possible and reinstalled.

Pay particular attention to these simple points:

1. Chances are that there is nothing seriously wrong with your engine. It is most important that you remain calm and analytical in your approach.

2. Take care to perform all the operations described, and don't close your mind to problems that you may not want to see.

3. If necessary, mark down results as you go along. If nothing else, this may help you locate the problem next time you have trouble.

Make sure the choke is operating correctly

31

Engine Does Not Start

For an engine to start, three basic conditions must be met: there must be compression, there must be a reasonably correct fuel/air mixture, and there must be a good spark arriving at the right time at the spark plug. Any engine starting problem can be attributed to one of these three things.

If your engine has not been serviced for a while, don't waste a lot of time trying to figure out why it won't start. The wisest thing to do in this case is perform a complete tune-up. It just could be that all of your engine systems are slightly out of adjustment and are conspiring together to keep the engine from starting. If the engine has been properly serviced, check for improper adjustment or faulty operation of components in the systems.

First, it can be assumed that if your engine was running yesterday, it still has good compression today. Compression may gradually disappear over many miles of use, but, over a short period of time, it will rarely decrease enough to cause hard starting—unless accompanied by unusual noises and a dramatic decrease in performance. If it takes the normal amount of effort to kick the engine over using the kick-start lever, you can be reasonably sure that there is sufficient compression present for the engine to fire. If in doubt, remove the spark plugs and place your thumb over each plug hole, using enough force to seal it, while turning the engine over. If there is enough compression to break the seal, there is enough compression for the engine to start.

To check for positive fuel flow, simply remove the fuel line at the carburetor and observe the amount of fuel that issues from it. If anything more than a restricted dribble comes out, the carburetor is receiving enough fuel for the engine to start. It would be a good idea here to check the tightness of the carburetor intake tube clamps. If these are loose, an air leak might be creating a fuel mixture lean enough to be sabotaging all your efforts.

Once you are satisfied that fuel is present, it is time to move on to the ignition system. The most effective and reliable

way to check the sparking system is to observe the spark at the spark plug. Remove the plug and replace it in its connector cap. Switch on the ignition and, while holding the base of the plug against the crankcase or cylinder, crank the engine over briskly. A fat, hot spark should be seen (and heard) across the plug electrodes. If the spark is weak, or there is no spark at all, elminate the plug and stick a nail or other metal object into the connector cap and rerun the test holding the nail about $\frac{1}{8}$ in. from the engine. If you have spark now, install a new set of plugs and your engine should start. If there is still no spark, the fault lies with some other ignition system component, which will be covered in the next section.

You should, by now, be aware of the problem area. Refer to the following sections for more detailed checks of each system.

CHECKING THE ELECTRICAL SYSTEM

A lack of spark at the spark plug high tension wire spells out problems in some other area of the ignition system. When checking ignition components, start with the most basic and obvious areas, and work from there. Don't overlook the obvious and the simple. In many cases you will find that your problem is so basic and uncomplicated that you'll feel like a fool after discovering it. Some of the obvious faults to look for are:

1. Kill switch in the OFF position.

2. Undercharged battery or loose or dirty battery terminals. On many machines, it is absolutely essential that the battery be producing nearly full voltage for the engine to start.

3. Faulty ignition switch. If the lights don't work or the horn doesn't blow, you can be pretty sure that this is your problem, unless . . .

4. The main electrical fuse has blown out. On most machines, the fuse is located near the battery in a plastic in-line holder.

5. Loose or dirty connections in the wiring. Check all the connections you can get to for tightness. If loose or dirty or wet, correct the condition and try starting the engine again.

6. On older magneto equipped bikes, a

blown taillight bulb can shut down all or part of the electrical system. Don't overlook this as your source of trouble.

If you haven't found your albatross in any of these obvious areas, it's time to look a little more closely at the spark generating components of the ignition system. At this point you will need a test light. If your bike has a battery, the test light need only consist of a small 6 or 12 volt light bulb (whichever is applicable) with two wires attached so that it will light when connected to a power source. If your machine doesn't incorporate a battery, a test light with a self-contained power source is necessary. The test light is used to determine where the flow of electricity has been interrupted. Start at the point where you should have juice but don't, and work back toward the power source. If, for example, you find that you have power at the coil but none at the points, check the wire connections and then check the continuity of the low tension wire using the test light. In this manner you can discover faults that are invisible and otherwise detectable only by trial and error replacement. Faults that should be checked for include:

1. Frayed or internally broken wiring.
2. Faulty or weak ignition coil.
3. Improperly grounded points base plate, due to looseness, oil or, on some machines, a broken ground strap or "pigtail."
4. Points shorted due to foreign matter on the contacts or grounding of the "hot" lead.

Once you have isolated the specific area of the trouble, refer to "Electrical Systems" for more detailed tests. Refer also to "Electrical Systems" for complete operational descriptions and information on CDI systems.

CHECKING THE FUEL SYSTEM

As mentioned earlier, delivery of fuel to the carburetor is the first thing to check for when hard starting is experienced and the fuel system is suspected. Disconnect the fuel line at the carburetor and check flow at this point while taking care not to dump gasoline all over the engine. On diaphragm petcocks, fuel will flow only in the "prime" position when the

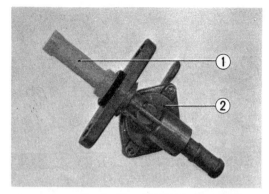

On some petcocks, the filter (1) is inside the gas tank

engine isn't running. Lack of flow can be caused by any of these conditions.

1. Empty gas tank.
2. Clogged fuel line.
3. Fuel tap not functioning properly or in OFF position.
4. Gas tank cap vent plugged.
5. Fuel strainer (in fuel tap or tank) clogged.
6. Fuel line kinked.

If your machine has been in storage, it is possible that the carburetor has gummed up from the fuel evaporating and leaving a residue. In this case the best thing to do is disassemble and clean the carburetor before going any further. In doing so, you can ensure that the jets are clear, that the float needle and seat are not sticking and causing flooding, and that all passages are clear. Flooding can also be caused by a hole in the float, which will allow the float to fill with gas and sink. To check for this condition, simply remove and shake the float. If there is any indication of fuel inside the float, it should be replaced with a new one.

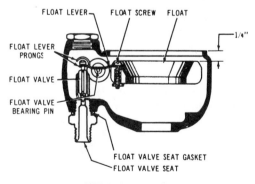

CROSS SECTION OF CARBURETOR
BOWL SHOWING FLOAT MECHANISM
AND FLOAT SETTING

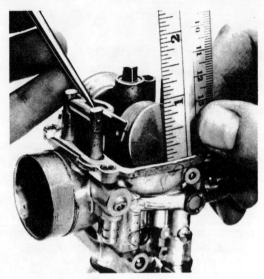

Checking float height

Some machines are quite sensitive to the float level setting; however, the float level will rarely vary from the correct setting unless the float arm or tang has been bent. If any doubt exists here, consult a repair manual applicable to your model for the correct setting specifications. Note also that on Mikuni carburetors equipped with an O-ring around the needle and seat unit, it is very important that the O-ring be in good condition.

As a final measure, make sure that the carburetor mounting screws are tight and that the throttle cables and starter jet cables (if applicable) are properly adjusted and not binding.

COMPRESSION CHECK

A compression check will tell you quickly and simply what condition the top end components of your engine are in. A quick test can be made by placing your finger over the spark plug hole, but the use of a compression gauge will give you far more accurate and convincing results. Be sure to hold the throttle wide open when using the gauge, and crank the engine over long enough to be sure that you are getting a maximum reading. Look for a minimum compression of about 110–120 psi, and a maximum deviation between cylinders of 10–15 psi. Low or varying compression readings mean either worn rings or cylinder bore, or a leak between the head and cylinder barrel or at the crankcases. In either case, the head and

barrel should be pulled for inspection. This is one area where the two-stroke has it all over the four-stroke. With fewer moving parts and generally less bulk, performing a top end overhaul on the usual two-stroke is quite staightforward and simple.

It should be noted here that after many miles of use, sometimes carbon buildup in the head and on the piston crown can increase compression to the point where the engine will "ping" even on quite moderate throttle openings, and have a tendency to run much hotter than normal. If this is the case, which a compression test can bear out, the head should be pulled for decarbonization and a look at the rings and bore.

Unlike the four-stroke engine, which does not have a pressurized crankcase and can tolerate leaks around the crankcase area, the two-stroke depends on crankcase pressure for the filling of the combustion chamber with fuel. In this way the two-stroke engine acts like a pump; as the piston travels downward it decreases the volume of space inside the crankcase and forces the fuel up through the transfer ports. Therefore, any crankcase leaks are disastrous for the performance of the two-stroke engine. In addition to this, the crankshaft throws in two and three cylinder two-stroke engines are spaced either 180 or 120 degrees apart (the pistons do not move up and down at the same time), and therefore, the individual crankchambers must be sealed off from each other. This poses the additional problem of possible internal leakage, not to mention the possibility of a leak into the transmission case area. Fortunately, the quality of the seals and the standards of machinework on the crankcase mating surfaces are excellent, which greatly reduces the chances of case leakage. Also, the labyrinth (metal spiral) seals used by some manufacturers last virtually forever.

If a crankcase leak is suspected, remove the carburetor and seal the intake port with your hand. Rotate the engine to position the piston at bottom dead center (BDC), and blow into the exhaust port with a steady pressure. If you don't pass out, you should be able to tell whether air is escaping from the crankcase. If it is, a piece of rolled up paper can help you to locate any leaks around the crankcase joint area. A leak into the transmission can be detected by listening at the transmission breather. An internal seal leak in a twin or triple will show up through the carburetor or exhaust of the adjacent cylinder. In any case, the engine will have to be removed and torn down for repair.

Poor Engine Performance

HARD STARTING OR ERRATIC PERFORMANCE

The first items to check for, as always, are the obvious ones. Is the gas tank at least ¼ full? Sometimes a machine will be hard to start if the fuel supply is very low. Is the battery at or near full charge? An easy way to check is to observe the intensity of the headlight. If it is dim when the engine isn't running, have it recharged before doing anything else. Make sure that all electrical connections are clean and tight, and that the battery ground strap or cable is secured properly. Check to see if the ignition switch is playing tricks on you by applying the brake while jiggling the key (ignition on) and watching to see if the brake light flickers. Ensure that you have a sufficient flow of fuel to the carburetor by pulling off the line at the carb and observing the flow.

If you've gotten this far and still not discovered the problem, remove and examine the spark plugs. Although not the problem that it has been in the past, spark plug fouling is still common in many two-stroke engines. Electrodes that are wet and black (gas fouled), or covered with a thick, soft deposit (oil fouled) should be cleaned or replaced. A gas fouled plug means that your engine is flooded or running rich, or that the plug heat range is too cold. An oil fouled plug indicates (unless the plug has been in use for some time) that either the engine is being over-oiled or, again, the plug is too cold for conditions. It may pay off, if your plugs become oil fouled often, to check and adjust the oil pump setting or be more careful when mixing your fuel.

The next area to investigate is the ignition timing. The timing can be off for one of three reasons: the contact breaker plate has come loose and allowed the timing to

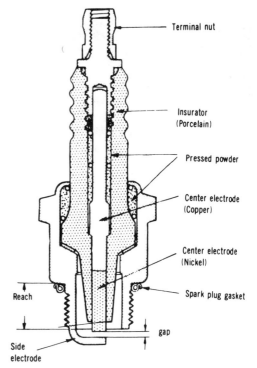

Spark plug construction

slip; the rubbing block that rides on the breaker cam has worn, altering the points gap and changing the timing; or the points have been gapped or replaced without also checking and adjusting the timing. All modern two-strokes are very sensitive to timing variations, and considerable care must be used to adjust the timing exactly to specification. If the engine kicks back when you are trying to start it or backfires at low rpm, suspect the ignition advance mechanism. Although it rarely happens,

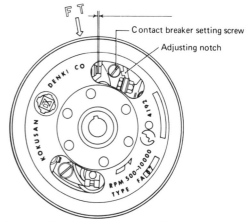

Contact breaker points gap (flywheel magneto type shown)

Removing an air filter for cleaning (a good thing to do once in a while)

you may find that the advance unit has weak or broken springs, or that the unit has frozen. Most electric-start two-strokes have timing advance mechanisms. Most others do not. Check the condition of the points, and replace or clean and gap them if necessary. If they are badly pitted, do not hesitate to replace the condenser at the same time. If oily, examine the distributor drive seal and replace it if any oil is leaking past.

If you can't remember the last time your air filter was serviced it should be checked. A dirty filter can cause hard starting, rich running, overheating, poor performance, plug fouling and excessive fuel consumption. This especially applies to dirt and desert driving. Even though you installed a well-known aftermarket brand, it still has to be cleaned now and again.

Finally, if you've just taken your bike out of storage and it was running well before you put it away, your carburetor is probably gummed up with residue from evaporated fuel and oil. This can usually be remedied by simply removing the jets and cleaning them thoroughly.

ENGINE DIES WHEN THROTTLE IS OPENED

Most cases of engine lag can be attributed to an extremely twitchy throttle hand. It must be understood that two-stroke engines nowadays produce lots and lots of power for their size, and that the carburetor throat size compared to the engine displacement is equally huge. This means that you can't crack the throttle wide open from low engine speeds without experiencing a slight lag, even with a finely tuned engine.

If the lag is exaggerated or overly obtrusive, chances are that the carburetor is at fault. Problems to look for are:

1. Clogged air filter.
2. Carburetors badly out of synchronization on twins and triples.
3. Starting jets not returning to fully closed position.
4. Idle speed set too low.
5. Air leak around carburetor intake tube flanges.

LOW SPEED MISFIRING

If your engine misfires on acceleration from low speed, the chances are, again, that carburetion is at fault. An overly rich mixture is generally the culprit and should be checked as follows:
1. Make sure that the air filter is not clogged.
2. Reset the idle adjustment screws to be certain that the idle circuit is as close to perfect adjustment as possible.
3. Remove the float bowl and examine the float needle and seat valve. If it is dirty or worn it could be hanging up and allowing the float bowl to overfill.
4. Make sure that the starting jets are returning to the fully closed position.

If none of this solves your problem and your machine can't exactly be considered a youngster, it may be time to rebuild the carburetors. One thing that you might try first, however, is to replace the plugs with new ones. Sometimes spark plugs can be awfully erratic, not firing at low voltage or short circuiting at high voltages, and it wouldn't hurt to see if new ones help.

RPM RELATED MISFIRE

In most cases, if your engine misfires at a certain rpm regardless of the gear you are in or the throttle opening used, it can be put down to a timing problem. Check and adjust the timing, and if this doesn't clear up the trouble, the ignition advance unit, if fitted, should be examined. If in doubt, replace the complete unit or, at the very least, the springs. This can also be caused by poor electrical connections, defective condensers or coils, etc.

THROTTLE OPENING RELATED MISFIRE

If a misfire occurs at a certain throttle opening, regardless of the gear you are in or the revs the engine is turning, the problem is caused by the mechanical parts of the carburetor. Carefully examine the needle and needle jet for wear and damage,

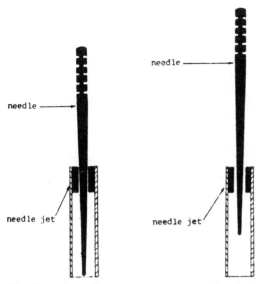

needle

needle

needle jet

needle jet

Needle and needle jet in operation: as the slide raises the needle, the tapered portion exposes more of the jet opening increasing fuel flow

and make sure that the slide is not worn and can move up and down freely. Fuel jets which are too large or too small may also cause this.

INCONSISTENT MISFIRE ON ACCELERATION

An inconsistent misfire, throughout the rpm range at various throttle openings, can usually be attributed to the ignition system. If your machine is about due for a tune-up anyway, now would be a good time to take care of it. At the same time, go over the whole electrical system, checking for loose connections, condition of the battery, deteriorated high tension wires, etc. Normally, you will find that it is something simple, like a loose condenser wire, that is causing your headaches. Take care to check everything in your search.

ENGINE MISFIRES UNDER LOAD

A load can be placed on an engine in many ways, such as running up a steep hill in high gear, riding at high speeds against a head wind, using maximum acceleration constantly, etc. All of these cases involve large throttle openings, and in each of them the misfire can usually be stopped by reducing the amount of throttle.

The first symptom to look for in this instance is overheating. Remove and examine the spark plugs, looking for a lighter than normal color and eroded electrodes.

If overheating is occurring, investigate the following possible causes:

1. Excessive carbon build-up in the combustion chamber and on the piston crown.

2. Improper timing or a faulty ignition advance unit. Note that timing becomes more critical at high engine load and rpm.

3. Air leak at the intake tube flanges between the carburetor and cylinder.

4. Too "hot" a spark plug. In many cases it is necessary to go to plugs that are one or two steps colder in heat range when cruising at high speeds or running in hot weather.

Rich running can also be considered when you encounter misfiring under load. Check first for a clogged air filter, and then check to make sure that the main jet is the right size. Although most two-strokes will run well even on a cheap regular grade of gas, it would be a good idea to check for contamination of the fuel. To do this, simply remove the float bowl (taking care not to dump the gas out) and smell the fuel in it. If it separates as if it had water in it, drain the entire system and refill with fresh gas.

HIGH SPEED MISFIRING

A high speed misfire is, in many cases, simply the first indication that a tune-up is necessary. If you need a tune-up do it, and if one was recently performed go back and check it because somebody probably fouled up.

If this isn't the case, rich running, as indicated by a black, sooty spark plug, could be causing the misfiring. Check again for a clogged air filter, and, if you've been fooling around with the main jet size, you have probably selected one that is too large. This condition can also be caused by a cold spark plug which has fouled during previous low-speed running.

If you experience spark plug electrode erosion which indicates overheating, check for lean running. You may have an air leak at the intake tube flanges (again), or the float level may be set too low causing fuel starvation at high speeds. Look also for leaking cylinder head and cylinder-to-crankcase gaskets or a leaking crankshaft oil seal (see "Compression Check" section), any of which can cause a lean running condition.

Finally, check the high tension components of the ignition system. The coil should be capable of producing a fat, hot spark, and the high tension (spark plug) wires must be clean and free of breaks or deterioration of the insulation.

One more thing: very often, clogging of the muffler baffles can lead to high speed misfiring in addition to fouled plugs, even when everything else is in perfect condition. The baffles should be removed and cleaned without fail at the manufacturer's specified intervals.

POOR LOW SPEED PERFORMANCE

Normal service items are usually at fault if you are experiencing poor or erratic performance in the lower third of the rpm range. Do not mistake a few seconds of unsteady or rough running, after long periods of slow running or idling, for poor low speed performance, because this is the quite normal result of combustion chambers being loaded with partially burnt fuel and oil due to slow running. If necessary, perform a complete tune-up first, then begin checking the following areas:

1. Make sure that the fuel tank vent is not clogged.

2. Make sure that the starter jet cables are correctly adjusted, and that the jets open and close fully.

3. Check and adjust, if necessary, the float level.

4. Disassemble and clean the carburetors, paying particular attention to the low speed circuit.

5. Check the ignition advance unit for free operation, and replace the springs if weak or broken.

POOR MID-RANGE OR HIGH SPEED PERFORMANCE

Again, after normal tune-up items have been attended to, look for the following:

1. Frozen ignition advance pivots or weak or broken springs.

2. Restricted fuel lines, clogged fuel tap or tank vent, or improper float level adjustment.

3. Incorrect carburetor alignment on twins and threes. (Loosen the carb clamps and rotate them so that their tops are level, using a small steel ruler to check.)

4. Incorrect main jet size.

5. Worn or broken piston rings or a leaking head gasket. A compression check

will reveal any top-end mechanical problems.

6. Weak battery. Don't be fooled into thinking that because the battery is strong enough for the engine to start, it is strong enough for the engine to fire properly at high speeds. With some machines the battery must be at or near full charge in order for the ignition system to work strongly at high rpm.

7. Carbon deposits, when they become excessive, will always cause a power loss usually noticeable in the higher ranges.

POOR GENERAL PERFORMANCE

A tune-up, spark plug check, and compression check will tell you just about everything you'd ever want to know about the condition of your engine. If one of these checks indicates that something bad is going on inside the engine, don't waste your time looking for trouble elsewhere. Wishful thinking won't help. If the engine checks out OK, however, and you're still not satisfied that performance is as good as it should be, look for other things like dragging brakes, a tight chain, a slipping clutch, etc.

*ENGINE OVERHEATING
AND SEIZURE*

Overheating to the point of seizure is much less common today than it was even ten years ago, thanks to the advent of oil injection systems and advances in metallurgy. However, mostly due to the fact that motorcycle engines require a stream of air passing through the fins for cooling, partial seizure still happens once in a while. Slow trail riding in hot weather, overloading a small bike, and extended periods of idling can all contribute to overheating which could cause a partial piston seizure. A brand new or rebuilt engine is particularly prone to overheating, and care should be taken in the first few hundred miles to use small amounts of throttle and a moderate rev range. If a mild seizure does occur, just letting the engine cool off for a few minutes will generally free it again, probably without any damage. Strange noises and a loss of performance, however, mean that you'd better pull the head and cylinder to have a look at the piston and bore.

If your bike is overheating (noticeable

as a drop in performance and an inordinate amount of heat radiating from the cooling fins), look for these causes:

1. Insufficient amount of oil, due to incorrect mixing or an out of adjustment oil pump.

2. Incorrect (lean) fuel/air mixture, caused by an intake air leak or incorrect carburetor jetting.

3. Improperly adjusted ignition timing or a faulty ignition advance unit. Two-strokes are very sensitive to timing variations, and overheating can easily result from a careless setting.

4. Carbon buildup in the combustion chamber. Excessive carbon buildup can cause an increase in the compression ratio, which will increase the amount of heat produced by the engine. In addition, the carbon tends to remain very hot, causing pre-ignition and adding to the overheating problem.

5. Clogged exhaust port and muffler baffles. This causes an increase in back pressure, which in turn increases the amount of heat retained by the engine, as well as the throttle opening necessary to maintain the same level of performance. (Engine heat produced is directly related to the amount of throttle opening being used.)

6. Too "hot" a spark plug, which can ultimately cause a holed piston. The heat range of a spark plug refers to the heat dissipating ability of a plug. Therefore, a hot plug retains (not produces) more heat than a colder plug will, causing more heat buildup in the cylinder head.

7. Oily or dirty cooling fins, which are prevented from performing their job of dissipating heat as quickly and over as large an area as possible.

ENGINE VIBRATION

Nearly all abnormal engine vibration can be attributed to three or four causes: loose or broken engine mounts, incorrect ignition timing or unsynchronized carburetors on twins or triples. If broken mounts are suspected, be sure to check the mounts under the bolt heads and nuts, where hidden fractures can occur. Although it happens only with high mileage engines, it is possible that worn crankshaft bearings can cause excessive vibration, which of course would show up more gradually than the other causes would.

ENGINE NOISES

Engine noises are often the first indication of component malfunction or excessive wear. It is important, however, that you don't confuse normal noises with those indicating a problem. Nearly all motorcycles produced today are air-cooled, and use a great deal of aluminum alloy in their engines. Both of these factors contribute to the transmission of normal noises and should not be cause for alarm.

Two-stroke engine noises are the most suceptible to misinterpretation because of the varying levels. An engine that has been run under load in extreme heat, for example, can emit some very frightening sounds but run quietly the next morning. This is not to say that you shouldn't be concerned when you hear these noises, but rather that you should learn the difference between the expensive thump of bad main bearings and the harmless piston slap of a cold off-road single.

Inconsistent Noises

A clicking or clattering under moderate acceleration is usually the result of carbon buildup on the rings which reduces the end gap, or it could be excessive side clearance of the rings.

A heavier clicking, sometimes heard as a double click in quick succession, is most often a sign of excessive clearance between the wrist pin and its bearing.

A definite knock heard under acceleration generally means that the connecting rod bearing is worn.

Pinging under hard acceleration is caused by incorrect ignition timing, cheap or contaminated fuel, excessive carbon buildup, or overheating.

A low rpm rattle, especially when the engine is cold, is normally attributable to piston slap. This is nothing serious, and is characteristic of some models, even when new.

Consistent Noises

A grating rattle, noticeable when the engine is idling in neutral, is clutch and primary drive noise. This is quite normal with some models, and not very serious in any case. The noise may be audible when running under a light load at low speed, and should disappear almost completely when the clutch is disengaged.

A sharp knock at all engine speeds could be the piston rings hanging up as they pass the ports, and is very serious.

A heavy thump throughout the rpm range is descriptive of worn main bearings. Worn mains are also sometimes noticeable as loud whirring or screeching from the bottom end.

Oil Injection Systems

OPERATIONAL DESCRIPTION

Kawasaki—Superlube and Injectolube

Both the Superlube and Injectolube systems include an oil reservoir, oil feed line, oil pump, and oil delivery lines. The pumps are of the plunger type and are driven by the end of the crankshaft through reduction gears. The amount of oil fed to the induction passage delivery line and crankcase drillway (Injectolube) is determined by two variables: the speed of plunger operation and the length of plunger stroke. These variables are set by the engine rpm and the degree of throttle opening, respectively. The pump effectively meters the amount of oil according to engine speed and load and, as a result, no more and no less than the required

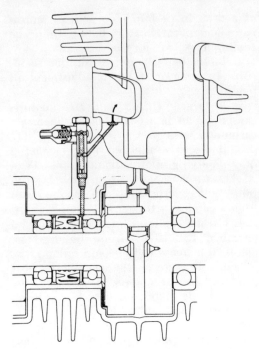

Interjectolube oil nozzle arrangement (H Series)

amount is consumed. The pump also houses a check valve that keeps the oil output pressure constant and seals the delivery line when the engine is not operating.

The essential difference between the Superlube and Injectolube systems is the extra lubrication to the crankshaft main bearings provided by the Injectolube type.

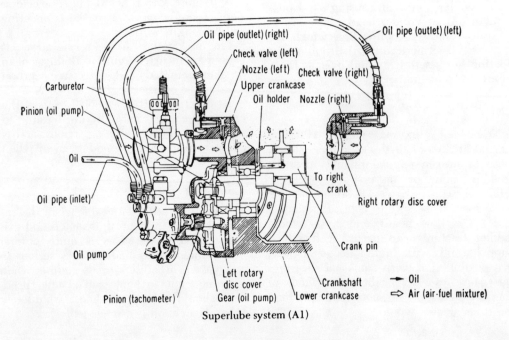

Superlube system (A1)

An additional output port in the oil pump leads to a drillway in the crankcase, which in turn leads to smaller passages to these critical points.

Suzuki—Posi-Force and C.C.I.

Called originally "Posi-Force Lubrication," later changed to "C.C.I.," this system is now used on all Suzuki two-strokes from the 50 cc bikes up to the 750 cc triple.

Direct oil injection has distinct advantages over the old oil-mist method, and indeed over other less sophisticated oil injection systems. Outstanding features include decreased engine wear at high rpm (particularly with the new C.C.I. modifica-

tions), less accumulation of carbon in the exhaust system and on the piston, much reduced exhaust smoke, and elimination of the chore of mixing the oil and gas.

Although variations in engine design require slightly different oil routing, accommodating direct port, reed valve and rotary valve configurations, the system works in basically the same manner for all machines.

On all twins, except the T-125, a plunger-type oil pump, operated by the crankshaft, supplies oil through tubes to both the right and left crankshaft bearings at a predetermined pressure. The volume of the pump is directly controlled by engine rpm

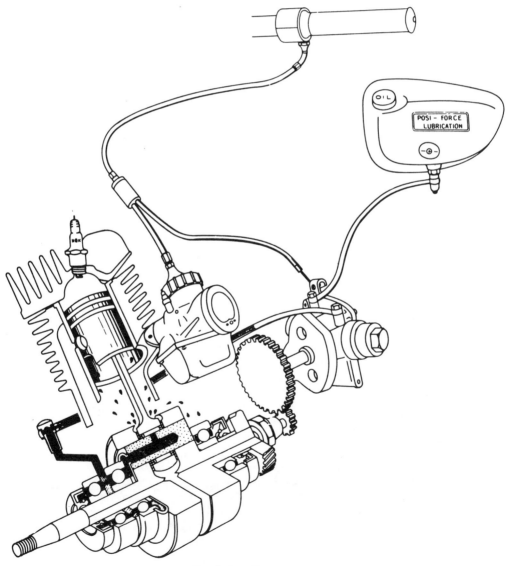

Suzuki Posi-Force system

and throttle slide opening so that just the right amount of oil is metered to lubricate without waste. The oil passes from the bearings through the crankpins and there lubricates the connecting rod needle bearings. From there, the oil is thrown off the crankpins by centrifugal force, atomized and blown up on the cylinder walls and connecting rod small end bearings. The C.C.I. system is almost identical to this, except that separate tubes spray oil directly onto the cylinder walls to add to the oil mist supplied from the crankpins. With both Posi-Force and C.C.I., the center crankshaft bearing is lubricated by the transmission oil, the drippings from which flow back into the transmission via a return hole in the crankcase.

On the T-125 twin, oil from two of the four injection tubes lubricates the left and center bearings and crankpins and is sprayed as a mist on the cylinder walls. The other two tubes inject oil into the carburetor inlet ports from where it is then drawn into the crankcase to lubricate the connecting rod small end and cylinder walls. On this model, the right crankshaft bearing is lubricated by the transmission oil.

The Posi-Force system used on singles is similar to that used on twins. A plunger-type pump, controlled by engine rpm and throttle opening, meters oil through one or two tubes to the engine. The left-side (or single if it has only one) tube supplies oil directly to the left crankshaft bearing, from where it passes through the crankshaft to the hollow crankpin to lubricate the connecting rod needle bearings. The oil is thrown off the crankpin, and is blown as a mist up over the lower cylinder walls and connecting rod small end bearing. Models having only one injection tube, such as the K-10P, K-11P, and B-100 P, have their right crankshaft bearing lubricated by oil mist from the crankshaft chamber.

On models with two tubes, the oil that is injected from the right-side tube enters the intake port (or the cylinder directly) and is sucked into the crankcase to help lubricate the cylinder walls. With this sytem, the right crankshaft bearing is lubricated by the transmission oil in the same manner as the center bearing on twins.

A variation of this system is used on models with rotary disc valves, such as the A-100, AS-100, TC-90, and TS-90. One tube supplies oil to the left crankshaft bearing, through the crankpin and is sprayed on the cylinder walls and connecting rod small end bearing. The other tube supplies oil to the rotary disc valve and the right crankshaft bearing.

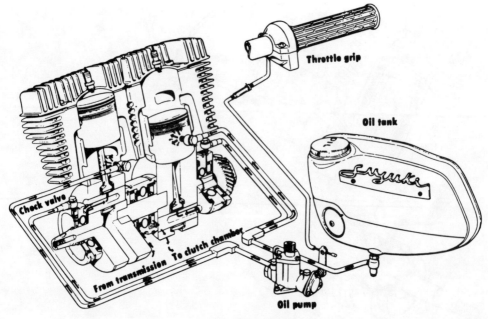

Suzuki CCI system

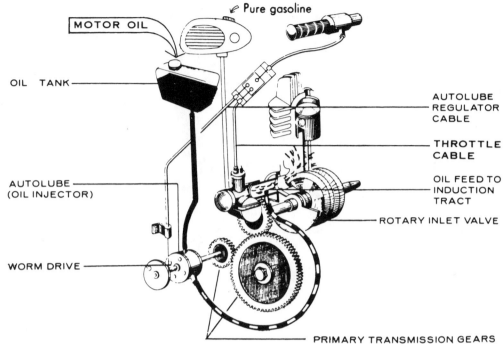

OIL TANK

MOTOR OIL

Pure gasoline

AUTOLUBE
REGULATOR
CABLE

THROTTLE
CABLE

OIL FEED TO
INDUCTION
TRACT

AUTOLUBE
(OIL INJECTOR)

ROTARY INLET VALVE

WORM DRIVE

PRIMARY TRANSMISSION GEARS

Yamaha Autolube system

Yamaha—Autolube

Yamaha was the first major manufacturer to offer an effective and reliable oil injection system. The Autolube system, introduced in the early 1960's, pioneered the throttle and rpm related injection of oil directly into the intake port. The Autolube pump is a plunger type and is driven by the crankshaft or clutch (early models) through reduction gears. The amount of oil fed to the crankcase delivery line is determined by two variables—the speed of plunger operation and the length of plunger stroke. These variables are set by the engine rpm and the degree of throttle opening, respectively. The pump effectively meters the amount of oil according to engine speed and load and, as a result, the precise amount of oil needed is delivered. The pump also houses a check valve that keeps the oil output pressure constant and seals the delivery line when the engine is not operating.

OIL PUMP TROUBLESHOOTING

It is inadvisable to attempt disassembly and repair of the oil pump. The internal parts are machined to very exacting tolerances and it is highly unlikely that the pump can be reassembled to factory speci-

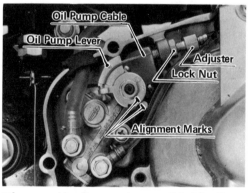

Oil pump cable adjustment is accomplished by aligning the marks. The manufacturer will specify throttle position

fications. In addition to this, oil pump failure rarely occurs due to internal malfunction.

The lubrication systems used on modern oil-injected two-strokes are extremely reliable and require little maintenance.

The first point which should be checked in the event of overlubrication (causing fouled plugs) or lack of oil (engine overheating or piston seizures) is the adjustment of the oil pump cable.

Procedures for adjusting the cable will be given in your owner's or shop manual. For most bikes, this cable works in conjunction

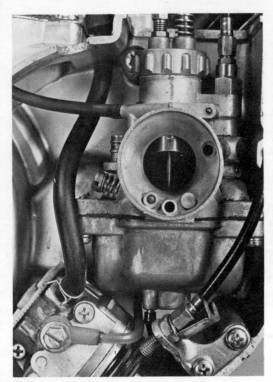

All oil line connections must be secure, but overtightening plastic banjos may cause leaks

On some models, the oil pump marks must align when the throttle slide mark is positioned at the top of the carburetor bore

with the throttle cable(s), and must therefore be adjusted any time the throttle cables or carburetors are attended to.

On most machines, the adjustment is checked by seeing whether an index mark on the oil pump lever aligns with a stationary index mark on the pump body. This alignment should take place at a certain throttle opening which will be specified by the manufacturer. Sometimes this alignment is checked with the throttle closed, but all slack taken out of the cable; on other machines, the marks will line up at the fully opened throttle position, while on still others, a punch mark on the carburetor slide will be aligned with an inspection hole or the top of the carburetor mouth when pump mark alignment is checked. Be sure you read your manual carefully before attempting this adjustment.

Any other lubrication system troubles which will arise should lead you to check ancillary systems other than the pump itself, which is rarely at fault.

Some items which may have to be considered are: poor quality injection oil, a blocked vent in the oil tank cap (if applicable), obstructions in the oil feed lines, and oil or air leaks in the lines or banjo connections.

Be sure that a sufficient supply of oil is in the tank. If applicable, check the oil tank banjo fitting, which is fitted with a filter on some machines, and may therefore become obstructed with foreign matter.

Check that all lines are in good condition, and not cracked or sharply kinked at any place. Be sure that all connections are tight and free of leaks.

Air in the feed lines is often a problem. If the oil tank has ever been emptied due to removal for cleaning or simply running out of oil, the lines should be bled of possible air bubbles before operating the machine.

Some oil pumps are fitted with a bleed screw for this purpose. By loosening this screw and turning the starter plate (if applicable), or by turning over the engine, the oil flow can be observed, and you should let the oil continue to flow out until it is free of air bubbles.

Bleeding can also be accomplished by allowing the engine to idle and holding the oil pump lever fully open for several seconds. This may foul the plugs, so proceed cautiously.

Some oil pumps, such as those used on Yamaha motorcycles have an adjustable stroke, and this may be checked as outlined in the shop manual.

Oil pump bleed screw

If none of the above operations seems to cure the problem, substitute a replacement oil pump. Pumps cannot be repaired.

Decarbonization

Decarbonization is a very important service procedure which must be done regularly and thoroughly if engine performance is to be maintained. The cylinder head, piston crown, exhaust port, and exhaust system should all be decarbonized at the same time.

Each manufacturer has their own recommended service interval for decarbonization, but this is only an approximation since the amount of carbon build-up on engine components is largely dependent upon carburetor settings, the type of two-stroke oil used, riding habits, and several other factors.

A substantial loss of power, especially in the higher gears, is usually a signal that decarbonization is necessary. Also, the presence of carbon deposits $1/16$ in. or more in depth on the exhaust system baffles indicates that service is required.

To perform a routine decarbonization, it is usually only necessary to remove the exhaust system baffle(s), the exhaust pipe(s), and the cylinder head(s). After an extended period, however, removal of the cylinder itself may be required to check or replace the piston rings. These may also become carbon-fouled.

The following items are needed for this procedure:

a. A blunted screwdriver, or broken hacksaw blade, or other unsharpened device for scraping off carbon;

b. A propane torch;

c. Some steel wool and a wire brush;

d. A quantity of solvent;

e. A torque wrench to refit the cylinder head;

f. Replacement parts: Exhaust pipe gasket(s), cylinder head gasket(s), and cylinder base gasket(s) if the cylinder is to be removed. If the cylinder is going to come off, it is recommended that the rings be replaced in any event. Piston rings not only wear rapidly on some machines, they often tend to become carbon-clogged after extended mileage. Rings in this condition are usually impossible to free without breaking them, and replacement is the only solution. The relatively small expense involved in fitting new rings makes this operation worthwhile from a maintenance standpoint.

1. Remove the set screw or bolt which secures the baffle at the rear of the exhaust pipe(s). Grasp the baffle with a large pliers and pull it out.

2. Unbolt the exhause pipe(s) from the cylinder and from the frame and remove it from the machine.

3. Loosen each cylinder head nut or bolt $1/4$ turn at a time, and in a cross pattern, until they are loose, then remove them and the cylinder head. If the head is stuck, tap it with a plastic mallet to free it. Remove the head gasket.

Removing an exhaust pipe baffle

Removing the baffle securing bolt

4. To clean exhaust pipe baffles, first heat them with a propane torch until quite hot. Grasping the baffle with a pliers, tap it against a wooden block to knock off heavy carbon deposits. After it cools, remove any remaining deposits with a wire brush and solvent.

5. Check the amount of carbon buildup on the inside of the exhaust pipe. If substantial, much of it can be removed on some types of exhaust systems by running an old length of drive chain back and forth inside the pipe. Alternatively, a bent up coat hanger should remove most deposits at the engine end of the pipe.

Carbon can sometimes be removed from exhaust systems which are not chromed by heating the pipe itself with a torch and tapping the outside with care with a plastic mallet to break carbon loose.

If exhaust pipe deposits are heavy, and especially if they show a wet, oily appearance, check the adjustments of the carburetor, oil pump, etc.

6. Remove carbon deposits from the combustion chamber using a blunt tool.

CAUTION: *Take care not to scratch the combustion chamber as this may cause localized "hot-spots" during operation.*

Remove as much carbon as possible, then finish up with steel wool and solvent. Leaving stubborn deposits in place is not recommended. Be sure to clean out any carbon chips which may have accumulated in the spark plug hole.

7. Remove carbon from the piston crown in the same manner. The piston must be placed at top dead center while this is done. Still, care must be taken to remove any particles which may become trapped between the piston and cylinder wall. Use compressed air to blow out such particles, or imbed grease between the piston and cylinder. When the piston is lowered in the bore, the grease will retain the particles which may then be wiped off. This procedure must be repeated several times to be effective.

8. To decarbonize the exhaust port, position the piston at the bottom of its stroke. Stuff a clean rag into the cylinder so that it covers the piston and blocks the exhaust port. Use a blunted instrument to scrape carbon from the exhaust port, being careful to prevent particles from entering the cylinder. If possible, parts can be decarbonized with a solvent specifically designed for this purpose, such as Gunk "Hydro-Seal."® Parts to be cleaned are immersed in the fluids for periods ranging

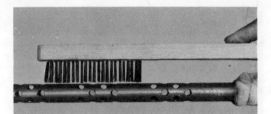

Removing carbon deposits with a wire brush

Scraping out exhaust pipe deposits

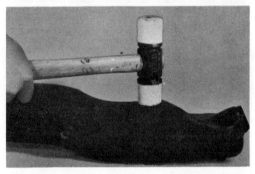

Otherwise inaccessible deposits can sometimes be removed by heating the pipe and tapping on the outside with a plastic mallet

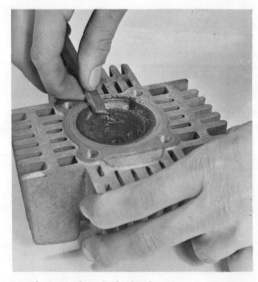

Decarbonizing the cylinder head

Removing deposits from the piston crown

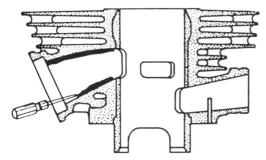

Decarbonizing the exhaust port

from 4 to 24 hours. Be sure the solvent you choose is safe for aluminum.

9. If the cylinder is removed, check that the piston rings are free to move. If they are stuck, they must be freed or replacement is necessary. If the old rings are removed, clean out the ring grooves with a thin screwdriver, once again being careful not to gouge the metal.

10. When assembling, be sure that the cylinder head studs or bolts are clean. Use a torque wrench to tighten the nuts or bolts to the recommended tightness. Tighten the nuts or bolts in a cross pattern and in increments of a few ft lbs.

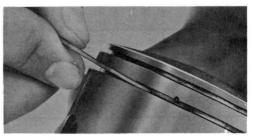

Clean out the ring grooves

Engine Troubleshooting

Problem	Possible Causes	Inspection/Remedy
Abnormal engine noise	Piston slap; piston-to cylinder clearance too great	Check clearance.
	Knock, especially noticable at idle: worn con rod big end bearing	Replace.
	Worn small end bearing	Replace.
	Rumble at idle developing into whine at high rpm: crankshaft main bearings worn or damaged	Replace bearing(s).
	Defective or worn transmission gears or shaft bearings	Inspect and replace worn parts.
	Pinging or spark knock	Timing too advanced; Low quality gasoline.
Engine fails to start (has spark at plug)	No gas in tank; fuel petcock turned off; fuel lines clogged	Refuel; turn on petcock; check for fuel at the carburetor; disconnect and blow out fuel line.
	Engine flooded	Remove spark plug and crank engine to clear it.
	Crankcase flooded	Remove spark plug; shut off petcock; crank engine.
	Ignition timing incorrect	Reset timing.
	Improper fuel/oil mixture	Drain fuel tank and refill with proper mixture.

Engine Troubleshooting (cont.)

Problem	Possible Causes	Inspection/Remedy
Engine fails to start (has spark at plug)	Low or no compression	Blown head gasket; warped head;
		Worn or damaged crankshaft seals; poor seal at crankcase mating surfaces.
		Worn piston rings; worn bore.
	Carburetor adjustments wrong, or carburetor flooded	Adjust carburetor. Check float height.
Engine fails to start (no spark at plug)	Ignition switched off	Turn on ignition.
	Kill button switched off	Reset.
	Spark plug too old; worn or fouled	Clean or replace plug.
	Spark plug heat range too cold	Replace with proper heat range plug.
	Spark plug gap incorrect	Reset gap.
	Spark plug cap resistor defective	Replace cap.
	Plug lead damaged or defective	Replace.
	Ignition coil defective	Replace.
	Condenser defective	Replace.
	Points dirty, pitted, worn, or improperly gapped	Clean and adjust or replace points.
	Breaker points wires disconnected; loose or corroded snap connectors	Check wiring; clean and tighten connections.
	Dead battery (battery-and-coil ignition)	Recharge or replace battery.
	Blown fuse	Replace.
	Loose or corroded battery terminals	Clean and secure terminals.
Engine is hard to start	Worn, dirty, or improperly gapped plug, or plug too cold	Clean or replace and gap plug or replace with correct heat range.
	Points dirty, pitted, or out of adjustment	Clean or replace and gap points.
	Carburetor idle settings wrong; pilot air or fuel passages clogged	Adjust idle settings or clean carburetor.
	Battery low (battery ignition)	Recharge or replace battery.
	Ignition timing out of adjustment	Adjust.
	Spark plug lead cracked or dirty	Replace plug lead.
	Loose or intermittently grounded wires at coil, points, or connectors	Check all connections and condition of wiring.
	Defective coils or condensers	Replace.
	Leaking of crankshaft oil seals or crankcase mating surfaces yielding low compression. Worn rings or cylinder bore	Rebuild.

Engine Troubleshooting (cont.)

Problem	Possible Causes	Inspection/Remedy
Engine idles poorly and misfires under acceleration	Incorrect carburetor adjustment	Adjust.
	Spark plug dirty, fouled, or improperly gapped	Replace or clean plug and set gap.
	Poor wiring connections in ignition circuit	Check connections at plugs, points, and coils.
	Defective ignition coils or condensers	Replace.
	Ignition timing incorrect	Adjust.
	Air leaks at carburetor manifolds	Check as described in Chapter 5.
	Water in carburetors	Drain float bowls and gas tank if necessary.
	Carburetor main jet clogged	Remove and clean.
	Gas tank cap vent clogged	Blow clear.
	Petcock clogged	Clean.
	Float bowl fuel level too low	Check float height.
Spark plugs foul repeatedly	Plug gap too narrow	Adjust to proper value.
	Plug too cold for conditions	Fit plug one heat range hotter.
	Fuel mixture too rich	Adjust carburetor.
	Too much oil in mixture	Check oil pump cable adjustment.
	Piston rings badly worn	Replace.
Engine surges or runs unevenly at standard throttle openings	Air leaks at carburetor manifolds	Refer to Chapter 5.
	Partial seizure occurring due to overheating	See below.
Engine breaks up or misfires while running	Battery dead (battery ignition)	Recharge or replace battery.
	Loose or intermittent connections in the ignition circuit	Check connections.
	Carburetor float level incorrect	Check that float needle is sealing properly; check float height.
Loss of compression or power	Holed or damaged piston	Replace.
	Piston partially seizing	Determine cause.
	Badly worn piston rings	Replace rings.
	Blown or leaking head gasket	Check gasket.
	Muffler or exhaust port carbon clogged	Decarbonize.
	Air filter clogged with dirt	Clean or replace.
Poor low-speed operation	Incorrect ignition timing	Adjust timing.
	Poor breaker point contact	Adjust or replace points.
	Defective coil or condenser	Replace.
	Carburetor float level incorrect	Adjust float level.
	Pilot screw not adjusted properly	Adjust carburetor.
	Spark plug gap too great	Adjust.

Engine Troubleshooting (cont.)

Problem	Possible Causes	Inspection/Remedy
Poor high speed operation	Ignition timing incorrect	Adjust timing.
	Spark plug gap too small	Adjust gap.
	Defective ignition coil	Replace.
	Carburetor float level incorrect	Adjust float level.
	Low compression	Check head gasket for leakage as well as crankcase mating surfaces. Check rings and cylinder for wear.
	Engine carbon fouled; exhaust pipe carbon-fouled or broken	Decarbonize engine and exhaust pipe; check exhaust pipe for leaks.
	Pipe loose at cylinder	Tighten.
	Weak breaker point spring	Replace points.
	Air cleaner dirty or clogged	Clean or replace element.
Engine partially seizes or slows after high-speed operation	Spark plug too hot	Use plugs one heat range colder.
	Piston seizure	Determine cause.
	Carburetor mixture too lean	Take plug readings. Adjust carburetor as needed.
	Insufficient lubricant in mixture	Check oil pump cable adjustment or gas/oil mixture percentage.
	Air leaks at carburetor manifolds	Check manifold.
Engine overheats	Heavy carbon deposits on piston, exhaust port, and muffler	Decarbonize.
	Ignition timing too retarded	Adjust timing.
Engine detonates or preignites	Spark plugs too hot for application	Replace with plugs one heat range colder.
	Ignition timing too advanced	Adjust.
	Insufficient oil in fuel	Adjust oil pump cable or fuel/oil mixture percentage. Bleed oil line if necessary.
	Carburetor mixture too lean	Adjust.
	Air leaks at carb manifolds	Refer to Chapter 5.
	Engine carbon-choked	Decarbonize head, piston, and muffler.
	Fuel octane rating too low	Use fuel with higher octane rating.
Engine backfires or kick-starter kicks back	Ignition timing too advanced	Adjust.
Rapid piston and cylinder wear	Ineffective or leaking air filter	Clean or replace filter element.

4 · Four-Stroke Troubleshooting

Starting the Engine

If you aren't familiar with the machine it may just be that you are doing something wrong. It's amazing how much trouble, for example, a big single can give to someone who's only used to riding twins.

Make sure you are going through the starting drill correctly. Turn the fuel tap to the ON position, provided you know that there is enough fuel in the tank, or to the reserve position. If you aren't sure which is correct, disconnect the fuel line and check for fuel flow. If the machine is equipped

Priming an Amal type carburetor

with Amal type carbs that have "ticklers," depress the button until gas begins to run out, then close the choke or air slide, or do what ever is necessary to enrich the mixture. Kick the engine through a couple of times with the key off and the throttle opened, or use the electric starter button (with the key on and the kill switch in the OFF position) to spin the engine through and loosen everything up. Now turn on the key, open the throttle ⅛ of its full travel and the spark advance (if applicable) about half-way, and get ready to do some kicking. Use all your weight on the lever, and straighten your kicking leg out on the way down. If you have a single with a compression release, depress the kick starter until the piston is felt to be approaching its strongest point of compression; then operate the release, while slowly

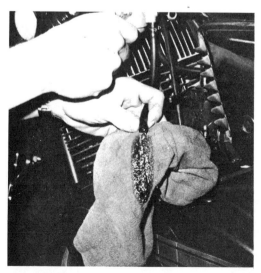

Checking for fuel flow at the petcock

moving the starter lever a couple of inches, until the piston is past compression. This should be done each time before you kick over a single, but don't worry, it will become like second nature in no time at all.

A lot of riders tend to yank open the throttle the first time the engine sounds like it may start, and they wind up with a flooded engine. To clear it out, just open the throttle wide and spin the engine through a couple times, or let it sit for a while; it will dry out faster if you remove the spark plugs. If the bike still won't start try to bump start it. Get a good run going, with the clutch pulled in and the transmission in the lowest gear that won't lock up the rear wheel; then hop on and pop the clutch as you hit the seat. If, after doing this for a while, you can't get it started, you better start troubleshooting.

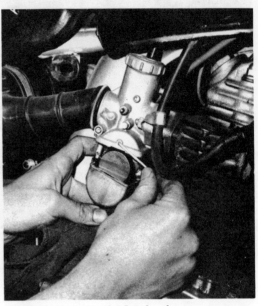

Checking for fuel in the float bowl

Engine Does Not Start

Systematically make sure that all the necessary systems are working, and do a tune-up if you are uncertain of the machine's state of tune. Is turning the key on completing the circuit and getting juice to the primary ignition circuit? If the bike is battery operated, the lights and horn

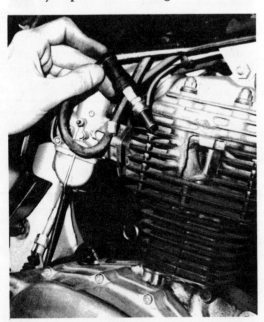

Checking for spark at the plug

should work; however, if the battery is discharged it may make starting difficult. If the machine doesn't have a battery you can ground a spark plug, while still in its cap, against the cylinder head and kick the bike over. Doing this isn't a bad idea with battery equipped machines as it removes all doubt. If you are getting juice you should be able to see a spark. If everything checks out and you are sure you are getting spark go on and check the fuel system.

If your machine has Amal type carbs equipped with ticklers you can be fairly certain the carburetor is doing its job if tickling produces a gas flow. If the carb has no provision such as this, remove the float bowl drain plug, or the whole float bowl, and see if there is gas there. If so, the chances are good that the carbs are alright, so the only remaining system is the mechanical.

Provided the machine has compression, and that the clutch is working so the engine turns over, the bike should start. If the clutch isn't working you should be able to tell just by kicking the bike over. To make sure, put the bike in gear and roll it to check the clutch. You should be able to hear the engine turn over when the clutch is engaged. The next thing to check is the compression. You should be able to tell if it has reasonable compression by kicking the engine through, or by putting

Compression tests provide a glimpse behind the cylinder walls

your finger over the spark plug hole and seeing if there is enough compression to push your finger away, but of course using a compression gauge eliminates much of the guesswork. A compression check will tell you whether or not you have trouble in the top end. Compression pressure in the cylinder should be about 140 psi. To obtain an accurate reading, make sure the compression gauge is properly seated in the spark plug hole and hold the throttle open all the way while cranking the engine until the needle on the gauge stops advancing. Low readings can indicate a leaking head gasket, valves that are too tightly adjusted, stuck, or burnt, or worn piston rings.

If you obtain a low reading, squirt oil into the spark plug hole and recheck the compression. If the pressure increases significantly, this indicates that the rings are worn. If it does not increase and there is evidence of a cylinder head gasket leak,

the chances are that the head gasket is blown and must be replaced. If there is no evidence of a bad head gasket or worn rings, the process of elimination points to the valves. To make certain that it is not merely insufficient valve clearance that is doing you in, back out the valve adjusters a couple of turns and recheck the compression. Do this even if you have adjusted the valves because you may have been mistaken. If you still don't have good compression, button it up and get ready for a top end overhaul.

By now you hopefully know which system is sabotaging your attempt to go riding, so now it's time to concentrate on finding exactly what is wrong.

CHECKING THE ELECTRICAL SYSTEM

Electrical problems are usually very subtle, and unless you get lucky and find something blatant like an electrical connector that's worked itself loose, you'll have to carefully check over every inch of wiring. You should have an appropriate wiring diagram and a test light that's suited to your needs. If your bike has a magneto ignition, or if it's stone dead (and

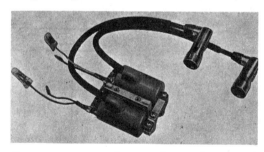

Snap connectors, such as on these coils, can work loose leaving you with no spark

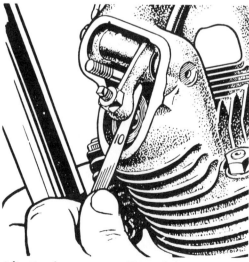

Adjusting the tappets on a Triumph

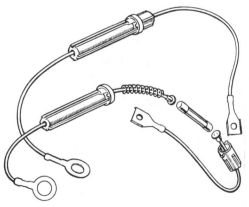

The fuse is usually located near the battery

of course you already checked the fuses now didn't you?) you'll need a light with a self-contained power source that can check for continuity. If you've got a battery ignition model you can get by with a simple test light since it will tell you where the current stops.

Always start at the point where you don't have juice and work toward the power source. Some of the things to look for are dirty, corroded, or loose connections; burn marks that may indicate a short; heavily pitted or burnt points (which probably mean a bad condenser); frayed wires at rubbing points (i.e. at the steering head and at the alternator or magneto); bad brushes (generator equipped machines); or poor grounding (many English bikes have the lighting circuit grounded to the frame). There may be hidden damage, such as a wire that has broken in the middle of the wiring harness. If something like this is suspected use a test light with a self-contained power source to test for continuity through the wire. Jiggle the wire to make sure it isn't an intermittent short that only occurs when the bike is vibrating. A word about switches—on many Japanese machines the switch assemblies are very delicate, and repeated removal and installation can loosen up the leads just enough to cause an intermittent short. If you get

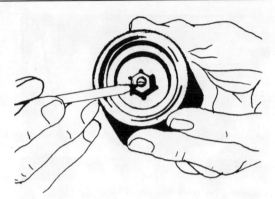

The carbon contact on this magneto's kill button disintegrated

power sometimes, and then sometimes it cuts out (like after you start the machine) suspect the kill switch. On multicylinder bikes like the Honda fours, such a situation can make it possible to have two cylinders firing normally, and the other two firing intermittently or not at all. In fact, whenever you have an ignition problem keep the ignition switch and kill button in mind.

To get an idea of how the electrical system operates, let's break it down. The ignition circuit runs from the power source to the spark plug and is the one which has failed when there is no juice anywhere on the machine. The lighting circuit feeds off the battery and directs the current to all of the accessories. On most battery equipped models this system can fail without affecting the ignition circuit.

The ignition circuit can be further broken down into the high and low tension systems. The high tension system consists of the coil, the spark plug's high tension lead, and the spark plug, and is called the high tension system because the coil boosts the relatively low voltage produced

Testing wiring harness for continuity

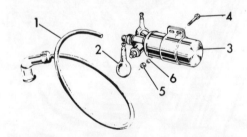

A H-D Sprint high tension system

1. Spark plug cable	4. Mounting screw
2. Terminal cover (2)	5. Nut
3. Spark coil	6. Washer

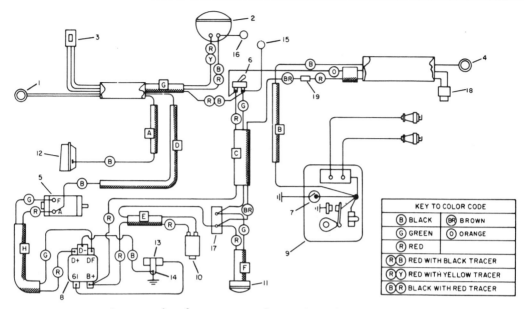

A magneto based system wiring diagram (1969 Sportster XLCH)

A. Conduit (one wire)—black
B. Conduit (one wire)—black
C. Conduit (two wires)—red and green
D. Conduit (one wire)—black
E. Conduit (two wires)—red
F. Conduit (two wires)—red and green
G. Conduit (three wires)—red wire with black tracer, red
   wire with yellow tracer, black wire with red tracer
H. Conduit (two wires)—green and red

1. Horn switch—two black wires
2. Headlamp—black wire with red tracer and red wire
   with yellow tracer
3. Headlamp dimmer switch—red wire with black tracer,
   red wire with yellow tracer, black wire with red
   tracer
4. Ignition cut-out switch—black wire
5. Generator
   F terminal—green wire
   A terminal—black wire

6. Light switch—red, green and red with black tracer
   wires
7. Ignition ground switch lock
8. Voltage regulator—
   DF terminal—green wire
   D+ terminal—red wire and condenser wire
   B+ terminal—two red wires
   D— terminal—black wire
9. Magneto—black wire
10. Stoplight rear switch—two red wires
11. Tail and stop lamp—red and green wires
12. Horn—black wire
13. Capacitor—black wire connected to regulator D—
    terminal
14. Grounding screw—black wire
15. Speedometer lamp
16. High beam indicator lamp
17. Terminal strip
18. Stoplamp front switch (late 1969)
19. Connector (late 1969)

by the alternator, generator, magneto, or whatever to the very high voltage necessary for a spark to jump the gap at the electrode. The low tension system starts at the battery, on battery equipped models, or at the magneto and runs to the coil. In between there may be an alternator or generator to recharge the battery (if applicable) and provide the current demanded by the engine's speed, and there may be other options such as an ignition switch, a kill switch or button, or an electric starter.

Somewhere along the line provision must be made to interrupt the flow of juice so the spark plug will fire at the correct time. Traditionally this is accomplished through use of a contact breaker and con-denser. The condenser stores up juice while the points are closed, and then when the breaker cam opens the points, the current is free to flow and the charge which has been building up in the condenser is released. When a condenser goes bad it leaks current and then the charge isn't strong enough to jump the plug gap effectively. It is this leaking current which burns and pits points because it is never cut off as it should be.

Try and localize the problem before you start tearing things apart. If you can, for example, determine that the problem is at the point plate you may find that it's just a bad ground or something cheap like that. If you work with a wiring diagram you

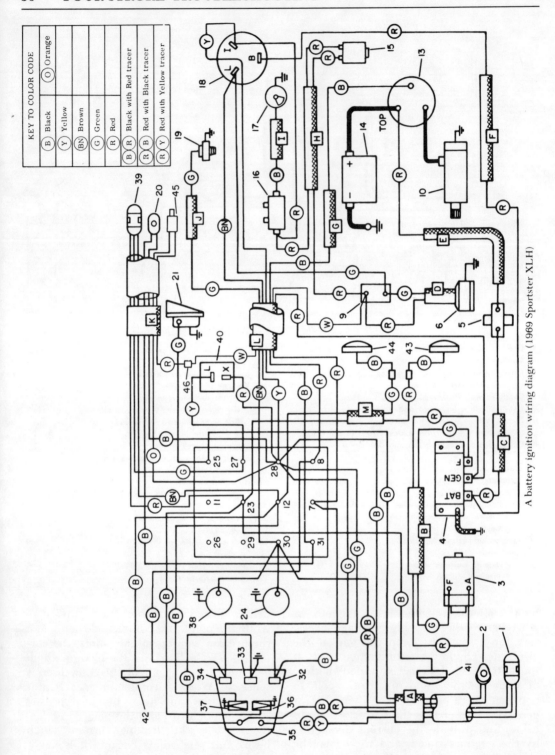

A battery ignition wiring diagram (1969 Sportster XLH)

KEY TO COLOR CODE

B	Black
Y	Yellow
BN	Brown
G	Green
R	Red
O	Orange
R·R	Black with Red tracer
R·B	Red with Black tracer
R·Y	Red with Yellow tracer

A. Handlebar (five wires)—red wire with black tracer, black wire with red tracer, red wire with yellow tracer, and 2 black wires
B. Conduit (two wires)—green and red
C. Conduit (one wire)—red
D. Conduit (two wires)—red and green

E. Conduit (one wire)—red
F. Conduit (one wire)—red
G. Conduit (one wire)—black
H. Conduit (two wires)—red
I. Conduit (one wire)—green
J. Conduit (one wire)—green

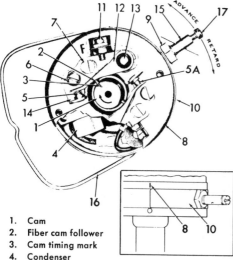

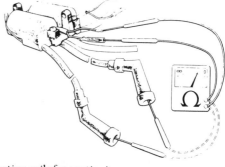

Testing coils for continuity

1. Cam
2. Fiber cam follower
3. Cam timing mark
4. Condenser
5. Front cylinder contact points
5A. Rear cylinder contact points
6. Lock screw
7. Adjusting screw
8. Timing mark
9. Adjusting stud lock nut
10. Timing adjusting plate
11. Wire stud screw
12. Circuit breaker lever
13. Pivot stud
14. Contact point and support
15. Timing adjusting stud
16. Cover retainer
17. Control wire lock screw

A contact breaker in use on Harley-Davidson Twins

should be able to figure out which component leads to attach the test light for testing continuity. If you can find out for sure which part is the troublemaker you can replace the part and see if the problem is resolved. Be sure before you start swapping parts though, because most parts men won't take back an electrical part once its been on the bike. Consult Chapter 6 for more detailed information on the subject.

CHECKING THE FUEL SYSTEM

As mentioned previously, the first thing to check for here is fuel delivery. Blockage of a fuel line or carburetor jet may come on suddenly if loose matter lodges in a passageway. If the bike is running when the problem comes on it will almost al-

K. Handlebar (5 wires)—red, brown, green and 2 black wires
L. Conduit (five wires)—brown, yellow, black, red and green
M. Conduit (2 wires)—red and green

1. Headlamp dimmer switch
2. Horn switch
3. Generator F and A terminals
4. Regulator
    BAT terminal
    GEN terminal
    F terminal
5. Overload circuit breaker
6. Tail lamp
7. Terminal
8. Terminal
9. Junction terminal board
10. Starter motor
11. Terminal—not used with standard wiring
12. Terminal
13. Starter solenoid
14. Battery
15. Stoplight rear switch
16. Ignition coil
17. Circuit breaker
18. Ignition-light switch
19. Oil signal light switch

20. Starter button
21. Horn
22. Terminal plate
23. Terminal
24. Speedometer light
25. Terminal
26. Terminal—not used with standard wiring
27. Terminal—not used with standard wiring
28. Terminal
29. Terminal—not used with standard wiring
30. Terminal
31. Terminal
32. Oil signal light
33. High beam indicator light
34. Generator indicator light
35. Headlamp
36. Left direction signal pilot lamp
37. Right direction signal pilot lamp
38. Tachometer light
39. Direction signal switch
40. Direction signal flasher
41. Left front direction lamp
42. Right front direction lamp
43. Left rear direction lamp
44. Right rear direction lamp
45. Stoplamp front switch (late 1969)
46. Connector (late 1969)

ways begin to sputter and wheeze before it cuts out, but if the machine has been in storage for a while it may have become blocked by deposits and consequently will fail to deliver enough fuel for combustion. Two items which often go unnoticed are the air cleaner and the gas cap vent. A clogged or oil soaked air cleaner will cause so excessively rich a mixture that the engine can't breathe well enough for combustion to occur, and if the vent is plugged, air can't get in to replace the gas which is used, and a partial vacuum is created which prevents the fuel from flowing.

The first thing to determine in instances of fuel starvation is at what point the fuel flow is blocked. Disconnect the fuel line at the petcock and turn on the tap. If the fuel won't flow at this time, remove and inspect the petcock. Many models have a fuel filter located on top of the petcock which can become clogged by impurities in the gas or by rust particles from inside the tank. The petcock should also be cleaned out with a suitable solvent or replaced if defective. Another possibility, although somewhat remote, is that the fuel line itself may be clogged. This of course can be easily remedied by poking something through it.

If the problem still eludes you it's time to pull apart the carburetor. Try tapping on the float bowl with a wrench before tearing into the carb because it may just

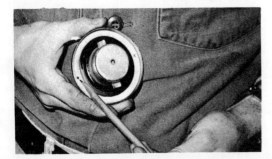

Check for a clogged gas cap vent

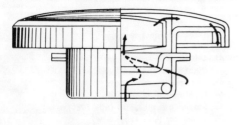

Air flow through a Honda gas cap

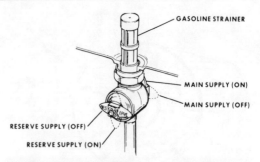

A diaphragm type petcock with fuel strainer

Removing the petcock sediment bowl

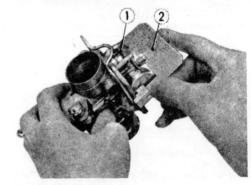

Adjusting the float level on a Keihin carb

1. Float
2. Float level gauge

be a hung-up float, and make certain the choke is working correctly. It helps to have an exploded diagram or a step-by-step list of procedures (such as is found in the individual Chilton *Repair and Tune-Up Guides*), but if you take your time and are attentive to how it came apart you shouldn't have any trouble. Use a light hand on the wrenches, especially on Japanese carbs, and avoid scoring, gouging, or in any way deforming the parts. Clean it out carefully with a suitable solvent and then put it back together using all the parts which come in a carb rebuilding kit. Take special care in adjusting the float level, and make sure the float and valve move freely. It's not necessary to install a kit, but once the gaskets are used they may leak and cause an excessively lean mixture. Consult Chapter 5 for additional information.

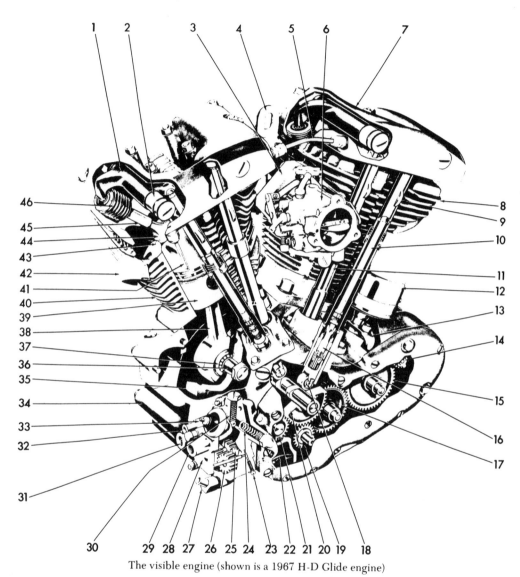

The visible engine (shown is a 1967 H-D Glide engine)

1. Rocker arm	17. Intermediate gear	33. Oil pressure switch
2. Rocker arm shaft	18. Tappet and roller assembly	34. Crankcase
3. Carburetor insulator	19. Pinion gear	35. Flywheel
4. Engine mounting bracket	20. Cam gear	36. Crankpin
5. Oil line	21. Breather gear	37. Connecting rod roller bearing
6. Carburetor	22. Breather screen	38. Connecting rod
7. Rocker arm cover	23. Chain oiler screw	39. Piston
8. Cylinder head	24. By-pass valve	40. Cylinder
9. Push rod cover keeper	25. Oil feed pump drive gears	41. Overhead oil line
10. Push rod	26. Oil scavenger drive gears	42. Exhaust port
11. Push rod cover	27. Oil feed nipple	43. Exhaust valve seat
12. Circuit breaker (timer)	28. Oil pump cover	44. Exhaust valve
13. Clamp	29. Oil return nipple	45. Exhaust valve guide
14. Generator drive gear	30. Check valve	46. Valve spring
15. Idler gear	31. Breather outlet	
16. Hydraulic lifter	32. Chain oil return	

CHECKING THE MECHANICAL SYSTEM

Mechanical problems generally come on slowly, and assuming your engine hasn't expired with the proverbial big bang, it probably indicated something was going wrong before it stopped running. An engine can't break down due to mechanical difficulties overnight if it was running the day before, unless it breaks while you're kicking it over, so try to remember if it was making any unusual noises when last run.

It should be very easy to localize the problem to one of the following areas; top end, bottom end, clutch, or transmission. Running a compression check, as described previously, should tell you what's happening in the top end, and cranking the bike over will let you know if the bottom end is free. Kicking the bike will let you know right away if the kick starter mechanism is damaged, and whether or not the engine turns over will say something about the state of the clutch. The gearbox, unless totally wiped out, shouldn't keep a machine from starting.

Poor Engine Performance

HARD STARTING OR ERRATIC PERFORMANCE

If you've got an old machine that has never run quite right, or if your machine is equipped with high performance parts this section is not for you. No amount of tuning can smooth out a rough idle caused by a worn carburetor slide, or make a machine with a hot cam idle well. What we're dealing with here is the machine that has been getting progressively worse, or one that suddenly becomes difficult to start, and consequently also probably runs erratically.

If your machine has a battery ignition and the battery is weak or poorly grounded you'll have trouble getting it started because the battery is supposed to provide the impetus to get things rolling. A quick trip to the gas station, and a subsequent check with a hydrometer, will indicate whether or not the battery is sufficiently charged. If the reading of any cell is below 1.200 at 68° F, the battery should be recharged using a low-output charger,

such as a trickle charger, according to the manufacturer's directions. A good battery should read between 1.260–1.280 at 68° F. Make sure the terminals are clean and secure.

Next, take a close look at the spark plug's condition and heat range. Maybe it's too cold a plug for the engine or climate, or possibly it wasn't even designed for use in your particular kind of engine.

How is the carburetor idle mixture screw (if applicable) adjusted? It is possible that the adjustment may have been changed by engine vibration, or the needle's seat may have been damaged by a heavy handed mechanic somewhere along the way. If the machine has a preset idle circuit it may be partially blocked by gum residues or foreign particles, and in this case an overhaul, or at least a thorough cleaning may be in order.

The next thing to check is the ignition timing which normally changes with wear of the points and the cam fiber rubbing block. Dirt or oil, or perhaps a cracked rubbing block may cause an intermittent miss so make sure the point plate is well grounded and clean. While you are at it take a look at the automatic advance unit (if applicable) and the cam itself. The springs on the advance mechanism may be worn or damaged, or the cam may be scored from many miles of use without sufficient lubrication. Even though the advance unit looks fine it may be slightly off, so you should first static-time the engine and then check the advanced timing with a strobe light. If the bike kicks back at you when you try to start it, look immediately to the spark advancer.

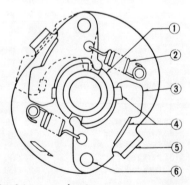

Spark advance mechanism

1. Breaker cam
2. Governor spring
3. Governor weight
4. Rubber bushing
5. Stopper
6. Governor weight support

While you're checking out the timing, how about the points? If they are burned, worn or pitted, they should be dressed up or replaced. If they are badly pitted or burned they should be replaced as a matter of course, and the condenser should be held suspect. You probably won't have access to a factory tester, so if you think the condenser is faulty you should replace it and note whether there is a difference in performance. If the points are oily it is necessary to locate the source of the oil leak and repair it, or the points are just going to act up again soon. All of the

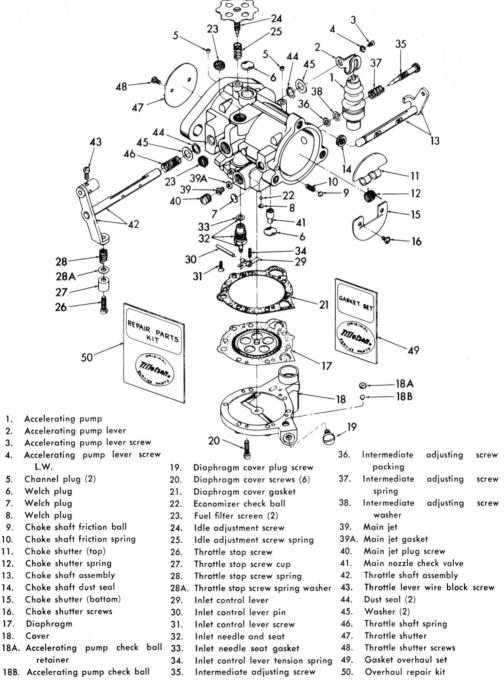

1.	Accelerating pump	
2.	Accelerating pump lever	
3.	Accelerating pump lever screw	
4.	Accelerating pump lever screw L.W.	
5.	Channel plug (2)	
6.	Welch plug	
7.	Welch plug	
8.	Welch plug	
9.	Choke shaft friction ball	
10.	Choke shaft friction spring	
11.	Choke shutter (top)	
12.	Choke shutter spring	
13.	Choke shaft assembly	
14.	Choke shaft dust seal	
15.	Choke shutter (bottom)	
16.	Choke shutter screws	
17.	Diaphragm	
18.	Cover	
18A.	Accelerating pump check ball retainer	
18B.	Accelerating pump check ball	

19.	Diaphragm cover plug screw
20.	Diaphragm cover screws (6)
21.	Diaphragm cover gasket
22.	Economizer check ball
23.	Fuel filter screen (2)
24.	Idle adjustment screw
25.	Idle adjustment screw spring
26.	Throttle stop screw
27.	Throttle stop screw cup
28.	Throttle stop screw spring
28A.	Throttle stop screw spring washer
29.	Inlet control lever
30.	Inlet control lever pin
31.	Inlet control lever screw
32.	Inlet needle and seat
33.	Inlet needle seat gasket
34.	Inlet control lever tension spring
35.	Intermediate adjusting screw

36.	Intermediate adjusting screw packing
37.	Intermediate adjusting screw spring
38.	Intermediate adjusting screw washer
39.	Main jet
39A.	Main jet gasket
40.	Main jet plug screw
41.	Main nozzle check valve
42.	Throttle shaft assembly
43.	Throttle lever wire block screw
44.	Dust seal (2)
45.	Washer (2)
46.	Throttle shaft spring
47.	Throttle shutter
48.	Throttle shutter screws
49.	Gasket overhaul set
50.	Overhaul repair kit

A Harley-Davidson model HD diaphragm type carburetor

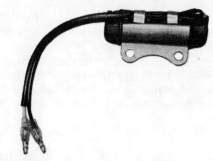

Condenser

A dirty air cleaner can rob your machine of horsepower

above information also pertains to magneto equipped machines, and in addition you should also pay attention to the condition of the slip ring. It too, like the points, must remain clean in order to properly perform its function.

By now you've hit on all tune-up points except the valves. Valves normally work themselves loose, not tight, so if the bike has begun to run progressively worse it's not valves. The valves could be slowly burning, or their seats or guides could be in need of attention; this should show up during a compression check. However, if you just tuned the bike and it has become hard to start, and it won't run at high revs, the valves may be adjusted too tight, so adjust them carefully and see what happens.

Another thing a compression check may indicate is that the rings are worn, the head gasket leaks, or the piston has a hole in it. Any one of these indicates that it soon will be time to do a top end job. If the rings are worn you'll know it by the voluminous blue smoke, and if the gasket leaks, the spark plugs will look burnt.

Overheated spark plugs may also indicate a leak at the intake manifold. An easy way to determine if this is the case, and to locate the leak, is to squirt some solvent on the manifold while the bike is running.

If the idle smooths out it was leaking, and the bubbles will reveal the leak.

Two more remote possibilities which would most likely only pertain to poorly maintained older machines are a clogged air cleaner or exhaust baffle. If the air filter element becomes oil soaked or filled with dirt it can restrict intake air flow so much that the machine becomes a hard starter and a poor performer. A clogged muffler can also cause hard starting because it creates excessive back pressure. The solution in either case is to remove the offending item and clean it thoroughly or replace it.

Lastly, if the machine has been stored for a while and then is put into service without being properly serviced, there may be gum deposits in the jets, or the float may hang up. The solution here is a thorough cleaning or an overhaul.

ENGINE DIES WHEN THROTTLE IS OPENED

Theoretically, you should be able to crack open the throttle of a well tuned machine as fast as you'd like without causing the engine to bog, but in practice this is not usually the case. On many machines, someone with an exceptionally fast throttle hand is going to have problems regardless of how well the machine is tuned, so these hints are more for the rider who notices that throttle response has become slower than normal.

The first thing to check is the state of tune of the machine. Although the problem is probably related to the carburetor, bogging or stumbling may be caused by retarded ignition timing. This would cause a decrease in performance, but still allow the engine to start easily. While you are tuning, take special care to get the car-

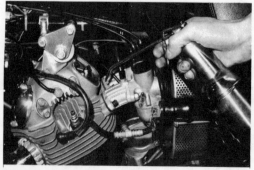

Checking for air leaks at the intake manifold

buretor settings as close as possible to factory specifications, because this symptom is often caused by too rich a mixture. Also, the idle speed of the engine is very important for fast throttle response.

Next, check the choke assembly for proper operation. If the linkage is improperly adjusted it may cause the engine to be partially choked at all times. Also, make sure nothing is holding the choke linkage in a partially choked position. This was found to be a problem on some Sportsters on which the air cleaner was keeping the lever from reaching its seat fully.

If you still haven't found the problem it's time to overhaul the carburetor. Maybe the idle jet is partially clogged or the needle is in the wrong position. It is possible that an air leak at the intake manifold has been compensated for by installing the wrong size jets, and therefore the vacuum is reduced too much to immediately provide enough fuel.

ENGINE MISFIRES

If your engine misses off the line, but runs fine the rest of the time, incorrect carburetion is probably the reason. Most likely the reason is too rich a low speed mixture which is indicated by a rough idle, black exhaust smoke, and misfiring upon application of the throttle. It is necessary to lean out the mixture to relieve this situation. If this problem presents itself only during the early stages of the day's ride it may be due to water in the float bowl or fuel strainer. What happens is that water is drawn into the carb before the gas, and this causes the engine to misfire since water won't burn. Misfiring at the low end can also be caused by a clogged air cleaner or a dirty spark plug, but in most cases this will result in poor performance throughout the engine's range.

If you have a miss that occurs at a certain rpm regardless of what gear you are in, the first thing to suspect is a defective automatic advance mechanism (if applicable) that operates correctly up to a certain point. Examine the springs of the advance mechanism carefully, and replace them, or the unit, if they appear stretched or damaged. If the machine is equipped with a battery ignition the problem may be improper timing. A simple adjustment will indicate if this was the problem. Static timing doesn't tell you anything about how the engine is timed once the automatic advance comes into play, so static time the engine, then strobe time it and compare results.

One other possibility is that an excessively rich mixture is causing "eight cycling," but this is unlikely. In any event your spark plug should tell you if the mixture is so rich that such a condition could exist.

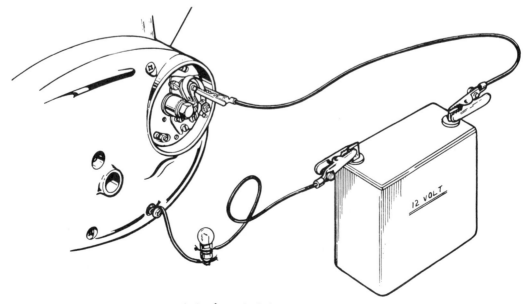

A simple static timing arrangement

Checking the advanced timing

Completely erratic misfiring is most likely due to an electrical problem somewhere. On machines with a battery ignition, look at the ignition system from the battery to the plugs, but don't overlook the ignition and kill switches, and on a magneto system check everything including the ammeter, turn signals, stop light switch, etc.

If the machine misfires while running uphill, it may be caused by several things. First, check the plug; it may be breaking down from overheating because the gap is set wrong or because it has the wrong heat range. Improper mixture caused by too large a main jet, or by a clogged air cleaner may be the reason, or the engine just may be really out of time. A more obscure possibility may lie in the octane rating of the gas you are using. High compression engines need high octane fuel to really get it on, so don't sell out your engine's performance for mere pennies.

High rpm misses, and by this we mean on the left side of the red line, are difficult to cure because there are so many possible contributing factors. In many cases the culprit will be a component that is losing its edge, and therefore only begins to act up when pushed to its limits. Plugs, condensers, coils, or leaking high tension leads are some of the more common causes, but the possibility of damaged parts shouldn't be overlooked.

One of the first things to check is the carburetion. The main jet controls mixture at high speeds, so if you've got the wrong size jet, or if the jet is damaged, you're going to have problems. Other carburetor related problems are a dirty air cleaner, improper float adjustment (probably too low), or an improperly adjusted choke. It is possible that the problem is caused by

air leaks at the intake manifold or by a stopped up exhaust pipe, but these sorts of things would show up at lower revs, and might even keep the machine from ever reaching high rpms.

If it is an electrical problem, arriving at a solution may be more difficult. A spark plug that has fouled before may never get it on at high revs again. Check the plugs and replace them if they are worn out or fouled. Is the heat range correct for the conditions? Is the gap too large for the spark to make the jump at high speeds?

If the problem is caused by a bad condenser, the points ought to tell you because they will probably pit quickly. The only way to determine if this is the case is to replace the condenser and see what happens. The same applies for a coil. Unless your dealer has a factory tester you'll probably have to substitute a new part and check the results. If the high tension lead is leaking, or if the plug cap isn't on tight, there might not be enough juice getting to the plug at high speeds. Run your fingers along the high tension lead while the engine is running. If your fingers tingle replace the lead and/or cap.

If you haven't found the solution yet it's got to be mechanical. A burnt or bent valve, a tired advance mechanism, or an air leak at the exhaust pipe could cause a high speed miss. If all else fails tune it up carefully again and make sure the valves aren't too tight.

One of the most annoying misses occurs when the engine is backing down from high revs. This sounds more like a pop in the pipes than a miss, and can be very difficult to solve. A slightly overrich mixture, lean, or unbalanced manifold vacuum (on the multi-cylindered super bikes) are the most common causes, but it also may be caused by a pinhole in the exhaust system or by a chipped valve seat. In any case, the plugs will probably look normal and it isn't dangerous—just a nuisance.

POOR GENERAL PERFORMANCE

Any machine which is left at idle too long, or which is run very slowly in traffic, will build up surpluses of fuel and carbon that will cause low speed stumbling. This can usually be cleared up by a couple of high rpm shifts, unless of course the plugs have become irrevocably fouled in which case they will have to be pulled and cleaned or replaced.

If your machine always runs poorly at low speeds, but runs fine once you open it up, look to the carburetor for the solution. A proper tune-up according to the manufacturer's specifications is in order, or, if the bike is loaded with high performance goodies, a little experimenting with the idle circuit may help some. Don't forget to check the needle adjustment.

If you've eliminated carburetion as the source of the troubles, check the timing. More than likely a good tuning will fix things up.

If the engine just doesn't have any punch at high speeds the first thing to do is to run through your maintenance and tune-up procedures. A machine with a clogged air cleaner, dirty points, a poor state of tune, or a weak battery is not going to give all it can, so check these things first.

If, after making sure everything is as it should be, the machine still doesn't want to get out of its own way, look for mechanical weaknesses. An older bike may have weak valve springs, worn rings or poorly seated valves that are robbing it of compression, or a clutch that slips when heavily stressed.

If the machine won't perform throughout the power range, and you've made certain that everything is just as it should be, look for the ridiculous like an oil pump that isn't clearing the sump, or brakes that are dragging. Other things that can slow you down are bad wheel bearings, a dry or overtightened drive chain, or something rubbing against the tires.

ENGINE VIBRATION

Vibration is a bad sign and its cause should be determined before everything falls apart. The most common cause, outside of those possibilities dealt with in Chapter 8 is loose or damaged engine mounts, so check these out carefully.

Other possible causes, and these will usually come on gradually (or immediately following some work that wasn't done right), are an incorrectly assembled clutch, improper ignition timing, a worn crankshaft, or bad main bearings. The solution should be sought immediately as all of these are serious, and will probably be

shortly followed by some sort of massive failure.

EXCESSIVE OIL CONSUMPTION

It is impossible to dogmatically place a limit on when oil consumption becomes excessive because each machine has its own characteristics. Some early Nortons, for example were oil burners because they did not use valve seals, but that doesn't mean they are less of a machine than a perfectly oil tight Honda. The oil we're concerned with here is that which is used up by the engine, not that which winds up on the garage floor or the rear wheel. You are alright until you begin to get a blue smoke from the pipes, an oil soaked spark plug, and amazing deposits on the exhaust pipe and baffle.

The first thing to consider is what kind of oil you are using. If you try to run a lightweight oil in a Harley during the summer you are going to burn up more oil than necessary. If the breather pipe is clogged you are going to use up a lot also. These things don't present any problem, but if it's bad valve guides or seals, bad rings, or a bad pump check valve, it's going to mean some work.

If all of a sudden you don't have any oil pressure, it's because either the pump is jammed, the pressure check valve is clogged, or the pump drive is broken. If the pressure drops off gradually it may be due to excessive clearances in the parts which are supplied under pressure. In either case you shouldn't try to run the engine as serious damage will result.

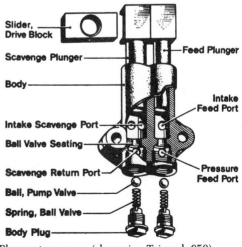

Plunger type pump (shown is a Triumph 650)

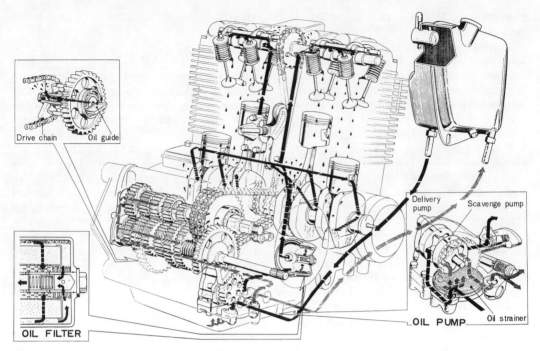

Drive chain   Oil guide

Delivery pump   Scavenge pump

OIL PUMP   Oil strainer

OIL FILTER

Dry-sump lubrication system (shown is a Honda 750)

The first thing to consider is what kind of oil you are using. If you try to run a lightweight oil in a Harley during the summer you are going to burn up more oil than necessary. If the breather pipe is clogged you are going to use up a lot also. These things don't present any problem, but if it's bad valve guides or seals, bad rings, or a bad pump check valve, it's going to mean some work.

If all of a sudden you don't have any oil pressure, it's because either the pump is jammed, the pressure check valve is clogged, or the pump drive is broken. If the pressure drops off gradually it may be due to excessive clearances in the parts which are supplied under pressure. In either case you shouldn't try to run the engine as serious damage will result.

A relatively common problem, especially with machines whose oil has not been changed as often as it should have been, is a lack of return to the tank. The causes of this will vary, but the symptoms, excessive consumption, heavy exhaust smoking, and a visible lack of return to the tank, are fairly universal.

Usually this is caused by a failure of the return pump, a blocked oil line, a stuck check valve, a blown gasket, or something else in the return system. Another possibility is that the feed pump has failed; this can be differentiated from a return failure because the smoking and consumption won't be present.

An intermittently stuck check valve is a fairly common problem, and can be caused by something as simple as a small piece of grit around the ball's seat. The only way to relieve a situation like this is to repeatedly flush the system. Generally this is not immediately dangerous, but may seem so because the oil trapped in the sump will be burned.

ENGINE OVERHEATING AND SEIZURE

These are interrelated because overheating causes, or usually immediately precedes, seizure. A bike usually seizes after being run with an insufficient amount of oil. What happens is that the piston expands because the oil isn't present to carry away the heat and to lubricate the cylinder walls. Eventually the piston expands so much that it can no longer move freely in the cylinder and the engine stops . . . suddenly. If you should ever feel the engine start to lose power, and if it should

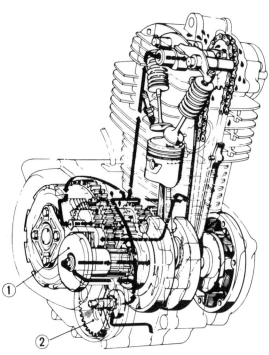

Wet sump lubrication system (shown is a Honda 100)

1. Oil filter   2. Oil pump

start feeling abnormally tight, move your hand over to the clutch lever and back off on the throttle. If you should hear a very metallic screech, pull in the clutch right away and look for a way out of the traffic; your bike is going to stop very soon. If this happens let the engine cool off for as long as possible before you try starting it again. In any case, be prepared to tear it down and have the cylinders honed at the very least.

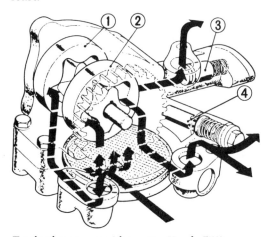

Trochoid type pump (shown is a Honda 750)

1. Delivery pump   3. Leak stopper valve
2. Scavenger pump   4. Relief valve

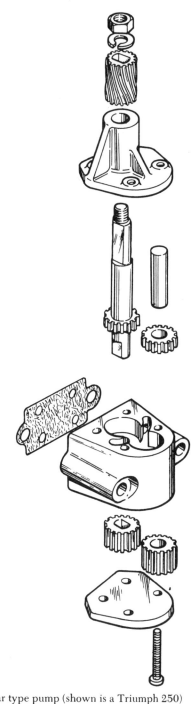

Gear type pump (shown is a Triumph 250)

Part of the cooling process is carried out by the fuel mixture because gas absorbs a lot of heat quickly, much more so than the air it gets mixed with. A lean mixture, in which there isn't enough gas to cool off the engine, causes the engine to run hot. If the mixture is too rich it doesn't burn efficiently and fouls the plugs. Therefore, if

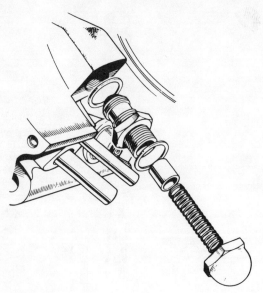

Oil pressure relief valve (shown is a Triumph Trident)

Pre-ignition holed this piston (Courtesy of Kiekhaefer Mercury, Fon du Lac, Wisconsin)

This damage was caused by detonation due to the use of poor fuel (Courtesy of Kiekhaefer Mercury, Fond du Lac, Wisconsin)

your carburetor is set too lean, or if you have air leaks at the intake manifold, the engine will overheat, and may even seize or hole a piston.

Ignition timing is also critical in keeping an engine running cool. The engine is timed for a spark to occur at a certain number of degrees before top dead center. If the spark is retarded, by the time the plug fires, the piston has moved too far and is subjected to excessive heat; this also can cause a holed piston.

Using too hot a spark plug can also cause overheating and a holed piston. For this reason, it is always recommended that you determine why a plug fouls and correct the situation, instead of using a hotter plug in hopes that it won't foul.

As was mentioned before, probably the greatest reason for overheating and subsequent engine seizure is running with an insufficient oil supply. Overheating can also be caused by using oil with too light a viscosity for the machine and the conditions. Rather remote possibilities are an overworked or dirty engine. Also make sure the bike isn't being forced to overwork because of increased resistance caused by too tight a chain, bad bearings, or rubbing brakes.

Finally, the subject of cleanliness. An air-cooled engine needs a cool air stream. If your bike is covered with caked-on grease and road grime it will run hotter than necessary.

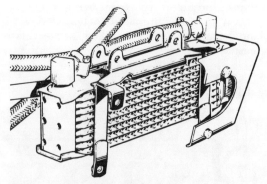

An oil cooler used on the BSA Rocket 3

ENGINE NOISES

One of the first indications of change in the condition of your motorcycle is the sounds that emanate from it. A thoughtful rider will know something is going wrong long before it happens and may be able to rectify the situation before it leads to costly repairs. Every machine has its own sounds and these sounds will remain constant until something begins to go wrong. Pay attention to this and whenever a new sound appears consult your local mechanic because he's the one who's heard them all before.

Valve Clatter

When tappet adjustment time comes rolling around you'll know it because the valves will let you know. They always make some noise, especially when cold, but will really get noisy when in need of attention. When listening to the tappets keep in mind that as long as you can hear them they're alright. If you can't hear anything as soon as you start the bike they're too tight and will cause damage to the valve train. One good way of listening to the valves is to place the metal tip of a screwdriver against the rocker box and listen through the handle.

Pinging

Poor quality gasoline, advanced ignition timing, incorrect spark plug heat range, or a piece of metal or carbon in the combustion chamber can be the cause of pinging (or pinking if we're talking about a British bike).

Pinging sounds are generally associated with the top end, and occur at mid throttle range during acceleration. Most of the time it is caused by pre-ignition due to the use of low octane fuel in a high compression engine. The unnecessary detonation causes undue strain on piston assemblies and bearings.

If the ignition timing is advanced too far, the force of the combustion will try to force the piston down before it completes its rotation. This is another type of pre-ignition and is as harmful as the use of poor fuel. When pistons end up with holes in them it is often due to this, but may also be due to using the wrong heat range spark plug.

If the plug in use is too hot it can't dissipate heat quickly enough and begins to act like a glow plug. This also causes pre-ignition and can be corrected by using a colder plug.

Carbon or metal pieces in the combustion chamber can heat up and act like a glow plug. This is less common than the others and only occurs when the engine is running hot. The only way to quiet this type of pinging is through top end overhaul.

Piston Slap

Slap occurs most often at mid throttle range during acceleration and requires a top end job to eliminate it. The noise is metallic and is caused by excessive piston-cylinder clearance. If the noise goes away after the engine warms up, the condition is not urgent but you'd better start planning on rebuilding the top end quite soon. One notable exception to this is in the case of big singles. These engines often slap even when in good condition, so perform all possible checks before tearing into things.

Knock

If you hear a mighty knocking noise coming from the bottom end while accelerating, you can be pretty sure the main bearings haven't long to go. It also may be a crankshaft problem and is remedied in either case by taking down the entire engine.

Rap

When the connecting rod bearings start to go, rap develops. This is most often heard during deceleration and increases in intensity with the speed of the engine.

Double Rap

This is caused by excessive piston/piston pin clearance and is most noticeable as a quick succession of raps at idle speeds.

Whine

In overhead cam engines an unusually loud whine often indicates a tight cam chain. It may also stem from primary or drive chains that are too tight or in need of lubrication.

Engines with ball or roller bearings in the bottom end don't thump when they go bad like plain bearings do, instead they may rumble. This rarely happens unless the machine has been run dry or really abused.

Lubrication

OIL

All manufacturers recommend a certain grade and viscosity of motor oil for their engines, and this recommendation should be adhered to in order to ensure long engine life.

All motor oil has a service rating stamped on the can. This rating comes from the American Petroleum Institute (API) and its code describes the oil's intended application and its constituents.

The oil you will purchase will be rated "SA," "SB," etc., down to "SE."

The "S" indicates that the oil is intended for use in gasoline engines. If it has a "C" prefix, this is for diesel engines.

The second letter lets you know the properties of the oil. "SA" oil indicates that the lubricate is for gasoline engines, and has no additives. "SB" oil has an anti-oxidation element added, "SC" has that and a detergent, and so on.

"SD" motor oil has antioxidants, high detergent qualities, and more. "SE" has all of the above, and is usable under still more severe conditions.

In general, all major motorcycles must use "SD" or "SE" motor oils. Others are simply not up to the job of providing sufficient lubrication in highly tuned air-cooled engines.

The second quality of oil which must be considered is the *viscosity,* which is nothing more than the thickness of the blend. Some motor oils are a "straight" viscosity such as 20W or 30W, while others are multi-grades, "20W-50," "10W-40," and so on.

The "W" in the oil's viscosity rating means that the oil has been rated at that thickness at 0° F. Therefore, a 20W-40 oil has a viscosity of "20" at that temperature.

Multi-viscosity oils do not change their thickness at different engine operating temperatures as some think. They do, however, have certain anti-thinning compounds added to them, so that the degree to which they thin out as engine temperature rises will be somewhat less than that of "straight" motor oil. For example, a "20W-40" motor oil will be rated at "20" thickness at 0° F, and at 212° F, its thickness will be not "40", but the same as a straight 40W oil would be at 212° F.

Many manufacturers will recommend a certain viscosity for normal air temperatures, as between 32° F and 80° F, with different recommendations for extremes on either side of this range. In general, multi-viscosity oils are good at all temperatures, while a straight grade should be changed to a thinner or thicker type as the air temperature falls below or rises above these extremes.

Since the bike maker knows a good deal more about the requirements of his engines than we do, it is foolhardy to experiment with different kinds of oil other than those he recommends.

A good grade of high-detergent multi-viscosity oil will have all that is needed to keep your engine in good shape for normal use.

Its multi-viscosity qualities will allow it to do a proper lubricating job under extremes of temperature, detergents will keep foreign matter in suspension so that they can be picked up by the filter(s) or drained off when the oil is changed, and the oil will also contain anti-oxidants to extend its useful life (oil oxidizes under exposure to air), and anti-acidic compounds to combat the inevitable metal-etching acids which are a by-product of combustion.

Oil additives are usually not necessary in an engine in good condition. We refer here to aftermarket magic cans or bottles which you add to the crankcase, not the additives which the oil company puts in their product. Such additives are not specifically called for in any manufacturers lubricant recommendations. In fact, several makers specifically warn against their use, not because they will harm the engine, but because they have been known to have an adverse effect upon the operation of "wet" type clutches.

OIL CHANGES

Oil changes should always be performed according to the recommended schedules.

An often overlooked fact about oil change intervals is that they depend not only on mileage, but upon *time,* that is, how long the oil has been in the crankcase, regardless of how much the machine has been ridden.

The time interval may be surprisingly short, so you should check what it is, and abide by it.

Oil wears out in time, as you know. This reduces its lubricating properties and the oil also begins to be filled with acids from combustion as well as the more widely feared particles of dirt or metal.

As noted above, oil oxidizes during exposure to air, and this naturally affects its efficiency. Acids get into the oil when the engine is started from cold. While the cylinder walls are not yet at operating temperature, the acids formed by the combustion process may condense on them, and then get into the oil. Unless the lubricant is changed, these acids may destroy the oil's lubricating properties in time.

The bike maker's oil-change interval is based upon normal usage, and should perhaps be accomplished more frequently if the bike is used under adverse conditions.

These include extended periods of high-speed riding at high air temperatures, operation in an extremely dusty environment, extended periods of stop-and-go riding, extended short hops (such as commuting a short distance), infrequent operation, especially during the winter months, and so on.

Always drain the oil from the crankcase or oil tank (on dry-sump machines) when the engine is at or near operating temperature. This will not only allow the oil to flow out more freely, but will help it carry out any particulate matter it may be carrying.

If you have a dry-sump motorcycle, such as a Norton or 750 Honda, be sure to drain the oil tank and the crankcase as well. If you can, kick the engine over slowly a few times to force out any oil remaining in the crankcases.

Oil filters come in many forms. Oil filters should be attended to at every oil change or every other oil change, depending on type. Refer to your owner's handbook for detailed information. Most motorcycles now have replaceable cartridge filters like autos. Others may have only wire mesh screen filters which

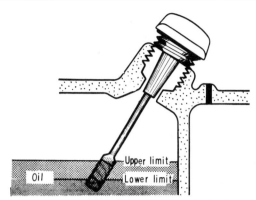
In many cases, oil should be checked with the dipstick resting on the threads of the hole

can be cleaned in solvent and reused, or rotating drums to catch and hold particulate matter with centrifugal force, like Honda Twins. Since many machines have more than one filtering device, be sure you know where they all are. Also, some bikes have magnetic-tipped drain plugs to attract metal particles in the engine, and these should be wiped off before they are installed.

Add the quantity of oil which the manufacturer recommends. Remember that in many cases the oil capacity given is an approximate value, and may vary slightly depending on how much of the old oil is left in the engine. Therefore, always check the oil level after the engine has been allowed to run for a few minutes, using the dipstick, sight glass, level screw, or whatever else is provided for this job. Any routine check of oil level should be done with the engine at operating temperature. This is especially true of dry-sump motorcycles whose level is checked at the oil tank. After the bike has been sitting idle for any length of time, the oil may seep from the tank into the crankcase, and lead you to believe that the oil level is much lower than it really is.

When checking oil, the motorcycle must be parked on a level surface and on the center stand for an accurate reading. If a dipstick is used, note that some types which screw into crankcases must be positioned to rest on the tops of the hole rather than being threaded in.

TRANSMISSIONS

Non-unit, semi-unit, or drive-shaft motorcycles such as Norton, Guzzi, Triumph, or BMW may require additional lubrication for items such as the primary chain, transmission, or drive box.

British motorcycles which use a primary

Removing the centrifugal oil filter cover plate circlip

chain will generally have special requirements for lubricating the chain. On Nortons, oil must be added to the chaincase, and the level checked periodically by means of the level plug. The same holds true for some Triumphs and BSAs. Other machines may incorporate automatic lubrication of the primary chain by oil blown through a crankshaft main bearing or crankcase breather hole. Primary chains are lubed with motor oil.

Separate transmissions ordinarily use 90W oil and the components are oiled by splash. The oil puddle in the gearbox is checked with a level plug in most instances, and once again, it should be checked on a warm engine. The same is true of drive boxes on shafties.

Since there is no combustion, and the forces involved are somewhat less violent than in the engine proper, lubrication intervals for drive line components are extensive, usually somewhere in the neighborhood of 6000 miles. Oil changes on these components must always be done with the unit at operating temperature, and the oil closely checked for particulate matter.

REAR CHAINS

Final drive chains are sometimes lubricated by excess engine oil, which may be randomly applied through an oil tank breather such as some Nortons and Triumphs, or through a transmission shaft as on some Hondas.

Strictly speaking, motor oil is not the ideal chain lubricant, even if it had some time to penetrate to the roller pins (which it doesn't since the chain is moving rapidly), and in consequence some supplimentary lubrication is always necessary.

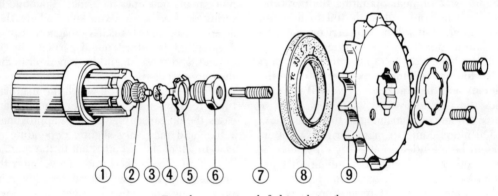

Typical transmission shaft drive chain oiler

1. Countershaft   4. Rubber orifice   7. Adjusting screw
2. Oil plug   5. Lockwasher   8. Oil seal
3. Oil stopper   6. Oiler plug   9. Countershaft sprocket

Engine Troubleshooting

Problem	Possible Causes	Inspection/Remedy
Abnormal engine noise (top end)	Excessive tappet clearance	Adjust.
	Piston knock due to worn cylinder	Inspect and have cylinder bored if necessary.
	Excessive carbon build-up in combustion chamber	Decarbonize.
	Worn wrist pin or con rod small end	Inspect and replace if necessary.
	Misadjusted or worn cam chain	Adjust. Replace if adjustment does not quiet the chain.
	Worn cam or crankshaft sprocket	Inspect.
	Pinging or spark knock	Timing too advanced; Low quality gasoline; drain and refill tank with fresh gas.

Engine Troubleshooting (cont.)

Problem	Possible Causes	Inspection/Remedy
Abnormal engine noise (bottom end)	Rumble at idle developing into whine at higher rpm: crankshaft main bearings worn or damaged	Inspect and replace if necessary.
	Knock, especially noticeable at idle, increasing with rpm: worn con rod big end bearing	Replace.
Noisy Transmission	Worn gears	Inspect and replace if necessary.
	Worn transmission shaft splines	Inspect; replace if necessary.
	Worn primary gear	Inspect primary gear.
	Noisy clutch	See Chapter 7.
Engine fails to start (no spark at plugs)	Ignition switched off	Turn on ignition.
	Kill button switched off	Reset.
	Battery dead	Charge battery.
	Blown fuse	Check fuse and replace if necessary.
	Loose or corroded battery terminals	Clean and secure connections.
	Spark plugs too old; worn or fouled	Clean or replace plugs.
	Spark plugs wet	Kick engine over after removing plugs to clear it. Blow plugs dry.
	Plug gap incorrect	Set to correct gap.
	Points wires disconnected; loose or corroded snap connectors	Check wiring; clean and tighten wire connectors.
	Points incorrectly gapped, pitted, worn or dirty	Inspect points. Replace or clean and adjust gap.
	Spark plug cap resistors defective	Replace spark plug caps.
	Plug leads dirty, damaged, wet, or defective	Replace leads and coils.
	Ignition coils defective	Replace.
	Condenser defective	Replace.
	Points grounding out against point plate	Inspect. Check that the point wire is insulated.
	Damaged insulators at points terminal	Replace.
Spark at one plug	Defective, worn, dirty, or fouled spark plug	Switch the nonfunctioning plug to the other lead. If spark is evident, the plug is not at fault. If no spark, replace the plug.
	Defective resistor spark plug cap	Replace.
	Defective, cracked, wet or dirty plug lead	Replace along with coil.
	Dirty, misadjusted, pitted or burned breaker points	Replace.
	Breaker point wire disconnected, broken; snap connector loose or corroded; insulation torn	Check point wiring; clean and secure connector.

Engine Troubleshooting (cont.)

Problem	Possible Causes	Inspection/Remedy
Spark at one plug	One set of points grounding out against point cover or mounting plate. Damaged insulators on point wire terminal	Check point assemblies.
	Defective condenser	Replace.
	Defective ignition coil	Replace.
Engine fails to start (has spark at plugs)	Lack of fuel	Make sure petcock is on; check for fuel in the tank.
	Fuel starvation: fuel lines clogged; petcock or filter dirty; vent in gas tank cap closed up; carburetor float valve closed off	Check for fuel at the float bowl and then back through the system.
	Carburetor adjustments incorrect	Adjust.
	Ignition timing incorrect	Adjust.
	Incorrect valve adjustment	Adjust.
	Carburetor float punctured	Replace.
	Low compression: worn rings or cylinder; bent or poorly seated valves; broken or worn valve guides	Inspect top end.
	Low compression due to blown head gasket, warped head	Rebuild.
	Incorrect valve timing	Reset.
Engine is hard to start	Worn, dirty, or improperly gapped plugs, or plugs too cold	Clean or replace and gap plugs or replace with correct heat range.
	Points dirty, pitted, or out of adjustment	Clean or replace and gap points.
	Carburetor idle settings wrong; pilot air or fuel passages clogged	Adjust idle settings or clean carburetor.
	Battery low	Recharge or replace battery.
	Ignition timing out of adjustment	Adjust.
	Valves adjusted incorrectly	Adjust valves.
	Spark plug leads cracked or dirty	Replace plug leads.
	Loss or intermittently grounded wires at coil, points, or connectors	Check all connections and condition of wiring.
	Defective coils or condensers	Replace.
	Worn or improperly seating valves	Perform top end overhaul; inspect and lap valves.
	Low compression due to worn or. damaged top end components	Overhaul top end.
Engine starts but refuses to run	Fuel feed problem	Check fuel supply; check fuel petcock, lines, carburetor for blocked passages; check gas tank cap vent.
	Spark plugs too cold or worn	Replace with proper heat range plugs.

Engine Troubleshooting (cont.)

Problem	Possible Causes	Inspection/Remedy
Engine starts but refuses to run	Valve clearance incorrect	Set valve clearance.
	Ignition timing incorrect	Adjust.
Engine idles poorly	Carburetor idle adjustments incorrect	Adjust idle circuit.
	Spark plugs worn, dirty, or gap too wide	Clean or replace and gap plugs.
	Spark plugs too cold	Fit the proper heat range plugs.
	Breaker point gaps incorrect	Adjust.
	Ignition timing incorrect	Adjust.
	Valves improperly adjusted	Adjust.
	Water in carburetors	Drain float bowls and gas tank if necessary and fill with fresh gas.
	Carburetor float levels wrong	Adjust.
	Air leaks at manifolds	Determine cause and rectify.
	Leaking valves	Lap valves.
	Worn valves, valve guides, valve seats	Check valve train.
	Weak spark	Check coils and condensers.
	Petcock clogged	Clean.
	Float bowl fuel level too low	Check float height.
Engine misfires when accelerating	Loose or intermittent connections in the ignition circuit	Check all connections; make sure that they are clean and tight.
	Ignition timing incorrect	Adjust.
	Gas tank cap vent clogged	Clear.
	Water in float bowls	Drain and refill with fresh mixture.
	Carburetor main jet clogged	Remove and clean.
	Air leaks at carburetor manifolds	Determine cause and remedy.
	Defective ignition coils or condensers	Replace.
	Carburetor settings wrong	Take plug readings and rejet carbs if necessary.
	Very low or dead battery	Recharge or replace battery.
Engine surges or runs unevenly at steady throttle openings	Carburetor fault; mixture too lean, erratic fuel flow	Remove and inspect carburetors.
	Air leaks at carburetor manifolds	Determine cause and remedy.
	Valves improperly adjusted	Adjust.
Engine breaks up or misfires while running	Battery very low or dead	Recharge or replace battery.
	Loose or intermittent connections in the ignition circuit	Check and secure connections.
	Battery terminal come adrift	Clean and secure battery connections.
Poor low-speed operation	Incorrect ignition timing	Adjust timing.

Engine Troubleshooting (cont.)

Problem	Possible Causes	Inspection/Remedy
Poor low-speed operation	Carburetor idle circuit poorly adjusted	Adjust pilot screws and idle speed.
	Spark plug gap too great or plugs too cold	Use correct heat range and gap to proper specifications.
	Poor breaker point contact	Clean or replace breaker points.
	Valves improperly adjusted	Adjust.
	Carburetor fault	See Chapter 5.
Poor high-speed operation	Ignition timing too retarded	Adjust timing.
	Spark plug gap too small	Adjust gap.
	Plugs too cold	Fit plugs of the correct heat range.
	Carburetor float level too low	Adjust float level.
	Partially blocked fuel lines or petcock	Clean.
	Dirty air cleaner	Clean or replace element.
	Weak breaker point arm spring	Replace points.
	Defective ignition coils or condensers	Replace.
	Weakened valve springs	Inspect springs.
	Incorrect valve timing	Reset.
Loss of power	Incorrect valve adjustment	Adjust tappets.
	Clogged or dirty air cleaner	Clean or replace the element.
	Incorrect ignition timing	Adjust.
	Dirty carburetors	Clean.
	Valves not sealing	Lap valves.
	Valve springs weakened	Replace.
	Rings or cylinder worn	Rebuild.
	Valve timing incorrect	Reset.
	Carburetor float level incorrect	Adjust.
	Spark plug gap incorrect	Adjust.
	Engine or muffler carbon choked	Decarbonize.
	Exhaust pipe broken or loose	Secure or replace.
Engine overheats	Insufficient engine oil	Top up.
	Too lean a mixture	See "Carburetor Troubleshooting" section, Chapter 5.
	Timing too advanced	Adjust.
	Oil pump defective; oil passage blocked	Clear system.
	Engine carbon choked	Decarbonize.
Engine backfires or kick-starter kicks back	Timing too advanced	Adjust.
	Advance unit stuck	Lubricate; check for free movement.
Popping at muffler after shutting off throttle	Air leaks in muffler	Secure clamps or nuts.

Engine Troubleshooting (cont.)

Problem	Possible Causes	Inspection/Remedy
Popping at muffler after shutting off throttle	Mixture too lean	Adjust idle circuit and float level. Check for air leaks.
Exhaust smoke accompanied by oil consumption	Too much oil in engine	Set to correct level.
	Worn rings or bore	Rebuild.
	Worn valve guides or seals	Replace.
	Scored cylinder	Bore to oversize.
Black smoke from exhaust pipes	Engine carboned up	Decarbonize.
Piston seizure	Low oil level	Maintain oil at proper level.
	Engine overheating due to too advanced ignition timing, insufficient tappet clearance, stuck valves	Check settings.
	Insufficient oil	Check oil pump.
Burned valves	Clearances adjusted too tightly	Replace valves; check guides; maintain adjustment.
	Timing too retarded	Adjust.
Bent valves or broken valve guides	Valve hitting piston because of incorrect valve timing, over-revving the engine, or weak valve springs	Check top end components.
Bad connecting rod bearings	Insufficient or contaminated oil	Check oil, filter, and oil pump.
	Overrevving engine	Abide by tachometer red line.
	Extended use of the engine with ignition timing too advanced, high-speed misfire, etc.	
Bad crankshaft bearings	Insufficient or contaminated oil	Replace bearings.
	Overrevving engine	Abide by tachometer red line.
	Extended use of the motorcycle with one weak or misfiring cylinder	
Worn cam lobes or bearings	Insufficient or contaminated oil	Maintain oil at proper level; change filter when directed.
	Failure to allow engine sufficient warm-up	Allow at least one minute of warm-up when starting cold engine.
	Defective oil pump or clogged oil passages in engine	Replace.
Worn cylinder and rings	Damaged or leaking air cleaner	Replace element; secure connections.
	Low oil level or contaminated oil	Maintain oil at proper level; change oil and filter at proper intervals.
	Defective oil pump	Replace.
	Failure to allow engine sufficient warm-up	Allow at least one minute for warm-up when starting cold engine.

5 · The Fuel System

With certain notable exceptions, the vast majority of modern motorcycles use the "slide throttle" carburetor, most of which are quite similar in outward appearance and operation, although they differ in detail according to make and application.

The most widely used carburetors today include the Keihin units found on Hondas and some models of the other Japanese manufacturers, Mikunis, which are used extensively by Suzuki, Yamaha, and Kawasaki, and Amals found on British and some Spanish machines.

Other makes currently in use include Dell 'Orto (Italian), Bing (German), and Bendix (USA).

For purposes of clarity, modern motorcycle carburetors may be divided into one of three types: the "direct control" type, the "CV" (constant velocity or constant vacuum) type, and the "throttle plate" type, the last being used only on Harley-Davidson V-Twins at the present time.

The ratio of fuel to air is a compromise value. For example, a mixture containing less fuel might allow more complete combustion and therefore more power, but might result in an overheated engine, since fuel entering the combustion chamber actually cools the internal components somewhat.

A very basic theoretical carburetor consists of a fuel reservoir or float bowl, a fuel nozzle (or jet) and a venturi tube. Fuel from the gas tank is gravity-fed into the float bowl in amounts determined by the float itself. The float is connected to a needle, and when the fuel reaches a certain pre-determined level, the float presses the needle into its seat, stopping the fuel flow. Then, as the gas is consumed by the engine, the float drops proportionally to allow more fuel to enter the bowl. In actual operation, the float rarely closes off the fuel supply completely, but reaches a balance in which the amount of fuel consumed matches that entering the float bowl.

Operational Description

The carburetor's purpose is to mix gasoline and air in the proper proportions and to deliver this mixture to the engine.

This mixture generally consists of one part fuel to fifteen parts air (by weight). At this ratio, the gasoline can mix completely with the air.

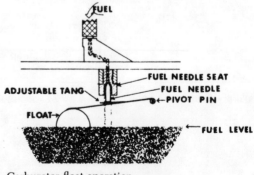

Carburetor float operation

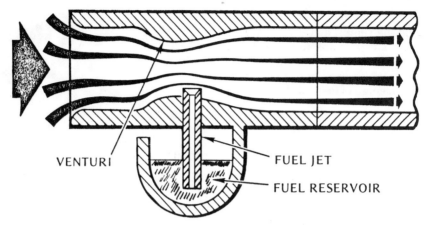

A basic "carburetor"

It is important that the fuel in the float bowl be maintained at the proper level, or the amount entering the engine may be excessive or insufficient depending on whether the level is too high or too low. Most floats are equipped with an adjustable tang which can be used to correct the fuel level.

It is the difference in pressure between the float bowl (which is at atmospheric pressure), and the pressure in the venturi, or carburetor throat, which causes the fuel to leave the bowl, rise through the fuel nozzle, and enter the venturi. The venturi is basically an air funnel which is narrower in the center than it is at the ends. When air rushes through it, pulled in by the suction of the piston, a low-pressure area is created in the narrow section. The higher the rpm of the engine, the faster the air moves through the venturi, and the greater the pressure drop in the narrow section. Since

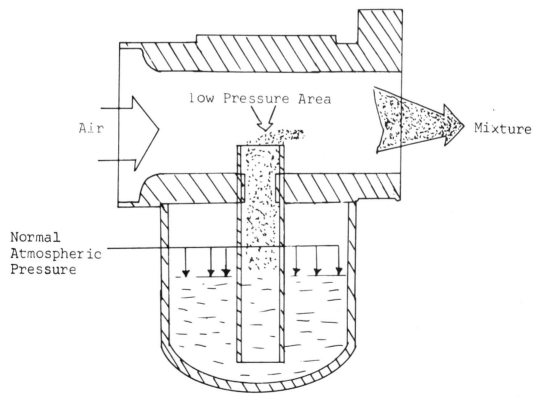

Float bowl and venturi operation. Air sucked into the carb intake by the movement of the piston causes a low pressure area above the jet tube. This causes fuel in the float bowl to rise in the tube and this fuel is atomized and mixed with the inrushing air in the venturi

the fuel in the float bowl is at atmospheric pressure, and the venturi above the fuel nozzle (or jet) is a low-pressure area, the fuel is forced up through the jet into the air flowing through the venturi in an effort to equalize the pressure. The amount of fuel which enters the venturi is dependent upon the size of the jet. The amount of air is determined by the size of the venturi.

Of course, in actual practice, carburetors are not quite that simple. The basic unit described above has no provisions for throttle control, cold starting, or the varying needs of the engine.

The operating stages of a "real" carburetor are described below.

CONSTRUCTION

Most carburetors consist of a one-piece body cast from cheap pot metal, although some "racing" units are made from more expensive materials such as magnesium. The body incorporates the venturi, a bore for the movement of the throttle slide, and provides a mounting point for various fuel and air jets.

In addition, the body is drilled with a number of fuel and air passages. Among these

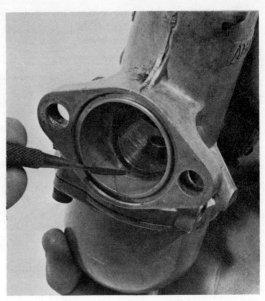

Pilot outlet and by-pass passages

are the primary air passage, pilot air passage, and pilot outlet or by-pass.

The *primary air passages* can usually be found just beneath the carburetor intake, and is drilled through to the needle jet. The air taken in through this passage helps to atomize, or mix, the gasoline passing through the needle jet before it enters the venturi. Unless the gasoline is atomized, raw fuel will reach the combustion chamber, resulting in wet-fouled spark plugs, inefficient combustion, and generally poor operation.

The *pilot air passage* is located alongside the primary air passage on most carburetors. The air taken in through this drilling is used for idle and low-speed operation.

The *pilot outlet* is a very small drilling which can be seen on the engine side of the throttle slide bore. The fuel/air mixture for idling pass through here and then to the engine.

The carburetor body also has a place for the attachment of the *float bowl*. The float bowl houses the float assembly and carries the carburetor's gasoline supply. A part of the float assembly is the float valve which usually consists of a small needle and a needle seat. The floats rise and fall according to the amount of gasoline in the float bowl, alternately pressing the needle against its seat and releasing it, thence controlling the fuel flow. The float bulbs may be made of various materials. Most early carburetors used brass bulbs, but plastic has been used more frequently in recent years. Float needles can be plastic, brass, or

Primary air passage, flanked by idle air passage on left

Float bowl components: float, needle, spindle, and needle seat

neoprene-tipped brass, the last proving most effective. Needle seats are almost always brass, and on most carburetors can be un-screwed for cleaning or replacement.

The great majority of modern carburetors

Mikuni SH-type carburetor: Floats (A), starter jet (B), float arm (C) and needle jet set bolt (arrow). The main jet is in the float bowl

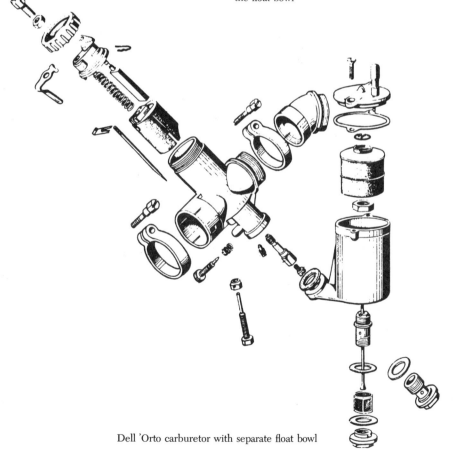

Dell 'Orto carburetor with separate float bowl

mount the float bowl directly beneath the carburetor body. In this position the fuel supply surrounds the main jet ensuring an accurately metered supply of fuel during acceleration, braking, or banking to either side. This type of carburetor is usually known as "concentric." Not all carburetors were constructed in this manner, and separate float bowl carburetors were the rule for many years.

On the Amal "Monobloc" carburetor, which was used on British and some Spanish motorcycles up to the introduction of the "Concentric" in 1967, the float bowl was cast in a single unit with the carburetor body and positioned off to one side. This arrangement was primarily a manufacturer's advantage, since the Monobloc could be mounted at almost any angle without modification. It was, however, adversely affected by tilting to the left or right, and could therefore produce lean or rich mixtures during severe banking of the motorcycle. Another interesting feature of the Monobloc was that, when used in pairs, usually only one was fitted with a float bowl, the other carb being fed by a balance tube.

The *throttle slide* is the chief metering component of the carburetor. It is controlled directly by the throttle cable which runs to the

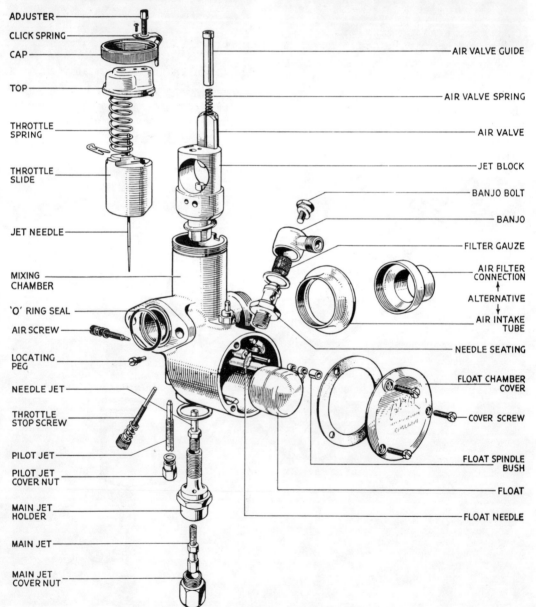

Amal Monobloc carburetor

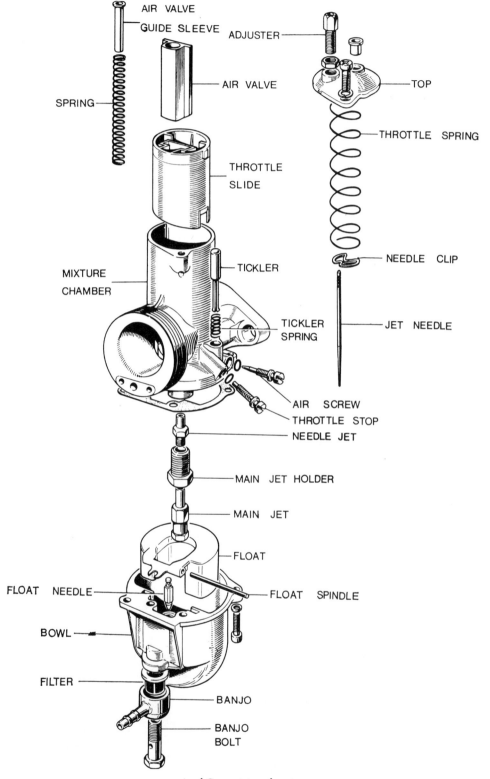

Amal Concentric carburetor

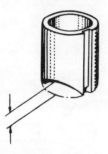

Throttle slide cutaway

twist grip on direct-control type carburetors. On "CV" units, the throttle cable opens and closes a throttle plate, and the slide proper opens and closes by venturi vacuum (this is explained later).

The throttle slide determines the size of the carburetor venturi and therefore meters the amount of air in the fuel/air mixture at most of the operating range. Additionally, the *needle* or *jet needle* is attached to the slide. This needle works in conjunction with the *needle jet* and determines the amount of gasoline allowed to pass into the engine primarily in the mid-range.

The throttle slide is cylindrical in most carburetors, although there are examples of "square slides" such as used by some Dell 'Orto carburetors. The slide has a cutaway at the intake side of the carburetor to allow the entry of air in sufficient quantities to mix with the gasoline when the throttle is closed. The higher the cutaway, the leaner the mixture will be when the slide is just opened. If the size of the cutaway is not matched to the other metering components and the particular needs of the engine, the transition from idle to the main metering system will be greatly impaired. This is a particularly critical period, since the load on the engine is changing as the clutch is engaged, and smooth starts from a dead stop must be considered a matter of safety in many cases.

Formerly, throttle slides were cast from the same material as the carburetor body, but this was found to cause greatly accelerated wear on both slide and body. Today, the slide is commonly steel, often chromed, bringing wear into more acceptable limits. In CV carburetors, where the slide must be moved by venturi vacuum, the slides must be light in weight so light alloys are used.

Dell 'Orto VHB-type "square slide"

CV carburetor slides are light in weight and must be closely fit to the carb bore

Operation

The operation of a practical carburetor can best be described by dividing it into five circuits, and the components which control each one.

DIRECT-CONTROL CARBURETOR

Starting Circuit (0 Throttle Opening)

The engine needs a rich mixture for starting when cold. Since this need is only temporary and the mixture must be balanced when the engine warms up, a manually operated "choke" is incorporated into most carburetors and is controlled by the operator.

There are various ways of creating this rich mixture. The most simple is to reduce the amount of air available to the carb by closing off the mouth with a plate. This method is most often found on Honda motorcycles and on some others as well.

On some units, notably the Amal Monoblocs and Concentrics, a temporary rich mixture is obtained by flooding or overfilling the float bowl. "Ticklers" are provided on the carburetor. When pushed, they depress the float, allowing the float needle to rise from its seat. The fuel level in the float bowl then exceeds its normal level and rises through the jets into the venturi where it provides a rich starting mixture.

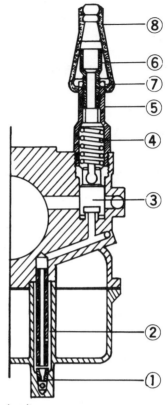

Starter circuit

1. Starter jet
2. Starter pipe
3. Plunger
4. Plunger spring
5. Plunger cap
6. Adjuster
7. Locknut
8. Dust cover

Other carburetors, such as Mikuni and Dell'Orto use a refined version of the tickler. A starter jet is fitted which is activated by a cable or lever. When activated, the jet is opened (in most cases a spring-loaded plunger does the opening and closing), and fuel from the float bowl can bypass the normal fuel jets and pass into the carburetor bore.

Once the engine is started and warmed up, the choke is switched off, and the fuel/air metering is turned over to the idle circuit components.

Idle Circuit (0–⅛ Throttle Opening)

At idle under normal operating conditions, the engine requires very little fuel and air. It does, however, require more accurate metering than pure venturi action can provide while the engine is turning relatively slowly and intake air velocity is low.

The idle circuit on most popular carburetors consists of a pilot jet, pilot air passage, and the throttle slide.

Fuel is provided by the float bowl. The

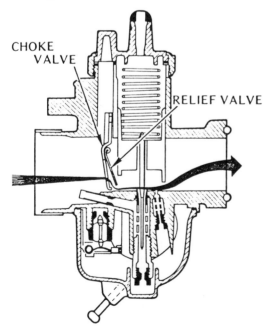

CHOKE VALVE

RELIEF VALVE

Typical choke plate operation

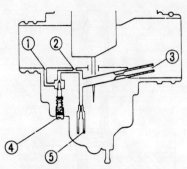

Idle circuit components: 1, 2 pilot outlets; 3, air passage; 4, pilot screw; 5, pilot jet

lowed to pass, and hence the mixture. On some carburetors the pilot screw is fitted directly to the pilot air passage and is sometimes called the "pilot air screw." On carburetors of this type, the amount of fuel entering the idling engine is determined by the size of the pilot jet alone, and the amount of air is varied to meet changing conditions.

On other types of carburetors, it is the amount of air which is fixed by the size of the pilot air passage. On these carburetors, the pilot screw changes the amount of *fuel* passing into the engine.

In operation, piston suction creates a low-pressure area behind the throttle slide. To equalize this low pressure, air rushes through the pilot air passage, mixes with fuel from the pilot jet. This mixture is bled into the carburetor's intake tract through the pilot outlet. The air coming in under the throttle slide is added to this mixture and delivers it to the combustion chamber.

amount of fuel is metered by the pilot jet, while air is taken in through the carburetor venturi and passes under the throttle slide (which is almost, but not quite closed at this point).

Because the idle mixture is so crucial, it is possible to adjust the mixture to compensate for changing conditions so that a good idle is always maintained. For this reason a pilot screw is fitted to most carburetors. The pilot screw is really a tapered needle and is fitted to an air or fuel passage. Turning the screw in or out will change the amount of fuel or air al-

Low-Speed Circuit (⅛–¼ Throttle Opening)

This circuit uses the same components as the idle circuit. There is, however, an increase in the airflow as the throttle slide rises,

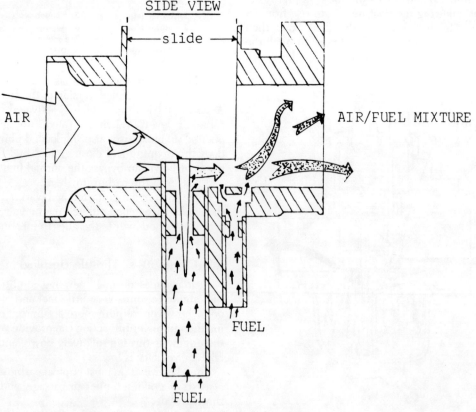

Carburetor low-speed operation

and in fuel flow as the needle begins to come out of the needle jet. This effects a transition to the mid-range circuit, since the increased amounts of fuel and air delivered by the needle jet and the venturi overshadow the smaller amounts coming from the pilot outlet, eventually eliminating the idle circuit from the metering system.

Mid-Range Circuit (¼–¾ Throttle Opening)

In this circuit, air is supplied by two sources: the venturi and the primary air passage. The more important reason for the air going through the primary air passage, however, is that it mixes with the gasoline in the needle jet (the needle jet has a number of holes drilled in it), and this helps to atomize the fuel before it enters the venturi.

Fuel is supplied by the float bowl and metered by the needle jet and needle. The needle jet on most carburetors is located just above the main jet and works in conjunction with the needle suspended from the throttle slide.

As the slide rises, the air flow through the carburetor is increased, and at the same time the tapered needle allows more and more fuel to pass through the needle jet.

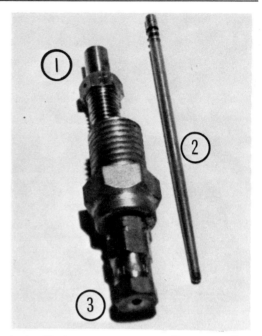

Mid and high-range metering: 1, needle jet; 2, needle; 3, main jet. (Amal Concentric)

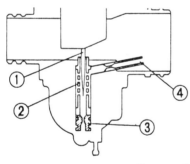

Mid-range circuit components: 1, needle; 2, needle jet; 3, main jet; 4, air passage

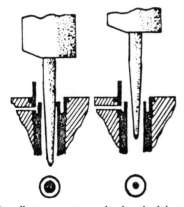

Needle/needle jet operation as the throttle slide is raised

High-Speed Circuit (¾–Full Throttle)

This circuit is close to that described for the hypothetical carburetor at the beginning of this section. The throttle slide has been lifted clear of the venturi, and no longer controls the amount of air. By the same token, the needle has lifted out of the needle jet, and no longer controls the fuel supply.

Venturi action takes over completely. The amount of air sucked into the engine is determined by the size of the venturi, and the amount of fuel delivered by the size of the main jet. The only other part of the system which still has a significant effect is the primary air passage which continues to aid fuel atomization.

It should be understood that the operating ranges of the various metering circuits overlap somewhat, so there is a gradual, rather than an abrupt, transition from one to another as the throttle is operated.

The relative independence of the various circuits, however, should explain why it is fruitless to make random changes in carburetor settings without first determining the nature of the problem, and the range in which it occurs.

ACCELERATOR PUMPS

Some direct-control carburetors now used on four-stroke motors incorporate accelerator

Accelerator pump on Dell 'Orto PHF carburetor

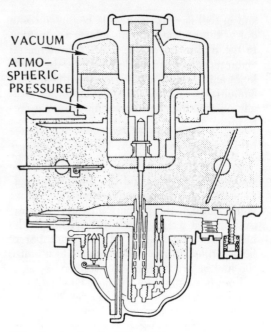

CV carburetor throttle slide operation

pumps which squirt a stream of raw gasoline into the venturi whenever the throttle is opened. The pumps usually consist of a throttle slide-activated plunger which takes fuel directly from the float bowl, bypassing the normal metering components.

Accelerator pumps are incorporated to aid the transition from the idle system to the main metering system. Throttle response is therefore much improved. One disadvantage of the system, however, is that it may have an adverse effect on fuel economy.

Accelerator pumps are widely used on Dell'Orto carburetors, and also on the Keihin units found on the Honda 750A. In this last case, the use of the pumps was necessary due to the unique (for motorcycles) problems of an engine working through an automatic transmission. Since no clutch is used here, smooth power transmission is entirely dependent on the throttle when starting out, and it was felt that a flat spot just off idle would have an unacceptable effect on rideability.

CONSTANT-VELOCITY CARBURETORS

The constant-velocity carburetor is basically the same as the direct-control type carburetor, except that the throttle twist-grip is not connected directly to the throttle slide. Instead, in the CV carburetor, the throttle grip and cable are connected to a throttle plate located between the intake manifold and throttle slide. As the throttle plate is opened, the manifold vacuum evacuates air from the top of the slide chamber through a passage in the slide. Consequently, on demand from the engine, the slide is raised and more air is admitted, and the tapered needle is proportionally lifted out of the jet tube to admit more fuel.

The term "constant-velocity" (or constant vacuum) refers to the speed of the air passing over the main jet tube and the vacuum in the carburetor throat which remains constant due to the movement of the piston in relation to the vacuum. As the engine demands more air and the manifold vacuum increases, the slide responds by lifting in proportion to the vacuum. Thus the carburetor air speed and vacuum remain constant, because an increase in vacuum means an increase in slide lift, which in turn increases the amount of air passing through the carburetor by altering the size of the air passage (venturi), and compensating for the increased engine demands with a larger flow of air. A constant vacuum indicates a constant-velocity, and vice versa.

THROTTLE-PLATE CARBURETORS

The "throttle-plate" carburetor is little different in theory from the throttle-slide types considered above except, of course, that there is no moving slide. In its place is a flat plate which pivots as the twist-grip is rotated to increase the size of the carburetor throat and allow progressively more of the fuel/air mixture to enter the combustion chamber.

Unlike the throttle-slide carburetors de-scribed above, the throttle-plate units do not usually have well-defined mid-range circuits, and are best described by breaking the operation down into "low-speed" and "high-speed" circuits.

The Bendix 16P12 carburetor is typical of this type and is used to illustrate the following

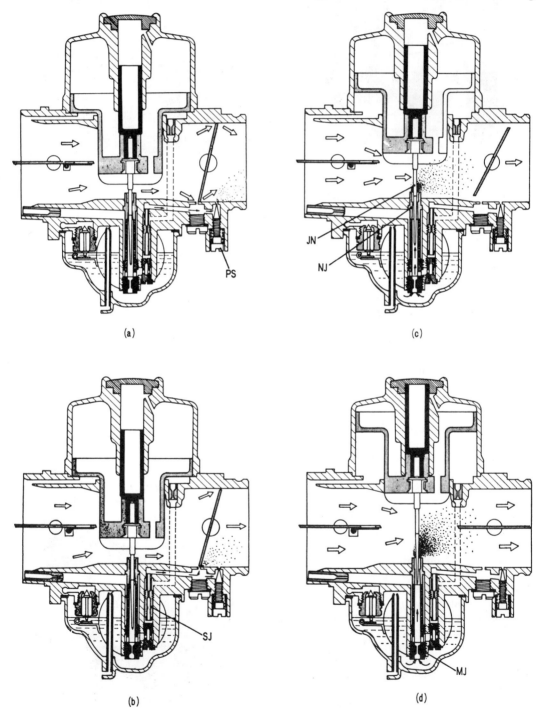

(a)

(b)

(c)

(d)

Operation of a constant velocity carburetor at various throttle openings

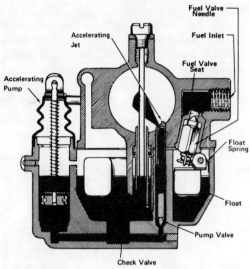

Starting circuit

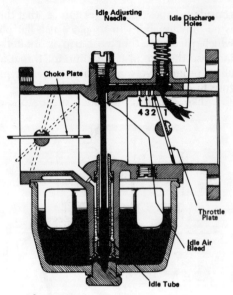

Low-speed circuit

explanation. This carburetor was used on most Harley-Davidson V-Twins after 1970, with the exception of late models fitted with a very similar Keihin unit.

Starting Circuit

A choke plate on the intake side of the carburetor closes off the mouth to yield a rich mixture needed for starting. A hole in the choke plate allows some air to enter to prevent flooding the engine. In addition, an accelerator pump is fitted which injects a stream of gasoline into the venturi when the throttle is opened.

Low-Speed Circuit

There are three or four idle discharge holes located at the top engine side of the venturi. The main idle discharge hole (No. 1 in the illustration) is variable in size as it works in conjunction with a tapered idle adjusting needle. At idle, the throttle plate stop screw holds the throttle plate open just enough so that this passage is able to discharge its fuel into the engine.

Drawn by piston suction, gasoline rises from the float bowl through the idle tube. As the fuel passes the idle discharge holes (Nos. 2, 3, and 4), air is drawn in and mixed with it. The mixture is then bled into the intake port through the idle hole No. 1.

The mixture is determined by the idle adjusting needle. If the needle is turned IN, the mixture will be leaned out, and it will be richened if the needle is turned out.

As the throttle is opened slightly, the other idle discharge holes are exposed in turn, each

allowing progressively more fuel and air into the intake port.

Eventually, the throttle plate is opened enough so that engine suction is powerful enough to draw gasoline from the main discharge tube and the transition to the high-speed circuit begins.

High-Speed Circuit

The high-speed circuit begins when all idle discharge holes are exposed, and can no longer supply sufficient gasoline and air for the engine's needs.

As the throttle plate is opened the velocity of the incoming air passing through the ven-

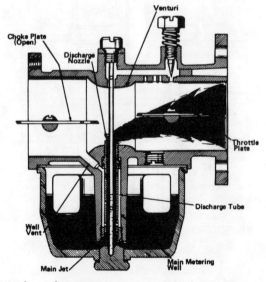

High-speed circuit

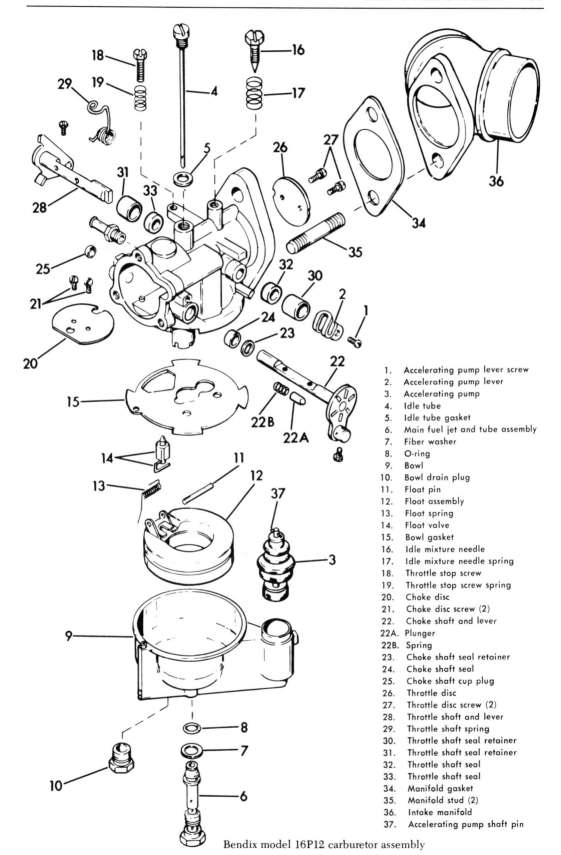

1.   Accelerating pump lever screw
2.   Accelerating pump lever
3.   Accelerating pump
4.   Idle tube
5.   Idle tube gasket
6.   Main fuel jet and tube assembly
7.   Fiber washer
8.   O-ring
9.   Bowl
10. Bowl drain plug
11. Float pin
12. Float assembly
13. Float spring
14. Float valve
15. Bowl gasket
16. Idle mixture needle
17. Idle mixture needle spring
18. Throttle stop screw
19. Throttle stop screw spring
20. Choke disc
21. Choke disc screw (2)
22. Choke shaft and lever
22A. Plunger
22B. Spring
23. Choke shaft seal retainer
24. Choke shaft seal
25. Choke shaft cup plug
26. Throttle disc
27. Throttle disc screw (2)
28. Throttle shaft and lever
29. Throttle shaft spring
30. Throttle shaft seal retainer
31. Throttle shaft seal retainer
32. Throttle shaft seal
33. Throttle shaft seal
34. Manifold gasket
35. Manifold stud (2)
36. Intake manifold
37. Accelerating pump shaft pin

Bendix model 16P12 carburetor assembly

turi is increased, and, as this happens, this air exerts an increasingly powerful suction on the gasoline in the discharge tube just below the venturi. This gasoline is already partially atomized by the air drawn through the well vent.

When the throttle is fully opened, the amount of air in the mixture is determined by the size of the carburetor venturi and the amount of fuel by the size of the main jet.

Carburetor Troubleshooting

For the most part, the carburetor(s) will become a troublespot when something occurs which upsets the balance of gas and air going into the engine.

When there is an excess of gasoline in the mixture, it is said to be "rich." An excess of air, and the mixture is said to be too "lean."

If you have read the "Operational Description" above, it should be obvious that it is possible for the mixture to be "lean" or "rich" at one throttle opening, but normal at others. This is often caused by the installation of the wrong size jets, rather than a defect in the components themselves.

Like all other aspects of troubleshooting, an approach to a carburetor problem must in large measure depend on the nature and the history of the ailment.

Probably the most common carburetor malady is simple dirt which has gotten past the fuel or air filters and has clogged or even partially obstructed the various passages in the carburetor.

Again, individual cases must be taken into account. If the trouble has developed slowly over a number of miles, this could be the cause. If the unit(s) have simply stopped functioning correctly, however, there is probably another reason. The following may serve as a rough guide to determine whether the mixture is lean or rich.

INDICATIONS OF A RICH MIXTURE

An excess of gasoline in the fuel/air mix is often indicated by one or more of the following:

a. Visible exhaust emissions without oil consumption. This refers primarily to four-strokes, since some visible smoke is charac-

teristic of two-stroke engines. These emissions will be black, as opposed to the blue-white color of burning oil.

b. Spark plug(s) black or carbon-fouled. When checking the plugs for mixture, the color of the side electrode is the key. The center electrode is more of a guide to plug heat range. If the plugs are too cold, however, it may seem that the fuel mixture is too rich.

c. Engine runs better when the air cleaner is removed. Since air filters are somewhat restrictive, removal will allow somewhat more air to enter the carburetor at any given throttle opening resulting in a slightly leaner mixture. This is only a check for a rich mixture, and should not be considered a solution.

d. Engine runs worse when hot. Since engines need a slightly rich mixture when they are cold, a faulty fuel/air mix may go unnoticed until the engine is at operating temperature.

e. Performance is sluggish.

f. Engine misfires at high rpm.

g. Excessive fuel consumption.

INDICATIONS OF A LEAN MIXTURE

a. Engine is hard to start when cold, or requires excessive choking.

b. Engine refuses to idle smoothly, or rpm fluctuates at steady throttle openings.

c. Engine runs hot.

d. Spark plugs are white or yellow in color. In extreme instances, the side electrode may be eroded or partially melted, both electrodes showing rounded edges.

e. Engine runs better when the choke is engaged.

f. Engine runs better at slightly less than full throttle than it does when wide open.

g. Engine runs worse when the air cleaner is removed.

In addition to determining whether the mixture is rich or lean, you should also analyze whether the imbalance occurs at all throttle openings, or just one in particular. If the malady seems to occur at one spot, it is probable that the trouble lies with the metering components which control that particular range of operation. For example, an overly rich mixture in the mid-range may be due to a worn needle and needle jet.

AIR FILTERS

Because it is designed to be replaced or cleaned at periodic intervals, the air filter is a likely source of trouble.

As it fills up with dirt, the air filter will cause the mixture to become increasingly rich. If it is not serviced, the mixture will become so rich that performance will be greatly impaired.

The oil-foam air cleaner is the most popular type in use today, although there are a multitude of different kinds.

The "metal mesh" air filter was a favorite for a long time. One type consisted of a series of steel screens one over the other. Filtering was accomplished by immersing the filter screens in motor oil. After the excess oil had drained off, a film remained which would trap impurities in the air passing through the filter. At least in theory. One advantage of this type of filter was that it could be cleaned by washing in a solvent, blown dry, re-oiled, and reused.

The dry "paper element" air filter has been standard equipment on most motorcycles until very recently. The paper is porous, and will therefore allow air to pass more or less freely, while retaining foreign matter.

Most paper elements are pleated to afford maximum intake area in a given space.

Paper elements can be serviced, after a fashion, by brushing dirt deposits off the outside and using compressed air to blow out remaining fine dirt from the inside of the filter box. This technique, however, is very limited in effect, and it makes more sense to simply replace the element after several thousand miles.

"Oil-foam" filter elements are now in wide use, and have many advantages over the paper filters they are replacing. First, the foam elements can capture much smaller bits of foreign matter, and yet are less restrictive to air. Secondly, the foam elements are easy to service and can be reused.

Like the metal mesh types described earlier, foam filters depend upon an oil film for filtering effectiveness.

Service oil-foam filters by first washing thoroughly in a solvent. Let the filter soak up the solvent like a sponge. Squeeze it dry. Repeat the procedure until the solvent being squeezed off ceases carrying off dirt. Be sure to *squeeze* the element: do not wring it out, as this risks tearing it, or at least damaging the close-knit pores.

Soak the cleaned element in the type of oil recommended by the manufacturer. In most cases, standard motor oil (20W/50 or 30W) can be used, but some filters specify 80W or 90W gear lubricant.

Squeeze off the excess oil, and the filter is ready to use again.

Another kind of air filter which is coming into use today can best be described as the "wet-paper" type. At the present time, this kind of filter is not standard equipment on any popular motorcycle, but is available as an ac-

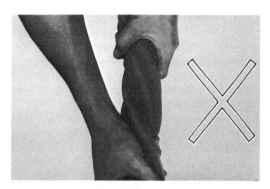

Do not wring out foam elements

Squeezing off excess oil

Blowing out the filter element

cessory item. This filter is composed of a special type of paper which offers almost no resistance to air but, when treated with a special oil supplied by the manufacturer, offers an extremely high degree of filtering. This filter must not be treated with motor oil or the like—only with the special oil. Cleaning is accomplished with lacquer thinner, and the filter is reusable.

Service Intervals

Air filter service intervals will depend entirely upon the environment in which the machine is ridden, although the owner's manual will give a guide to service under routine conditions. This is usually about 5000 miles for road bikes, and about 2500 miles for off-road machines, but this can be far too long if there is a lot of dust in the air.

The outward appearance of the air filter element is no reliable indicator of its condition. Some oil-foam filters tend to take on a dirty appearance after only a few miles, while their filtering ability is unimpaired. Some paper elements never look too bad, but may be almost fully clogged.

Fitting Accessory Filters

Non-Stock or accessory air filters are a popular item, and may benefit your machine. Often, such filters claim less intake restriction as well as improved filtering properties, and, if this is true, it may be necessary to rejet the carburetor(s) to avoid a lean mixture. Generally, the manufacturer of the accessory air filter will provide this information.

The filter you choose should be made specifically for your machine, as this will help you avoid numerous troubles in adapting and mounting the new filter. Even a reputable element may cause a decrease in performance if it is incorrectly mounted or simply too small to do the job. Additionally, foam air cleaners depend on a wire mesh or a coil spring to keep their shape. If incorrectly installed, engine suction can cause them to contract at high rpm, effectively cutting down the amount of air supplied.

FUEL FILTERS AND FUEL FEED

Another common cause of carburetor trouble is lack of fuel caused by clogging or damage to one of the components of the fuel feed system.

Like air filters, fuel filters require periodic service.

There are one or more fuel filters in the system, depending on the motorcycle involved. Prior to 1975, when Federal edict redesigned the fuel petcock, most motorcycles had a sediment bowl fitted to the petcock with a wire mesh filter just above it. This kind of filter is easy to clean. After shutting off the gas, unscrew and remove the sediment bowl. Pull out the o-ring and filter screen. Wash the screen and bowl in gasoline, and reinstall.

If the petcock has no sediment bowl, the filter is probably located on the petcock intake pipe inside the gas tank. Some petcocks with sediment bowls have an additional filter here as well. Access to these filters can only be gained by first draining all gasoline in the tank. Removal of the tank from the motorcycle first is the quickest and safest way to do this.

Petcocks are secured either with a single large nut which screws onto a fitting on the tank, or by two or more screws. In either case care must be taken on removal, since certain sealing devices are in use, such as rubber O-rings.

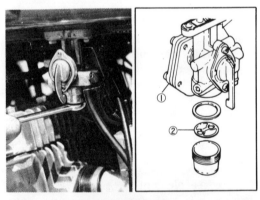

Sediment bowl removal and filter (2)

Petcock filter screen and O-ring

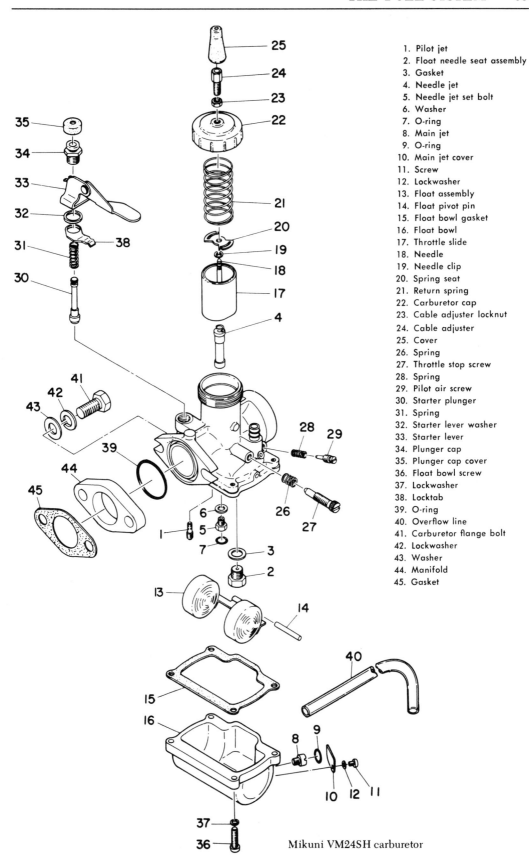

1. Pilot jet
2. Float needle seat assembly
3. Gasket
4. Needle jet
5. Needle jet set bolt
6. Washer
7. O-ring
8. Main jet
9. O-ring
10. Main jet cover
11. Screw
12. Lockwasher
13. Float assembly
14. Float pivot pin
15. Float bowl gasket
16. Float bowl
17. Throttle slide
18. Needle
19. Needle clip
20. Spring seat
21. Return spring
22. Carburetor cap
23. Cable adjuster locknut
24. Cable adjuster
25. Cover
26. Spring
27. Throttle stop screw
28. Spring
29. Pilot air screw
30. Starter plunger
31. Spring
32. Starter lever washer
33. Starter lever
34. Plunger cap
35. Plunger cap cover
36. Float bowl screw
37. Lockwasher
38. Locktab
39. O-ring
40. Overflow line
41. Carburetor flange bolt
42. Lockwasher
43. Washer
44. Manifold
45. Gasket

Mikuni VM24SH carburetor

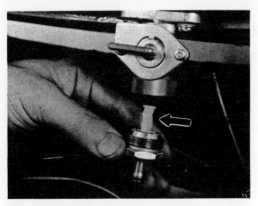

Fuel filter in gas tank

Clean the fuel filter(s) is gasoline and check condition. If the filter is very old, enough foreign matter may have accumulated on it to make thorough cleaning impossible. In this event, replace it.

Clogged fuel filters may cause a lean running condition at high speeds, since the engine may be using gasoline faster than it can flow through the filters. In addition, if clogged badly enough, the filters may cause hard starting, especially when the supply of fuel in the tank is low.

Some models have an additional fuel filter in the carburetor(s). This is considered under "Carburetor Cleaning," following.

FUEL PETCOCKS

Aside from their fuel filters, petcocks are seldom the cause of trouble.

Petcocks are generally of three types: electric, manual, and diaphragm, which refers to the method by which the fuel flow is started.

Electric petcocks are not in general use but are found on such machines as the Moto Guzzi. To check operation, simply disconnect the lines at the petcock with the ignition turned off. There must be no fuel flow. Placing a suitable container beneath the petcock, turn on the ignition. Fuel should commence flowing.

Manual petcocks are the rule at the present time. The petcock has three positions in most cases: "off," "on," and "reserve." This refers to the widely used single-lever type. Before Federally-mandated standardization, Harley-Davidson used a two-lever petcock.

The petcock must allow free fuel flow in the "on" and "reserve" positions, but no gasoline must pass through when the petcock is "off." This is probably the most common petcock fault: allowing gasoline to pass all the time. This can be very harmful for the engine—

especially four-strokes. If the gas is left on when the engine is not running, it can rise by capillary action into the carburetor throat, and eventually into the intake port and the combustion chamber. If enough raw gasoline collects in the combustion chamber, there can be an hydraulic lock the first time the engine is turned over. That is, there may be so much incompressibile fluid in the combustion chamber, that it may stop the piston dead. This often causes a bent connecting rod. Even if this does not happen, however, the gasoline may flow past the piston and contaminate the oil in the crankcase.

Therefore, petcocks which will not stop the fuel flow completely in the "off" position must always be replaced.

Fuel flow from the petcock in the "on" and "reserve" positions must be free and substantial. If flow seems weak or intermittent, open the gas cap. If flow increases, the gas cap vent is clogged and should be blown clear. If the flow does not increase, check the fuel filters as outlined above.

Diaphragm petcocks are used on Suzuki Triples and some other two-strokes. This petcock usually has three positions: "on," "prime," and "reserve." Fuel is allowed to flow through the petcock in the "on" position only when the diaphragm is activated by engine vacuum, which is only when the engine is running. To check fuel flow, turn lever to the "prime" position.

If no gasoline is getting to the carburetors, check that the vacuum line from the petcock to the engine is firmly secured at both ends, and is not cracked or dry-rotted. Vacuum leaks will cause the petcock to shut off the fuel flow. The second check is for a torn or punctured diaphragm, which would be very rare. The diaphragm is accessible after disassembling the petcock.

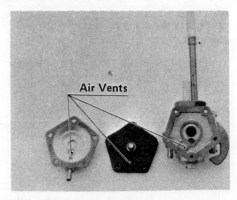

Construction of diaphragm petcock

CARBURETOR CONTROLS

One often-overlooked cause of poor fuel system operation can be found in the throttle controls: twist-grip, cables, and the linkage arrangements found on multi-carburetor motorcycles.

Proper lubrication of the carburetor controls is essential.

Twist-grips are usually of the split type in which the drum is contained in a two-piece housing. The housing top half can be removed for lubrication. Since many machines incorporate various electrical switches in the twist-grip, exercise care when removing to avoid damage to wiring and connections. Use a light grease in the throttle twist-grip. Apply some lubricant to the part of the grip which contacts the handlebar to ensure smooth movement. When putting the housing back together, note that on most motorcycles, there is a locating pin somewhere on the twist-grip to prevent it from rotating around the handlebar. This pin fits into a hole in the handlebar. Be sure it is engaged before tightening the housing.

When installing the top of the housing, tighten the fasteners slowly and evenly, checking for free throttle movement as you go along.

Throttle cables are arranged in many ways depending on whether the engine is a two or four-stroke, single, twin, or multi, and so on.

On most two-strokes, a main throttle cable

Separating the throttle drum for lubrication

enters a junction block beneath the gas tank, where it is split to operate one or more shorter carburetor cables and the oil pump cable.

Many machines now use a "push-pull" type cable arrangement whereby two cables at the twist-grip operate a pulley at the carburetors. Actually, the name is a misnomer since a cable cannot be "pushed" as it is flexible. In actual practice, the two cables are connected to opposite sides of the twist-grip, so one of them pulls the throttles open, and the other pulls them shut when the grip is released.

All throttle cables should be lubricated periodically in accordance with your owner's manual.

In addition, cables must be adjusted to the recommended free-play, an adjustment which is usually performed in conjunction with a tune-up.

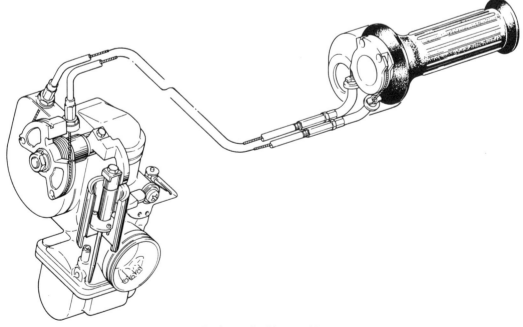

Dual-control cable assembly

Throttle cables must be arranged as the manufacturer intended. The cables must not be bent sharply or kinked anywhere along their length. Ensure that the cables are clipped to the frame only at those points determined by the factory. Removal and installation of the gas tank is one instance at which the cable(s) may be disturbed.

Check that cables are long enough, especially if new ones have been installed, or handlebars changed. With the engine idling, turn the handlebars from lock-to-lock. Any rise in the idle speed indicates that the cables are either too short, improperly adjusted, or are improperly installed.

On some motorcycles, especially multi-cylinder ones, the throttle cables must be routed in specific ways over or under the top frame tubes. Altering this arrangement even in a seemingly minor fashion can cause improper operation. Memorize the original cable routes before any work is done on the system.

Throttle linkages at the carburetors, such as the pulley arrangements now in wide use, are in most cases best left alone. Some of these linkages have grease fittings which should be lubricated with a light-weight grease at intervals recommended by the manufacturer. Systems of this sort also have the adjustments for throttle slide synchronization, and should

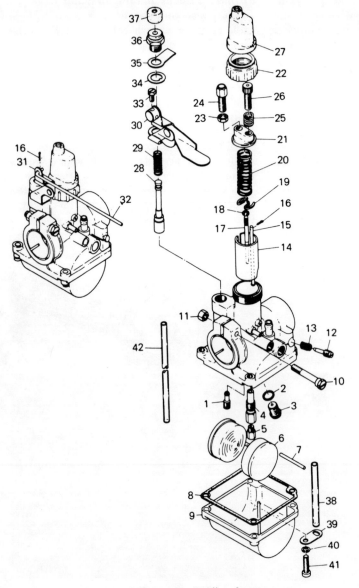

1. Pilot jet
2. Float needle seat washer
3. Float needle seat
4. Needle jet
5. Main jet
6. Float assembly
7. Float pivot pin
8. Float bowl gasket
9. Float bowl
10. Carburetor clamp screw
11. Nut
12. Pilot air screw
13. Spring
14. Throttle slide
15. Throttle stop rod
16. Cotter pin
17. Needle
18. Needle clip
19. Spring seat
20. Throttle return spring
21. Carburetor cap
22. Carburetor cap ring nut
23. Cable adjuster locknut
24. Cable adjuster
25. Throttle stop rod spring
26. Idle adjusting screw
27. Rubber cap
28. Starter plunger
29. Spring
30. Starter lever
31. Starter lever
32. Starter lever rod
33. Screw
34. Washer
35. Plate
36. Plunger cap
37. Plunger cap cover
38. Breather tube
39. Plate
40. Washer
41. Screw
42. Overflow tube

Mikuni type "SC" carburetor

therefore be approached with caution, unless you have the proper vacuum gauges to synchronize the slides.

Throttle slides must snap closed from any position except in those rare instances in which the linkage is the non-return type.

Pulley linkages as found on many machines are usually not prone to trouble in this regard. If the throttle slide(s) will not close when the twist-grip is released, first check that the tensioner sometimes fitted to the twist-grip for touring is not in play. Next, check cable lubrication. Inner cables which are sharply bent or kinked can cause the slide(s) to hang up.

Also, check the condition of the inner cable. A cable which is frayed or has even a single broken strand must be replaced at once.

The most common troublespot for throttle cables is at the twist-grip. Since on most motorcycles the cable is bent around the throttle drum when the twist-grip is turned, metal fatigue is only natural and the cable will eventually suffer one or more broken strands at this point. A broken strand can seize in the cable housing making it impossible to close the throttle slide(s). The frequency of cable damage at the twist-grip is dependent to some extent upon the diameter of the drum. A cable which must be bent around a small diameter drum will be more likely to break eventually than one which is not bent to such a great degree. Some machines which suffer frequent cable failure at this point may benefit from the installation of a "quick throttle," which has a large diameter drum.

Luckily, the sophisticated throttle linkages in use on many machines today have in some measure eliminated throttle failures of this sort. Another system which was used on some motorcycles such as Ducati and BMW was a throttle drum with a short length of miniature roller chain attached. The throttle cable was attached to the other end of chain. The result was that when the throttle was opened the chain would be bent around the drum, and not the cable itself.

Another problem which might cause control malfunction is seizing of the slide in the carburetor. Although relatively rare, this can happen on some models. Especially prone to this phenomenon are carburetors which are bolted to their manifolds with a flange. Uneven tightening or overtightening of the mounting nuts or bolts can warp the carburetor body and cause the slide to stick.

On carburetors of this sort, it is sometimes helpful to install the complete slide assembly with carburetor cap in the carb before bolting the unit to the manifold. Constantly operating the slide while tightening the fasteners is recommended. If the slide sticks suddenly, the nuts or bolts are either over-tight, or the carburetor body is warped. This presents a problem, since the fasteners must be relatively tight to form an effective seal at the manifold. If the body is warped, it should be replaced.

CARBURETOR CLEANING

Very often carburetor trouble can be cured by simply cleaning the unit, since the finely calibrated fuel and air passages can become clogged or partially obstructed by bits of foreign matter which get by the filters, thus altering the mixture. Most often a dirty carburetor will malfunction at idle or low speed, since the jets and passages which control these ranges are naturally smaller and more liable to be blocked.

Some carburetors, such as Amals and Dell 'Ortos, are equipped with an additional fuel filter mounted on the carburetor. This is most often located in the fuel feed banjo on the float bowl or carburetor body. This filter may be a finer mesh than that found in the petcock, and it is therefore more easily clogged.

Fuel filter in carburetor body

Early Amal Concentric carburetor had a final filter surrounding the main jet as well.

For cleaning purposes, solvents are readily available under several brand names. Be sure to choose one which is safe for plastic parts, since some carbs have non-removable plastic pieces in them.

Strip the carburetor body of all removable parts: float assembly, jets, idle and throttle screws, o-rings, gaskets, etc. Follow the solvent manufacturer's instructions for the cleaning process.

Fuel jets should be blown clear with compressed air if blocked. Never insert anything, such as wire or the like, into a jet to clean it out. The jet bore is calibrated to deliver exactly the correct amount of fuel, and the bore will be damaged if a sharp object is forced through.

Air and fuel passages in the carburetor body must be cleaned with compressed air as well. Pilot outlet and bypass holes are extremely small and can easily be blocked by impurities in the gasoline.

CARBURETOR FLOODING

Flooding of the carburetor will cause an overly-rich mixture at all throttle openings if not too severe, or leakage of fuel from the float bowl if it is really bad.

Minor flooding, which may not be immediately recognizable as such, can be caused by an incorrect float level. Another cause can be a worn float needle. Checking and adjusting the float level varies from carburetor to carburetor and procedures and specifications should be obtained from a shop manual. As a rule, two-strokes are somewhat more sensitive to float level than are four-strokes.

Major flooding of the carburetor(s) is usually indicated by the discharge of gasoline. Most carburetors are equipped with float bowl overflow tubes, and if fuel is being discharged from here after the machine has been sitting for a few minutes with the petcock open, there is undoubtedly something amiss with the float assembly.

On models which do not have overflow tubes, removal of the air cleaner hose may give an indication of excess fuel in the float bowl. If raw gasoline appears at the air passages in the carburetor mouth, either the float level is far too high, or the float needle and seat are not forming an effective seal.

The most common float malady is caused by the failure of the float needle to form an effective seal with its seat. The float bowl then becomes overfilled with gasoline. Often, a routine cleaning of the float needle and seat is all that is required, assuming that the needle is being held off the seat by a transient bit of foreign matter.

On older machines, however, this problem can be caused by corrosion built up on the needle or the seat. If this is the case, both components should be replaced. The needle seat on most carburetors can be unscrewed for replacement. Never attempt to reform a seal by lapping the needle against the seat. This will cause wear on one or the other, and will change the float level. Needle seats are almost always brass, and therefore highly resistant to corrosion. Long periods of disuse, however, can cause the build-up of foreign matter which is almost irremovable. Float needles can be brass or plastic, or neoprene-tipped. Any foreign matter on the tip of the needle can be removed with solvents (on neoprene needles only gasoline should be used to clean the tip) and compressed air, but no attempt should be made to scrape the tip clean.

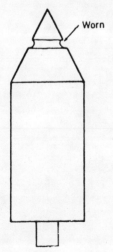

Check float needle condition

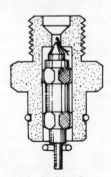

Float needle seat blocked by foreign matter

High-mileage machines may show wear of the needle tip. However, wear must be severe to be easily noticeable, and can be present though scarcely visible. If flooding is a problem, replacement of the needle is advisable.

On carburetors on which the float assembly is mounted on the carburetor body and the fuel feed is on the body as well, the efficacy of the float needle and seat can be checked as follows:

Remove the float bowl. Place a suitable container beneath the carburetor to catch any gasoline which may spill.

Carefully raise the float bulbs with your finger until the needle is gently seated. Do not use excessive pressure.

Turn on the fuel. No leakage should be apparent. If fuel leaks from the needle seat, replace or clean the needle and seat. When the needle is seated, fuel flow must be entirely cut off.

A less common cause of flooding, but one which should be checked, is failure of the float bulbs. If gasoline leaks into the bulbs, they will allow float level to become higher. Eventually, enough gasoline may leak in to "sink" the bulbs; at which time the needle will remain open at all times.

It is easy enough to check for a defective

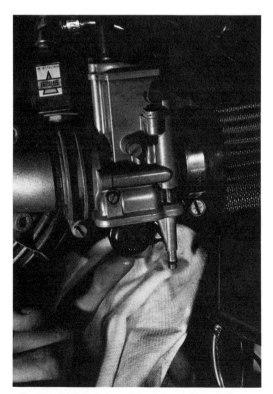

Checking sealing ability of the float needle and seat

float: just shake it next to your ear and listen for trapped gasoline. Alternatively, semi-transparent plastic floats can be held up to a strong light and any gasoline inside will become visible.

Punctured or leaking floats must always be replaced. No repairs are possible.

Troubles of this sort have been largely sorted out by modern carburetors, many of which use solid buoyant float bulbs of plastic or resin as distinguished from older floats of brass or hollow plastic.

AIR LEAKS

Carburetor air leaks are a very serious matter since they will cause an extremely lean mixture which can and will damage the engine due to the heat generated in the combustion process.

The most common area in which air leaks occur is at the manifold. Balance tubes between the manifolds of some twins and multis should be checked for tightness of connection and general condition.

Air leaks very often cause an extremely erratic idle which cannot be smoothed out by any degree of adjustment. Also, the mixture may vary depending on how hot the engine is. Therefore, settings which let the engine idle smoothly when it is cold will cause erratic operation as it heats up, and vice-versa.

To check for air leaks, warm the engine up to operating temperature and allow it to idle. Squirt motor oil carefully around potential areas of leakage such as the carburetor mount on the manifold or where the manifold mounts to the engine. If the idle changes, there is an air leak at that spot.

CARBURETOR REBUILDING

Sometimes, carburetor troubles arise from normal wear of the parts (such as the float needle, needle jet, or throttle slide), or from deterioration of seals, gaskets, o-rings.

When the carburetor is disassembled for cleaning after extended intervals, all gaskets and o-rings should be replaced. Some manufacturers offer rebuilding kits which contain all necessary parts.

O-rings are especially important. They can be easily damaged by removal or installation, and they do not have long service lives in general. On some carburetors, o-rings are used as the main seal at the carb mounting flange. This is one place where the o-ring must function perfectly, or an air leak will be apparent.

Mounting flange O-rings are critical to proper operation

EFFECT OF ALTITUDE ON CARBURETION

Increased altitude tends to produce a rich mixture; the greater the altitude, the smaller the main jet required. Most standard jetting is suitable for use in altitudes up to approximately 3,000 feet. If you use your machine constantly in altitudes between 3,000 and 6,000 feet, the main jet size should be reduced about 5 percent. A further reduction of 4 percent should be made for every 3,000 feet in excess of 6,000 feet altitude. No adjustment can be made to compensate for the loss of power due to rarefied air.

Carburetor Troubleshooting

Problem	Possible Causes	Inspection/Remedy
Carburetor floods repeatedly	Float set too high	Adjust. Refer to "Tune-Up" Chapter.
	Float needle sticking	Remove float bowl and clean needle and seat.
	Float needle or seat worn or damaged	Replace as necessary.
	Float sticking due to misalignment	Correct.
	Fuel petcock left open with engine shut off	Shut off the fuel after you stop engine.
	Float punctured	Replace.
Idle mixture too lean	Pilot jet too small	Replace with larger jet.
	Worn throttle slide	Replace.
	Pilot screw out of adjustment	Adjust.
Idle mixture too rich	Pilot jet too large	Replace with smaller jet.
	Dirt or foreign matter in idle passage	Dismantle and clean carburetor.
	Pilot screw out of adjustment	Adjust.
Lean mixture at sustained mid-range speeds	Jet needle set too lean	Reset needle clip at lower notch.
	Needle or main jet clogged	Remove and clean jets.
	Intake manifold air leak	Find leak and rectify.
Lean mixture at sustained high-speeds	Main jet too small	Replace with larger jet.
	Main jet clogged	Remove and clean.
	Float level too low	Remove float and adjust level.
Lean mixture during acceleration	Jets clogged	Remove and clean.
	Damaged or worn throttle slide	Replace.
	Float level too low	Adjust float height.

Carburetor Troubleshooting (cont.)

Problem	Possible Causes	Inspection/Remedy
Lean mixture throughout throttle range	Fuel filters clogged or dirty	Remove and clean.
	Gas cap vent blocked	Blow clear.
	Damaged or worn throttle slide	Replace.
	Air leaks at carb manifold	Find leak and rectify.
Rich mixture at sustained mid-range speeds	Air cleaner dirty	Clean or replace.
	Main jet too large	Replace with smaller jet.
	Carburetor flooding	See above.
	Needle or needle jet worn	Replace.
Rich mixture at sustained high-speeds	Main jet too large	Replace with smaller size jet.
	Carburetor flooding	See above.
	Air cleaner dirty	Replace or clean.
Rich mixture throughout throttle range	Carburetor flooding	See above.
	Air cleaner dirty	Replace or clean.
Erratic idle	Air leaks	Determine source and rectify.
	Dirty or blocked idle passages	Clean carburetor.
	Idle settings incorrect	Adjust to specifications.
	Damage to pilot screw	Replace.
	Worn or damaged air seals such as o-rings or gaskets	Rebuild carburetor.
	Unsynchronized carburetors on multi-carb machines	Adjust and synchronize carburetors.
	Defective auto timing advancer	Repair or replace.
	Mixture too lean	Adjust carburetor.

Motorcycle electrical systems vary widely in design and application.

Most of the large displacement road-going machines use either a battery/coil or CDI system for ignition, and an alternator to charge the battery. There are exceptions; early British motorcycles used a magneto ignition, the magneto being completely self-contained and separated physically and electrically from the alternator. Other machines continue to use a DC (direct current) generator as opposed to the AC output of an alternator.

Smaller machines and off-road or dual-purpose motorcycles may use either CDI or a flywheel magneto. Flywheel magnetos are primarily intended to spark the plug(s), but may have a provision for charging the battery if one is fitted.

Electric-start two-strokes most frequently use a DC starter/generator, which incorporates the functions of an electric starter and a DC generator in one unit.

The main power producer will also determine what other electrical components are needed to complete the system. An alternator, for example, requires a *rectifier* to change the alternating current output to direct current in order to charge the battery. Additionally, if the output of the power producer is great enough, as it is in the majority of instances, a *regulator* is necessary to prevent the battery from overcharging or discharging under varying conditions.

Any of these components may take on a variety of forms. Regulators, for example, may be mechanical (in which the current to the battery is switched off or on by electromagnetic switches), or electronic (in which case the switching function is handled by electronic components and semi-conductors). Rectifiers may be half-wave or full-wave depending upon the job they have to do, and so on.

Even though DC generators are all very similar, alternators may take on a number of forms. Some use permanent magnets, others use electro-magnets which require field windings, carbon brushes and the like, which still others use a rotating device to make and break the magnetic field around the armature to produce current.

Apart from CDI units and regulators using sophisticated solid-state electrical components, most motorcycles electrical parts work according to a few simple rules.

One of the basic rules is that current flowing in a wire creates a magnetic field around that wire, the direction of the field determined by

104

the direction of current flow, and its intensity by the rate of current flow.

Now magnetism is a mysterious phenomenon, but the field produced by the current flowing in a wire is of the same nature as that produced by a magnet.

If a loop of wire is placed in an already existing magnetic field, such as between two magnets, and then rotated, a current flow will be *induced* in the wire. The rate of flow of this current will depend upon the strength of the magnets and the speed of rotation, increasing as these two variables are increased. Of course, the resistance of the wire will play a part as well, but this is not significant in this discussion. This is known as *electro-magnetic induction.*

Furthermore, the direction of current flow in the wire will reverse itself once during each rotation of the wire loop as it cuts through the "North" and "South" poles of the magnets. This is alternating current, and the principle described is that upon which magnetos and alternators are based.

If commutators are added to each end of the wire loop and so positioned as to allow current flow at only a certain portion of the loop's rotation, direct current can be obtained, and the device is known as a generator, or more precisely, a DC generator.

In this example we have shown a wire loop rotating in a magnetic field. This is not the only method. If the loop was stationary, and the *magnets* rotated around it, the same effect would be produced. In fact, this is how most alternators and magnetos are designed.

As noted, the current flow from the loop of wire can be increased either by increasing the strength of the magnetic field or the speed of rotation of the wire. This can be easily correlated if you have had any experience with magneto-powered machines by noting that the headlight becomes brighter or the horn goes to a higher pitch when the engine is revved up. (Since most newer bikes have a battery to power these parts, don't be dismayed if this doesn't happen on your bike.) The higher engine rpm, obviously, is increasing the speed of the wire loops through the magnetic field and increasing the current flow.

Another way to obtain more current from this set-up is to increase the number of wire loops. In actual practice, no working magneto or alternator has only one loop of wire, but many.

We mentioned that power output can also be varied by changing the intensity of the magnetic field. This cannot be done with flywheel magnetos which use permanent magnets. Some alternators, however, do not use permanent magnets, but *electro-magnets* which are nothing more than coils of wire around an iron core with current running through them. The degree of magnetism is directly proportional to the current passing through the wire, so if this current is varied, the output of the alternator will vary. In fact, this is a common method of regulating the output of the alternator.

So far we have discussed one electro-magnetic phenomenon and seen how it applies to such things as generators and alternators. We have noted how a loop of wire moving in a magnetic field has a current flow induced in it. Now this current flow is not caused directly by the motion of the wire or magnets, but rather because the strength of the field is greater in some places and less powerful in others, and it is the change in magnitude of the field which causes the current to flow. This is a very important principle, since we will see that a rising or falling magnetic field will cause current flow in a wire, whether or not there is motion involved.

A good example of this phenomenon of electromagnetic induction is the construction of the common ignition coil. Most ignition coils consist of a winding of wire around an iron core. Under this winding is another, of much thinner wire, and consisting of several thousand more turns of wire than the first.

Now, a series of closely wound coils of wire will produce a very powerful magnetic field around themselves when current is allowed to pass through. In an ignition coil, this magnetic field will also surround the second coil over the first. When the current flow through the first (or primary) coil is stopped (which is what breaker points do), the magnetic field will rapidly collapse. This rapid change in field strength will induce a current flow in the second coil. The amount of current flow will be dependent upon the number of turns of wire in the two coils. For example, if the first coil had ten turns of wire, and the second coil ten thousand turns, the amount of current which was flowing through the first will be multiplied a thousand times in the second. This is why a simple twelve-volt battery can produce through the coil the 20,000 or so volts necessary to fire a spark plug.

Operational Descriptions

MAGNETO GENERATOR

The magneto generator, mounted in the flywheel, is one of the simplest types of charging systems and is commonly used on two-strokes that do not require much electrical power. The magneto base is usually mounted on the left side crankcase and is surrounded by a flywheel with symmetrical, cast-in magnets. The flywheel rotates around the ignition coils in the magneto base and, as the coils pass in and out of the magnetic field of the flywheel magnets, electricity is created. A cam on the flywheel opens and closes the contact breaker points as it turns. The alternating current (AC) generated by the magneto is used to power the ignition, headlight, and taillight directly on most machines. On bikes equipped with a battery, horn, and turn signals, a rectifier is used to convert the alternating current to direct current (DC).

When the contact breaker points are closed, the induced current in the magneto coils reaches approximately 3–5 amps, a relatively low figure. When the contact breaker is opened by the action of the flywheel cam, the current generated by the magneto coils passes through the primary ignition coil, which produces about 200–300 volts, and then through the secondary coil, where the voltage is greatly stepped up to fire the spark plug. A condenser is used in conjunction with the contact breaker to prevent premature spark discharge and to protect the breaker points from burning.

In order to supply the greatly varying needs of the charging and lighting system, two separate electrical supply wires are normally tapped from the magneto. The light-load wire supplies the lesser needs of

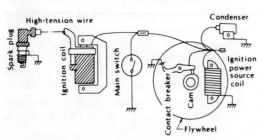

Magneto ignition circuit

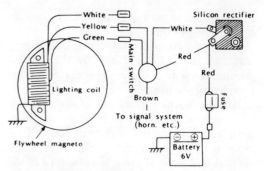

Magneto lighting circuit

day (lights off) riding, while the heavy-load wire supplies a greater amount of current to meet the demands of night riding. On a few models, a voltage regulator is used instead of the double supply system, and in this way the regulator, which senses battery voltage, automatically and efficiently controls voltage output of the magneto.

DC GENERATOR

The DC generator produces current in the same manner as an automobile generator. An armature made up of many looped wires around an iron core revolves within an electromagnet. The strong magnetic field of the magnet induces a voltage in the armature which is then picked up by carbon brushes that contact the commutator (where the looped armature wires meet). The current picked up by the brushes then passes through a voltage regulator and to the condenser, points, ignition coil, spark plug, and the lighting system. Very few machines today use the DC generator system, which is more complicated and less reliable than the alternator systems now used.

STARTER GENERATOR

The starter generator operates similarly to the DC generator except that it usually has an additional electromagnet and an extra pair of brushes, which serve to convert the generator to a starter when necessary. Current from the battery is sent to the windings of the electromagnet and to the armature via the carbon brushes. This current flow sets up a magnetic field in the armature and another surrounding the armature. The position of the north and south poles of these fields are contrasting, however, and since like poles repel and unlike poles attract, the armature (secured

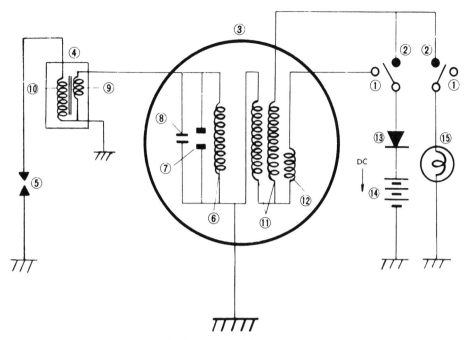

Flywheel magneto wiring diagram

1. Daytime running	6. Magneto coil	11. Lighting coil
2. Nighttime running	7. Contact breaker	12. Differential winding coil
3. Flywheel magneto	8. Capacitor	13. Rectifier
4. Ignition coil	9. Ignition primary coil	14. Battery
5. Spark plug	10. Ignition secondary coil	15. AC lamp load (head lamp and tail lamp)

to the crankshaft), spins around and turns the engine.

ALTERNATOR

The alternator (AC) system consists of the alternator, battery, rectifier, and, on some models, a voltage regulator or zener diode type regulator. The AC charging system is the most common system on to-day's machines.

The alternator consists basically of a sta-tor and rotor, which is bolted to the end of the crankshaft. Electrical current is in-duced in the stator as the magnetic fields

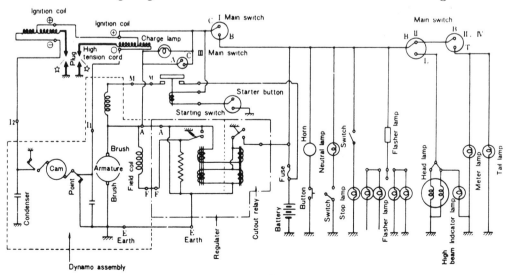

DC generator schematic

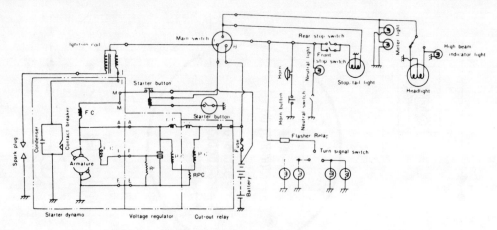

Starter generator schematic

of the rotor magnets cut through the stator windings. The advantages of an alternator over a DC generator are that it is less bulky and has fewer moving parts, and it produces a larger voltage at low speeds.

Since an alternator produces alternating current and the battery requires direct current for recharging, it is necessary to employ some means of converting the AC to DC. The selenium rectifier accomplishes this by allowing the alternating current produced by the alternator to pass through it in one direction only, thus converting it before it reaches the battery.

On most smaller displacement machines, alternator output is balanced against the normal electrical needs of the bike, and a voltage regulator is not used. The alternator is matched to the electrical system so that during day running (lights off) the battery will be receiving a normal charge, and during night running, the battery, with the additional load, will (hopefully) be receiving enough current to keep it from discharging. Frequent battery maintenance may be necessary if your bike is used almost exclusively for either day or night riding, or other abnormal conditions.

Most larger displacement Japanese machines (350 and up) are equipped with a silicon type voltage regulator which is non-mechanical and cannot be adjusted. With the addition of the regulator, a higher capacity alternator, which is capable of supplying a strong charge at full electrical load, is also used. As long as battery voltage is within the normal range, the regulator does not function, and alternator supplies its total output to the battery. When the normal battery voltage is

exceeded and the battery is being overcharged, the regulator functions to ground the excessive current and maintain a normal charging rate.

On most British bikes, a zener diode serves the function of a voltage regulator, tapping off excess alternator current output and rerouting it to a heat sink, where it is grounded to the frame. A zener diode is very efficient as long as it is kept clean, tight on its mounting, and free from obstruction in the cooling airstream at all times.

On Honda fours, an automotive type three phase excited field alternator is used in conjunction with a mechanical regulator. The advantage of this type of alternator is that the amount of current output can be precisely controlled to suit the needs of the machine. The alternator supplies the battery with the amount of charge it requires, which is monitored by the regulator. When the battery voltage drops below 13.5 volts, the upper regulator contact closes and battery voltage is routed directly to the alternator field coil.

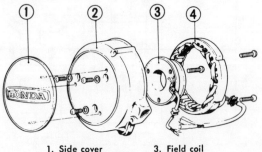

1. Side cover   3. Field coil
2. Alternator cover   4. Stator coil

Alternator components (Honda Fours)

Since the field coil is excited in proportion to the amount of voltage fed into it, alternator output increases and the battery recieves a stronger charge. When battery voltage is within the normal range, current through the regulator coil is great enough to open the upper point set, but not great enough to close the lower points. Battery voltage is then routed through a 10 ohm resistor which lowers voltage input to the alternator field coil, consequently lowering alternator output. When battery voltage

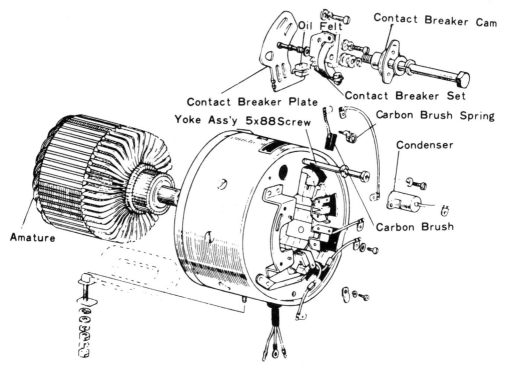

Starter / generator components (Kawasaki B1L-A shown)

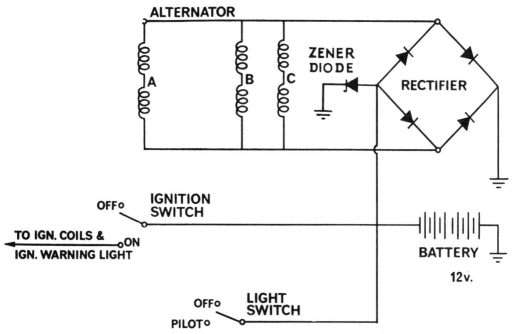

Lucas 12-volt charging system

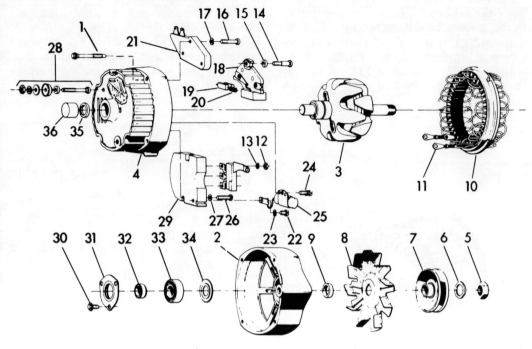

Alternator components (H-D Servi-car)

1. Thru bolt (4)	13. Washer (3)	25. Condenser & bracket
2. Drive end frame	14. Screw	26. Screw
3. Rotor	15. Insulator	27. Washer
4. Stator	16. Screw (2)	28. Battery terminal parts
5. Shaft nut	17. Washer (2)	29. Rectifier bridge
6. Shaft nut washer	18. Brush holder	30. Retainer screw (3)
7. Pulley (sheave)	19. Brush (2)	31. Ball brg. retainer
8. Fan	20. Spring (2)	32. Ball brg. seal spacer
9. Fan spacer washer	21. Regulator	33. Ball bearing
10. Stator coil	22. Screw	34. Ball brg. shield
11. Stator coil terminal	23. Washer	35. Needle brg. spacer
12. Nut (3)	24. Screw & lockwasher	36. Needle bearing

exceeds about 14.5 volts, the lower regulator contact closes, routing the battery voltage through a 10 ohm resistor and then to ground. This eliminates voltage input to the field coil, which consequently eliminates alternator output. In this way, the alternator supplies just the right amount of current needed for each situation, and is capable of handling any accessory demands that might be made on the bike.

CAPACITOR DISCHARGE IGNITION (CDI)

The capacitor discharge ignition system is basically a modification of the magneto system. In the CDI system, the primary winding of the ignition coil is supplied with current from the capacitor, in response to a timed signal at the time of ignition. Because the capacitor discharges current to the primary windings instantly, high voltage is induced in the secondary windings of the coil and a very strong spark is produced at the spark plug. Self induction in the primary winding occurs faster in the CD ignition system and this short-rise time is why a good spark can be produced across even a fouled spark plug.

Contact breaker points are not used with the CDI system. Instead, an electronic timing detector and electric switch are used to fire the spark plug at the right moment. The signal coil (timing detector) generates a small amount of voltage at every crankshaft revolution and sends it to the electric switch (silicon controlled rectifier, or SCR), which triggers the capacitor.

Capacitor discharge ignition is used on some of the high performance two-strokes currently being produced (notably Kawa-

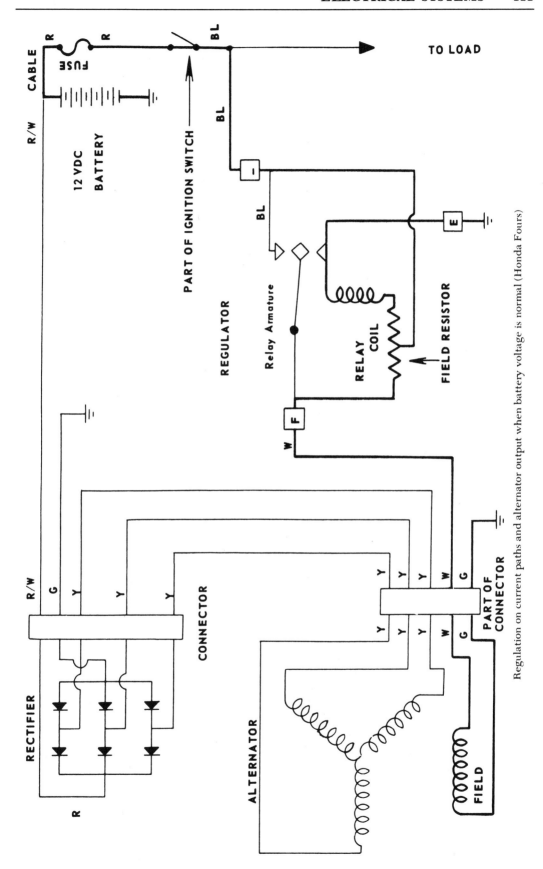

Regulation on current paths and alternator output when battery voltage is normal (Honda Fours)

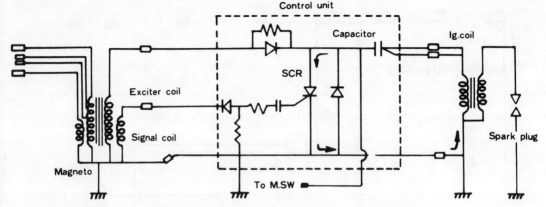

Schematic diagram of the capacitor discharge ignition system

saki). Its advantages are that it produces a very hot spark at any rpm, greatly reduces plug fouling, and because it doesn't use contact breaker points, maintenance is cut down and ignition timing (extremely critical on a two-stroke) tends to stay where it is set.

CONSTANT LOSS IGNITION

The constant loss ignition system is basically an alternator system minus the battery. Instead of the battery a capacitor is used, which results in a significant weight reduction for machines used in competition. In operation, the capacitor stores the current from the alternator and releases it at the moment of contact breaker opening. This produces an adequate spark for starting, although not as healthy a spark as is produced by the battery. When running, the capacitor also helps to reduce DC voltage ripple. The lighting system will also operate normally, except that the lights will not function when the engine is not running.

In addition to the obvious advantage of not requiring a battery, this system has several other points in its favor: alternator timing is not nearly as critical as on battery powered machines; cold weather does not affect the capacitor, and the system requires less maintenance. However, no street machines are currently being produced with the constant loss system because in most states it is illegal to license a bike that cannot operate its lights with the engine off for a specified interval of time.

BATTERY IGNITION

Battery ignition, also called battery-and-coil ignition, consists of a power source, the

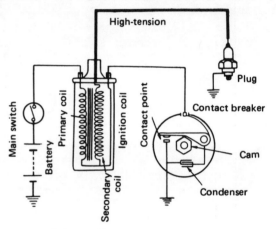

Circuit diagram of battery system.

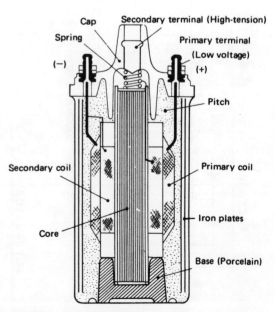

Ignition coil construction.

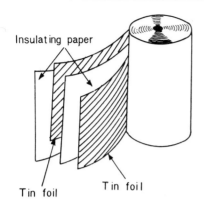

Insulating paper

Tin foil   Tin foil

Internal construction of condenser

battery, the contact breaker points, the ignition coil, and the spark plug(s).

When the ignition switch is turned on, current from the battery is directed through the primary winding of the ignition coil, creating a magnetic field which incompasses the secondary winding. The current then flows through the contact breaker points which are closed, thus grounding the current.

The breaker points are opened and closed by a cam which may be mounted on the end of the camshaft, the crankshaft, or any other rotating shaft of the engine. When the piston moves into the correct position, the breaker cam opens the points which in turn stops the current flow through the ignition coil's primary winding. The resultant collapse of the magnetic field induces high voltage in the secondary windings of the coil, and this voltage potential grounds itself by jumping across the air gap of the spark plug, igniting the fuel/air mixture.

In order to prevent sparking, and resultant reduction in spark voltage, at the points when they just begin to open, a condenser is fitted in parallel with the points. As they open, the condenser absorbs a portion of the voltage and feeds it back to the ignition coil almost instantaneously.

If the condenser is defective, the current passing through the points will tend to jump the narrow gap as the points just open, which will reduce the voltage at the spark plug (causing misfiring), and burn and pit the point contact surfaces making them unserviceable in a short length of time.

Motorcycles usually have one set of breaker points and one ignition coil for each cylinder, although there are many exceptions.

It is possible to have a single point set and coil serve two cylinders, in which case two spark plugs will fire at the same time. This is acceptable providing pistons are properly positioned: one on the compression stroke, and the other on its exhaust stroke. The spark in the cylinder not on the compression stroke is called a "waste spark." The Kawasaki KZ400 is a twin with one coil, while the Honda Fours use two coils for four cylinders: same principal.

This type of system is easily recognizable, and has two high tension leads coming from the ignition coil. It is important to note that the two spark plugs involved are interdependent. That is, both must fire at the same time. If one plug lead is disconnected, neither plug will fire, in most cases.

Troubleshooting the Charging System

If a charging system fault is suspected, the first thing to do is check the overload fuse, usually located near the battery. If it is not burned out, inspect the charging system wires and connectors. Make sure that the rectifier (if applicable) is securely mounted to the frame. If no obvious fault can be found, refer to the following sections for test procedures applicable to your machine.

BSA

Alternator Output Test

SINGLES

1. Disconnect the alternator output leads.

NOTE: *Earlier machines have three leads; later machines have two.*

2. Start and run the engine at 3000 rpm.

3. Connect a 0–15 volt AC voltmeter with a 1-ohm load resistor in parallel with each of the alternator leads as described below.

4. Three-lead-type stator:

a. White/green and green/black leads—minimum voltmeter reading 4.0 volts.

b. White/green and green/yellow

leads—minimum voltmeter reading 6.5 volts.

c. White/green and green/black with green/yellow leads—minimum voltmeter reading 8.5 volts.

5. Two-lead-type stator:

a. White/green and green/yellow leads—minimum voltmeter reading 8.5 volts.

6. If low or no readings are obtained, inspect the leads for damage and make sure that they have tight connections. Check the alternator output again, and if the same results are obtained, the difficulty lies in the alternator itself and must be referred to a qualified repair shop.

7. To check for grounded coils within the stator, connect the voltmeter to each terminal and ground. If a reading is obtained, the coil connected to the lead being tested is grounded.

TWINS

Test the alternator output as described for the single-cylinder models. Correct output. Readings are given in the chart.

Stator Number	System Voltage	Alternator Output Minimum AC Volts @ 3000 rpm		
		A	B	C
47162	6V	4.0	6.5	8.5
	12V			
47164	6V	4.5	7.0	9.5
47167	6V	7.7	11.6	13.2
47188	6V	5.0	1.5	3.5
47204	12V	N.A.	N.A.	8.5
47205	12V	N.A.	N.A.	9.0

A—Green/White and Green/Black
B—Green/White and Green/Yellow
C—Green/White and $\left\{ \begin{matrix} \text{Green/Black} \\ \text{Green/Yellow} \end{matrix} \right\}$ connected
NOTE: On machines fitted with two-lead-stator, only test C is applicable.

TRIPLES

Check alternator output for the triple in the same manner as described for the three-lead-stator on single-cylinder models.

Correct output readings are on the following page.

Alternator Output Minimum AC Volts @ 3000 rpm		
RM20 stator 47209 (12 volt)	green/white and green/black connected 5.0	green/white and green/yellow connected 8.0	green/white green/black and green/yellow connected 10.0

HARLEY-DAVIDSON

Generator Output Test

1. Remove the wire from the generator "F" terminal and connect a jumper wire from the "F" terminal to ground.

2. Remove wire(s) from "A" terminal and connect the positive lead to a 0–30 amp ammeter.

3. Run the engine at 2,000 rpm (40 mph in fourth gear) and briefly connect the negative lead of the ammeter to the positive battery terminal.

NOTE: *Avoid running the engine for long periods with the generator field grounded, and always disconnect the ammeter lead from the battery before stopping the engine so the battery doesn't discharge through the generator.* CAUTION: *Disconnect the wires from the regulator before grounding the regulator "F" (XLH) or "BT" (XLCH) terminals to check output, or regulator will be damaged.*

4. If the ammeter reads 15 or more amps for a 6 volt generator or 10 amps for a 12 volt generator, the generator is good and the trouble is in the voltage regulator or wiring circuit.

5. When installing generators or batteries and whenever the generator or regulator wires have been disconnected, flash the field coils to make sure the generator has correct polarity. Do this by briefly touching a jumper wire between "BAT" and "GEN" terminals on the regulator before starting the engine and after connecting all of the wires. The momentary surge of current from the battery to the generator will correctly polarize the generator.

Alternator Output Check

Consult the Alternator Check Chart for test specifications and connect the test equipment as shown in the illustration.

Alternator Check Chart

Component	Connection	Reading	Result
Rotor	Ohmmeter from slip ring to shaft	Very low	Grounded
	110 volt test lamp from slip ring to shaft	Lamp lights	Grounded
	Ohmmeter across slip rings	Very high	Open
	110 volt test lamp across slip rings	Lamp fails to light	Open
	Battery and ammeter to slip rings	Observe ammeter reading	1.9 to 2.3 amp
Stator	Ohmmeter from lead to frame	Very low	Grounded
	110 volt test lamp from lead to frame	Lamp lights	Grounded
	Ohmmeter across each pair of leads	Any reading very high	Open
	110 volt test light across each pair of leads	Fails to light	Open
Diodes	12 volt (or less) test lamp across diode, then reverse connections	Lamp fails to light in both checks	Open
		Lamp lights in both checks	Shorted
1970 and earlier Output	Run under load, adjust rheostat across battery to 14 volts and read ammeter	Ammeter	Rated @ 32 amp 18 amp @ 2000 28 amp @ 5000 (minimum)
1971 and later Output	Run under load, ground field, adjust rheostat across battery to 14 volts and read ammeter	Ammeter	Rated @ 37 amp 22 amp @ 2000 32 amp @ 5000

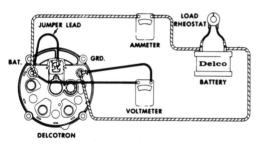

Wiring for testing output

Make sure that the negative battery terminal is grounded to the frame.

Magneto Spark Check

1. Hold the end of the spark plug lead, with the plug cap removed, about 1/8 in. from the spark plug terminal. When the engine is running a blue spark should appear twice in every 360° rotation of the engine between the end of the lead and the plug terminal. If the spark is constant, the engine should not misfire. Do this on both plugs.

2. To test for spark with the engine off but the ignition on, hold the lead not more than 1/4 in. from the plug terminal while kicking the engine over. Perform this on both plugs.

3. An easier test method is to remove the plug, reconnect the wire, and ground the plug tip against the cylinder head. Rotate the engine and watch for a blue spark at the plug tip.

4. If no spark is present, the kill button should be checked for a grounded condition before the magneto is removed for service.

HONDA

Alternator Output Test

125 AND 175

1. Check the state of charge of the battery. If necessary, recharge the battery before proceeding with the test.

2. Connect an ammeter between the positive (+) battery terminal and the input (alternator) side of the rectifier. Start the engine and compare the readings obtained with those in the table.

3. If alternator output is insufficient, the fault lies either in the wiring between the alternator and rectifier or in the alternator itself. If the alternator is producing a sufficient amount of current, it can be assumed that either the rectifier or the wiring between the rectifier and battery is at fault.

Alternator Output Table, 125 and 175

Model	Item	Charging Start	Charging Current /3,000 rpm	Charging Current /5,000 rpm	Charging Current /10,000 rpm
CB 175	Daytime	Max 2,400 rpm	——	Min 0.5 A	Max 3.0 A
	Nighttime	Max 2,800 rpm	——	Min 0.5 A	Max 3.0 A
	Battery voltage	12.3 V	——	13 V	16.5 V
CL 175	Daytime	Max 2,400 rpm	——	Min 0.5 A	Max 3.0 A
	Nighttime	Max 2,800 rpm	——	Min 0.5 A	Max 3.0 A
	Battery voltage	13.2 V	——	14 V	16.5 V
CB 125	Daytime	Max 1,300 rpm	Min 2.0 A	Min 2.7 A	Max 4.5 A
	Nighttime	Max 1,900 rpm	Min 1.2 A	Min 2.0 A	Max 4.0 A
	Battery voltage	6.3 V	6.7 V	7 V	8.3 V
CL 125	Daytime	Max 1,300 rpm	——	Min 1.7 A	Max 3.0 A
	Nighttime	Max 2,000 rpm	——	Min 1.7 A	Max 3.5 A
	Battery voltage	6.3 V	——	7 V	8.3 V
CD 175	Daytime	Max 1,300 rpm	Min 3.0 A	Min 4.0 A	Max 6.0 A
	Nighttime	Max 1,800 rpm	Min 1.2 A	Min 2.0 A	Max 4.0 A
	Battery voltage	6.3 V	7 V	7 V	8.3 V
SS 125	Daytime	Max 1,300 rpm	Min 2.0 A	Min 2.5 A	Max 4.5 A
	Nighttime	Max 2,100 rpm	Min 1.2 A	Min 1.5 A	Max 4.0 A
	Battery voltage	6.4 V	6.7 V	7.5 V	8.3 V

NOTE: *Remember that these models do not have a regulator, and running constantly with the lights on or under other heavy electrical load can cause slow battery discharge, which should be considered normal.*

350 AND 450

1. Check the state of charge of the battery. If necessary, recharge the battery before proceeding with the test.

2. Connect the positive lead of an ammeter to the yellow alternator lead and ground the negative lead on the engine. Start the engine and run it at a steady 5,000 rpm. The ammeter should read 1.5–2.5 amps (350) or 4.0–5.0 amps (450). Excessive amperage indicates a bad regulator.

3. Next, switch the ammeter lead from the yellow wire to the white alternator wire. Start the engine, turn the headlight on (high beam), and run it at 5,000 rpm. The ammeter should read approximately the same as before, 1.5–2.5 amps (350) or 4.0–5.0 amps (450). Battery voltage at 5,000 rpm in either case should be 14.8 volts.

4. If output in steps two and three is sufficient, chances are that the rectifier or wiring between the rectifier and battery is at fault.

5. If alternator output in steps two and three is insufficient, disconnect the yellow wire from the regulator, making sure it does not touch ground, and check the output again at 5,000 rpm with the lights on. If a good reading is obtained, the regulator is at fault (assuming there are no breaks in the wiring). If output is still insufficient, the problem lies in the alternator itself.

500 AND 750 FOURS

1. Check the state of charge of the battery. If battery voltage is less than 12 volts, or if specific gravity is less than 1.26, recharge the battery before proceeding with the test.

2. The test is performed using an ammeter and a voltmeter. Connect the ammeter as follows: Disconnect the positive (+) battery cable and connect it to the positive side of the ammeter. Connect the negative side of the ammeter to the positive battery

Engine RPM / Charging current	1,000	2,000	3,000	4,000	5,000	6,000	7,000	8,000
Day riding	6.5	0	2.4	1.3	1.0	1.0	0.8	0.6
Night riding	2-3	1	1	1	1	1	1	1
Battery terminal voltage (v)	12	12.4	13.2	14.5	14.5	14.5	14.5	14.5

Alternator output rate, Honda Fours

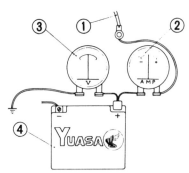

1. Red/white lead   3. Voltmeter
2. Ammeter   4. Battery

Test connections

terminal. Connect the voltmeter as follows: connect the positive side of the voltmeter to the positive battery cable, and ground the negative voltmeter lead on the engine.

3. Start the engine and check the amperage and voltage output of the alternator under both day riding (lights off) and night riding (lights on) conditions. If the readings obtained are noticeably greater or smaller than those in the accompanying table, adjust the regulator. Slight variation is acceptable due to the effect of the state of charge of the battery on alternator output. If alternator output is satisfactory, refer to the section on testing the rectifier.

KAWASAKI

Flywheel Magneto Component Tests

G Series, F6, and F8

Magneto Ignition Coil

Place a strip of paper between the breaker points to insulate them. Perform the following resistance tests using an ohmmeter.
1. Coil resistance:
a. Measure the resistance between the black lead and ground. The coil is good if the ohmmeter reading is approximately 0.5 ohm.
2. Insulation resistance:
a. Disconnect the ground wire from the coil to the magneto base.
b. Measure the insulation resistance between the iron core and the coil. The reading should be over 5.0 megohms.

Condenser

1. Capacity:
a. The condenser capacity should be between 0.18–0.25 microfarads.
2. Spark quality:
a. Connect the positive and negative wires of the condenser to a 6 volt DC power source for a few seconds to charge it.

Flywheel Magneto Specifications (G Series, BIL-A, and F Series)

Model	Type	Manufacturer	Cut-in rpm		Battery
			Day time	Night time	
GA1-A GA2-A	FE101	KOKUSAN	1400	1600	6V 4AH
G3SS-A G3TR-A	FE109	KOKUSAN	s.t.d. 1800 spare 2700	2100	6V 4AH
G4TR	FE109	KOKUSAN	s.t.d. 1800 spare 2700	2100	6V 2AH
G31M-A	NJ101	KOKUSAN	—	—	—
F6	F6079BL	MITSUBISHI	s.t.d. 2000 spare 3000	3000	6V 4AH
F7	HM-01	KOKUSAN	s.t.d. 2000 spare 3000	1800	6V 4AH
F8	FP6309	KOKUSAN	s.t.d. 1600 spare 3000	2000	6V 2AH
F81M	X016	KOKUSAN	—	—	—
F5	HM-01	KOKUSAN	1000	1800	6V 2AH

Lighting and Charging Coil Specifications (G Series and F Series)

Model	Lighting coil Yellow	Pink	Charging coil Blue	Yellow/Green
GA1-A GA2-A	0.41 Ω ± 10%	—	0.36 Ω ± 10%	—
G3SS-A G3TR-A G4TR	0.55 Ω ± 10%	0.55 Ω ± 10%	1.20 Ω ± 10%	0.29 Ω ± 10%
F6	0.48 Ω ± 10%	0.48 Ω ± 10%	0.60 Ω ± 10%	0.54 Ω ± 10%
F8	0.30 Ω ± 10%	0.30 Ω ± 10%	0.58 Ω ± 10%	0.57 Ω ± 10%

b. Disconnect the power source and touch the two wires together. If a spark is produced, the condenser is good.

3. Insulation resistance:

a. Disconnect the ground wire of the condenser.

b. Measure the insulation resistance between the outer case and the positive terminal. The reading should be above 5.0 megohms.

Lighting and Charging Coils

1. Coil resistance:

a. Measure the resistance of each coil with an ohmmeter and compare the readings with the specifications in the accompanying chart.

NOTE: *The lighting coil for the GA1-A and GA2-A models also serves as a charging coil when the headlight is turned on.*

2. Insulation resistance:

a. Disconnect the ground wire.

b. Check insulation resistance between the iron core and the coil. The coil is good if the reading is above 5.0 megohms.

Starter / DC Generator Fault Diagnosis

1. Starter does not turn engine over:

a. Check battery terminal connections and state of charge.

b. Switch on the headlight and press the starter button. If the headlight goes dim, it is likely that current is getting to the starter and the starter itself is faulty. If the light does not dim and a click can be heard at the regulator as the button

is pressed, then the starter brushes or contact points of the starter switch are at fault. If a click is not heard at the regulator and normal voltage is available at the starter switch, it is probable that the starter switch coil is bad and the switch will have to be replaced.

2. Undercharging, as indicated by the charge light staying on, or overcharging:

a. Disconnect the D and F wires from the engine and start the engine.

b. Ground the F wire on the frame and measure the voltage between the D wire and ground. If the reading is above 13 volts at 2,200 rpm, the voltage regulator is probably at fault. Refer to the preceding section for regulator tests and adjustments.

c. If a low reading is obtained, it is likely that the field coil of the starter/dc generator is broken off or short-circuited.

3. Charge light dimly lit:

a. Regulator cutout points fail to close fully due to break-off of the coil, grounding of the regulator, or short-circuiting. It is also possible that the cutout points are damaged or out of adjustment.

4. Charge light flickers:

a. Most often due to the imminent destruction or short-circuiting of the generator or regulator coil.

SUZUKI

Testing the Magneto

1. The magneto lamp coil can be tested with a continuity tester in the same way

as the magneto primary coil is tested. The resistance of the lamp coil is so low that testing it requires a sensitive ohmmeter. Between the yellow/green and red/green wires, resistance should be 1.9Ω; between the yellow/green and green/white, 0.45Ω. No reading should be attainable between the wires and stator housing.

2. The best way to test the lamp coil output is using the voltmeter and ammeter (or milliammeter). First, check out the battery voltage using the voltmeter, hooked up as per the magneto test schematic. It is important that the battery be fully charged before testing output, otherwise the results will not be accurate.

3. If the battery is fully charged, hook up the milliammeter, or better yet 0–5 DC ammeter if your tester has this range, as illustrated.

4. Start the bike and allow it to idle. No current will be shown at idle as a rule.

5. Speed the engine up to 2,000 rpm. At this speed, the output should be about 0.15 ampere, or 150 milliamperes, DC. If you don't have a 0–5 scale, you will have to stop here, otherwise the sensitive milliammeter will be damaged.

6. If you have this scale, speed up the engine to maximum rpm (about 8,000 rpm). The output should be 2.5–3.5 amperes DC.

7. Now, turn on the headlight high beam, or place the ignition switch in the headlight or night position. If all is well, output should be 100 milliamperes at about 2,500 rpm.

8. To check the light coil output, hook up an AC voltmeter as illustrated. Place the electrical system in the night mode, with all lights on. At 2,000 rpm, output should be at least 6.0 volts, and at 8,000 rpm should be not more than 9.0 volts. If these figures are not attainable, check out the wiring, connectors, rectifier, and coils in that order. Sometimes the ignition switch itself is corroded or not making proper contact, so don't overlook it.

Testing the Alternator

1. Hook up a 0–5 ammeter between the positive battery terminal and the wire removed from that terminal.

2. With the lights off, start the engine and gradually run it up to 2,000 rpm while watching the meter. The meter should be-

gin to show a slight charge at this speed.

3. Run the engine up to 5,000 rpm and observe the meter. Charging current should be 1–2 amperes.

4. Turn on the lights and again observe the meter at 2,000 rpm and 5,000 rpm. Readings should be 100 milliamperes and 1.5–2.5 amperes respectively.

5. If the charging current is not to specifications, check the battery, rectifiers, and no-load voltage.

6. To measure no-load voltage, disconnect the wires from the alternator green/white, red/green and yellow/green wires. Connect an AC voltmeter of at least 0–100 volts between the alternator red/green and yellow/green wires.

7. Start the engine and check the output. With the rectifier out of the circuit, some idea of its condition can be ascertained.

Engine rpm	Normal	Minimum	Maximum
2,000	23	17	33
5,000	49	40	60
8,000	82	70	95

These figures may vary for different bikes, but the ratio between them should be approximately the same or the alternator could be defective.

TRIUMPH

Refer to the BSA section. Test procedures and specifications are the same.

YAMAHA

DC Generator Voltage Output

1. Disconnect the generator wiring from the other components.

2. Connect a voltmeter to the armature terminal A (red) and ground field terminal F (black).

3. Run the engine up to about 2500 rpm and check the voltmeter reading. If within reasonable bounds of the necessary output (6 or 12 volts), the generator is not likely to be the source of your problem. If the output is minimal, the cause will likely be found in either the carbon brushes or the field winding insulation.

Troubleshooting the Ignition System

BATTERY AND COIL IGNITION MODELS

The ignition system consists of the contact breaker assembly and one, two, or three ignition coils. The coils are comprised of primary and secondary windings around a laminated, soft iron core—the secondary being closest to the core. When voltage is supplied to the primary winding, it sets up a magnetic field around its turns (approximately 300). This magnetic field induces a voltage in the turns (approximately 20,000) of the secondary winding, resulting in a voltage step-up.

To determine whether an electrical problem is located in the high-tension circuit (secondary winding to the spark plug) or the low-tension circuit (contact breaker to primary coil winding) perform the following check:

NOTE: *On multi-cylinder engines, this test should be performed individually at each coil.*

1. Make sure that the contact points, battery terminals, and main wiring harness fuse are all in good condition.
2. Connect the negative lead of a 0–15 volt DC voltmeter to the "CB" or "+" terminal of the coil, and connect the positive lead to ground.
3. Turn the ignition on and turn the engine until the points open. The voltmeter should read battery voltage.
4. No reading indicates a fault in the low-tension circuit. If the points are suspected of being at fault, you can quickly confirm this by disconnecting the points (CB) wire at the coil. If the voltmeter then reads battery voltage, the points are shorted out (usually caused by incorrect assembly of the insulating washers).

Low-Tension Circuit Test

If the above test shows that the fault exists somewhere in the low-tension circuit, isolate the problem source in the following manner:

NOTE: *Disconnect the zener diode center terminal (12 volt BSAs, Triumphs, and Nortons) or the regulator input terminal.*

1. Place a piece of nonconducting material, such as a strip of rubber between the contact breaker points. Turn the ignition switch on.
2. Using a 0–15 volt DC voltmeter (0–10 volts for 6v machines), make point-to-point checks as described below.
3. Check the battery by connecting the voltmeter between the negative terminal of the battery and ground (frame). No reading indicates a blown main fuse, or a faulty battery lead; a low reading indicates a poor ground.
4. Connect the voltmeter between the ignition coil negative terminal and ground (one at a time on multis). No reading indicates a faulty lead between the battery and coil terminal, or a faulty switch connection.
5. Connect the voltmeter between ground and one ammeter terminal at a time (if applicable). No reading at the "load" terminal indicates either a faulty ammeter or a break in the lead from the battery; no reading on the battery side indicates a faulty ammeter.
6. Connect the voltmeter between the ignition switch input terminal and ground. No reading indicates a break or faulty terminal along the ignition switch input lead. Check for voltage readings between ground and the input lead terminals at the rectifier, ammeter, and lighting switch (if applicable).
7. Connect the voltmeter between the ignition switch "load" terminal and ground. No reading indicates a faulty switch. A positive reading at this point, but not in step 4, indicates a break or faulty connection along the lead.
8. Disconnect the ignition coil lead from the positive terminal and connect one voltmeter lead in its place. Connect the other voltmeter lead to ground. No reading indicates a faulty primary coil winding.
9. Reconnect the ignition coil lead(s) and connect the voltmeter across the contact breaker points one set at a time. No reading indicates a faulty connection, faulty insulation, or a faulty condenser.
10. Reconnect the zener diode center terminal or regulator input terminal and connect the voltmeter to this terminal and ground. The meter should read battery output voltage.

High-Tension Circuit Tests

If the preliminary ignition system checks showed that the problem lay in the high-tension circuit, check the following:

1. Test the ignition coil(s) as described in component tests. If the coils are in satisfactory condition, either the high-tension cables or spark plug cap(s) are at fault.

2. Remove the spark plug cap(s) from the cable(s) and turn the ignition switch on. Hold the cable ⅛ in. away from the cylinder cooling fins and kick the engine over. A bright blue spark should jump across the gap; if not, the cable is defective. If the spark does appear, the spark plug cap is faulty.

CAUTION: *High-tension cables are so called because they carry very high voltage.*

Troubleshooting the Starting System

The starting system consists of the starter motor and clutch, the solenoid, and the handlebar-mounted starter switch (except for starter/generator systems, covered in a preceding section). When the button is pressed, the electrical circuit to the solenoid is closed and the solenoid is activated, sending the battery current directly to the starter motor. The starting system is quite reliable and it is unlikely that you will experience any major problems.

Testing

If the starter will not operate, switch on the headlight and observe its intensity. If it is dim when the starter is not being operated, check the battery connections and recharge the battery. If the headlight doesn't light, check the fuse, the battery connections, the ignition switch and its connections, and check the continuity of the wire between the ignition switch and the battery.

If the headlight is bright, press the starter button momentarily and watch the light. If it remains bright, touch a screwdriver blade between the two starter solenoid terminals. If the starter operates, connect a test light between the small wire on the solenoid and ground. If the test light comes on as the button is pushed, the solenoid is faulty. If it does not light, look for defective wiring between the starter button and solenoid or between the starter button and ignition switch, or simply a burned out starter button switch. If the starter does not operate and the headlight dims as the main solenoid terminals are bridged, the starter motor is faulty. If the headlight does not dim, look for a bad connection at the starter. If the starter motor operates freely but will not turn the engine over, the starter drive is not functioning (a rare occurrence).

STARTER SOLENOID

The solenoid is an electromagnetic switch that closes and completes the circuit between the starter and battery when activated by the starter button. The solenoid is a necessary addition to the start-

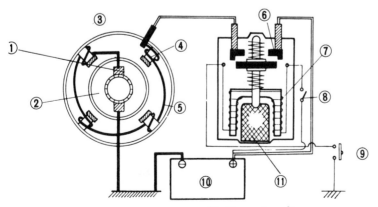

1. Brush
2. Armature
3. Starter motor
4. Pole
5. Field coil
6. Solenoid switch
7. Solenoid electromagnet
8. Ignition switch
9. Starter button
10. Battery
11. Solenoid plunger

Starting system diagram

ing circuit because the starter button switch is not capable of handling the amperage load required to operate the starter and mounting a heavy-duty switch on the handlebar, with the large cable needed to handle the load, is quite impractical.

If the solenoid does not work, check the continuity of the primary coil by connecting a multi-tester or test light and battery to the two small solenoid leads. Lack of continuity indicates an open circuit, and the solenoid must be replaced. If the primary coil winding is continuous, disassemble the solenoid and clean the contact points with emery paper or a small file. The points, after long use, have a tendency to become pitted or burned due to the large current passing across them.

NOTE: *Be sure to disconnect the battery before disconnecting the cables from the solenoid when it is to be removed.*

Replace the solenoid if cleaning the points fails to repair it.

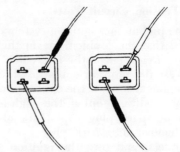

Reversing tester connections to check rectifier

run a length of wire off one of the battery terminals and connect one of the test light leads to the other terminal. The two free wire ends will be used to check electrical continuity of the diodes.

Connect one of the test leads to one of the diode wires at either end of the pack, and touch the other test lead to each of the other diode wires (except for the one at the other end), in turn. Now, reverse the leads and repeat the procedure. The test light should light (or the gauge needle respond) in one test direction only. If all is well so far, connect one of the test leads to the diode wire at the other end of the pack, and repeat the test as outlined above. Continuity in both directions (when reversing the test leads) indicates a defective diode, in which case the rectifier unit must be replaced.

The diodes are quite susceptible to failure from excessive heat and electrical overload. Observe the following precautions:

1. Do not reverse battery polarity.

2. Do not use high-voltage test equipment to test the rectifier diodes.

3. Do not run the engine with the rectifier disconnected.

4. Do not quick-charge the battery (high output charging equipment) without first disconnecting one of the battery cables.

Component Testing

JAPANESE MACHINES

Rectifiers

If alternator output is satisfactory but the battery discharges as the engine is running, it is quite possible that the rectifier is not functioning properly. (This is assuming, of course, that the battery is not old and tired or has one or more bad cells.) Before removing and testing the rectifier, make sure that it is solidly mounted on the frame. The rectifier is grounded through its mounting and will not operate without a good ground.

CAUTION: *Do not loosen or tighten the nut that holds the rectifier unit together, as this will adversely affect operation of the rectifier.*

To test the rectifier, pull off the connectors, unscrew the nut, and remove the rectifier unit. Inside the rectifier are a number of diodes which, if functioning properly, will allow the electricity to pass only in one direction. To check the diodes, you can use either a multi-meter or test light and the motorcycle battery. If the test light and battery are to be used, simply

BRITISH MACHINES

Rectifiers

1. Disconnect and remove the rectifier. Observe these precautions:

    a. When removing or installing the rectifier, hold the wrenches as shown in the accompanying illustration. This is to prevent any possibility of twisting the rectifier plates, which could result in broken internal wiring.

Removing and installing the rectifier

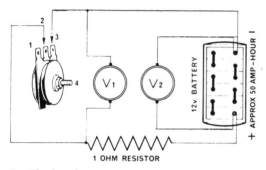

Rectifier bench test set-up

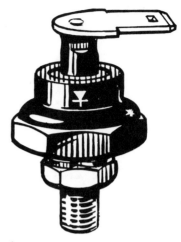

Zener diode

b. Never disturb the nuts that secure the rectifier plates together.

2. Connect the rectifier to a 12V battery and a 1-ohm load resistor.

3. Connect a DC voltmeter in the V_1 position as shown in the accompanying illustration. The meter should read 12 volts.

4. Disconnect the voltmeter and, using the accompanying illustrations for guidance, test each of the diodes with the voltmeter leads. Keep the testing time as short as possible so that the rectifier does not overheat. No reading should be greater than 2.5 volts in Test 1, and no reading should be more than 1.5 volts less than the battery voltage in Test 2 (i.e., 10.5 volts minimum).

5. If the rectifier does not meet specifications, it should be replaced.

Zener Diodes

The zener diode serves the function of a voltage regulator, tapping off excess alternator current output and rerouting it to a heat sink. It is very important that the diode be kept clean and free from obstruction in the cooling airstream at all times. Other than this, if you make sure that the base of the diode and heat sink have firm metal-to-metal contact, the diode is a maintenance free item.

NOTE: *Before making any of the following tests, make sure the battery is in a full state of charge.*

1. Disconnect the zener diode cable and connect a 0–5 amp (minimum) ammeter in series between the diode connector and the disconnected cable. The ammeter positive lead must be connected to the diode terminal.

2. Connect a DC voltmeter between the

Heat sink assembly

TEST 1 CHECKING FORWARD RESISTANCE

TEST 2 CHECKING BACK LEAKAGE

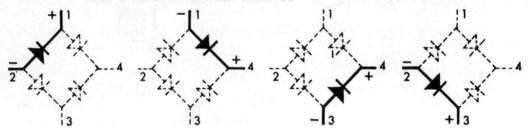

Rectifier diode test sequence

zener diode and the heat sink. The red or positive lead of the voltmeter must be connected to the heat sink, which is grounded to the frame.

3. Make sure all lights are off, then start the engine and slowly increase its speed while observing both meters.

4. Until the voltmeter reaches 12.75 volts, the ammeter should read zero.

5. Continue increasing the engine speed until the ammeter reads 2.0 amps, at which time the voltmeter should be reading 13.5 to 15.3 volts.

6. If the ammeter registers before the voltmeter reaches 12.75 volts in step 4, or if the voltage is higher than stated in step 5 when the ammeter reads 2.0 amps, the zener diode should be replaced.

Contact Breaker Condensers

A faulty condenser is usually indicated by burning or arcing of the points. To check the condenser(s), first turn the ignition switch on, then take readings across the contact breaker(s) (open position) with a voltmeter. No reading indicates that the condenser insulation has broken down, and the unit should be replaced.

Capacitors (Constant Loss Ignition)

The capacitor has a limited storage life of approximately 18 months at 68° F, or 9 to 12 months at 86° F. Therefore, it would be wise to check its condition regularly if it is not in use.

1. Connect the capacitor to a 12 volt battery for approximately 5 seconds. Make sure the terminal polarity is correct or the capacitor will be ruined.

2. Let the capacitor stand for at least 5 minutes, then connect a DC voltmeter to the terminals. Note the *steady*, not instantaneous, reading of the meter. A good capacitor will register at least 9 volts.

H1 AND A SERIES KAWASAKIS

CDI Components

Contact breaker points are not used with the CD ignition system. Ignition timing is detected electrically and converted into a pulsing voltage, which is transmitted to an amplifier. It is then routed through a trigger amplifier, which adjusts the voltage pulse to a suitable signal wave. The signal is then passed through a semiconductor switch (thyristor) which acts as a one-way gate to the capacitor. Since the capacitor discharges current to the primary coil windings instantly, high voltage is induced in the secondary windings and a very strong spark is produced at the spark plug. Self-induction in the primary winding occurs extremely rapidly in the CD ignition system, and this short-rise time, along with the amplified timing signal, is why a good spark can be produced across even a fouled spark plug.

SERVICE PRECAUTIONS

1. Do not reverse battery polarity.
2. Do not run the engine with the battery disconnected.
3. Take care to connect any wiring correctly. Improperly connected wiring can damage the CDI components.

4. The battery and ignition coil are matched to the CDI system. When replacement is necessary, use identical parts.

5. Make sure to install any rubber insulators correctly when a component has been removed and reinstalled.

6. The igniters (amplifiers) are sealed

CDI Troubleshooting

No Start

Possible Causes	Inspection and/or Remedy
1. No high frequency sound from Unit B	
a. Damaged ignitor Unit B	Replace.
b. Insufficient battery voltage	Charge battery.
2. Strong spark at plugs	
a. Reversely connected high-tension leads	Switch.
b. Insufficient battery voltage	Charge battery.
c. Loose battery terminals	Clean and tighten.
3. Weak spark at plugs	
a. Leaking high-tension leads	Check high-tension circuit and repair as neccessary.
b. Faulty ignition coil	Test and replace if necessary.
c. Faulty ignitor Unit B	Replace.
d. Faulty wiring harness	Test continuity and repair as necessary.
4. No spark at plugs	
a. Faulty ignition coil	Test and replace if necessary.
b. Faulty ignitor Unit A or B	Replace.
c. Faulty signal generator	Replace.
5. Spark without kick-starting	
a. Faulty ignitor Unit A	Replace.

Hard Starting

1. Strong spark at plugs	
a. Incorrect ignition timing	Readjust.
b. Insufficient battery voltage	Charge battery.
c. Loose terminal connections	Clean and tighten.
2. Weak spark at plugs	
a. Leaking high-tension leads	Check high-tension circuit and repair as necessary.
b. Faulty ignition coil	Test and replace if necessary.
c. Faulty ignitor Unit B	Replace.
d. Faulty wiring harness	Test continuity and repair as necessary.
3. No spark at plugs	
a. Faulty ignition coil	Test and replace if necessary.
b. Faulty ignitor Unit A	Replace.
c. Faulty signal generator	Replace.

Poor Running Performance

1. Incorrect ignition timing	Readjust.
2. Faulty spark plugs	Replace.
3. Faulty ignitor Unit A	Replace.
4. Faulty ignitor Unit B	Replace.

with epoxy and cannot be disassembled. Disassembly will invalidate a warranty claim if the ignition system is defective.

H2 SERIES KAWASAKI

The H2 model is equipped with an electrical system different from any of the other models. What Kawasaki has done is combine the best features of both magneto ignition and pointless capacitor discharge ignition to provide a simple, reliable circuit.

Whereas conventional CDI takes a low battery voltage and raises it to 370–500 volts with a converter, magneto CDI taps its high voltage directly from a special generator winding and then rectifies it. Another advantage is that magneto CDI can use the signal generator voltage directly, without amplification.

Magneto CDI also differs from conventional magneto ignition in that two primary ignition coils are used: one contains a high number of windings so that high voltage can be tapped at relatively low rpm, the other contains a low number of windings so that, as rpm rises, voltage can be produced quickly enough to fire the plugs properly.

In addition to the above, magneto CDI differs from the CDI used on other Kawasaki models in that 3 separate CDI units, one for each cylinder, are used.

The system is quite simple and very reliable, so it is highly unlikely that you'll ever run into trouble. If a problem does develop, however, it is best to refer it to a qualified Kawasaki mechanic.

Use the following chart for determining specific areas of fault if you are experiencing trouble with a CDI system.

COILS

1. Check the coil in the machine by removing the spark plug cap and holding the high-tension cable end about ⅛ in. away from the cylinder cooling fins. Turn the ignition on and kick the engine over. Observe the caution given in "High Tension Circuit Tests."

2. Check primary winding resistance by removing the coil and connecting an ohmmeter to the low tension terminals. The readings obtained should be:

   6 volt coils—1.8–2.4 ohms
   12 volt coils—3.0–3.8 ohms

Battery

GENERAL MAINTENANCE

1. The battery electrolyte level should be checked about once every two weeks, more often in warm weather.

2. Maintain the electrolyte level between the maximum and minimum marks on the battery case. This refers to batteries with transparent plastic cases which are found on the majority of motorcycles today. If the battery does not have this type of case, check level by removing the caps from each cell. Maintain the electrolyte level just above the tops of the plates.

3. Never add acid to a battery. Add *distilled water* only. Tap water in some areas contains chemical or mineral impurities which may shorten battery life.

4. Do not overfill the battery. This may cause spillage of the electrolyte while riding.

5. Check the condition of the battery terminals. On some small batteries, the terminals are sealed and need no service. On most batteries, however, this is not the case. Terminals must be free of corrosion. Check that the connections are tight.

6. Check the battery overflow tube. It must not be blocked or pinched at any point, and must be arranged to that it will discharge any electrolyte well below any painted or plated surface. On most late models, a plate is provided on the motorcycle showing the correct routing of the overflow tube. Follow the manufacturer's instructions.

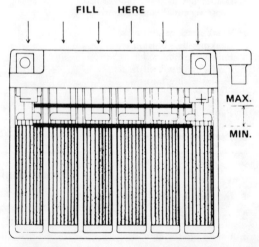

Maintain electrolyte level between the maximum and minimum marks

7. Check that the battery is securely mounted and that any and all straps, rubber pads, etc. provided by the manufacturer are in place and in good condition.

8. Any battery service such as cleaning, charging, etc., should not be carried out with the battery in the motorcycle. See following sections for procedures.

9. During cold weather, keep the battery fully charged. A low battery will freeze much quicker than one with a charge. Freezing will ruin the plates even if it doesn't harm the case.

CHARGING

1. Battery state-of-charge is checked with an hydrometer. These are available in several sizes and prices, and range from professional models which provide a numerical specific gravity reading to less expensive units which check battery condition by indicating how many colored balls will float in the hydrometer tube.

The measure of battery state-of-charge is the *specific gravity* of the electrolyte, which is nothing more than the weight of the electrolyte relative to an equal volume of water. Electrolyte with a specific gravity of 1.230, for example, is 1.230 times as heavy as water.

Note the following relations between specific gravity and battery state-of-charge, these figures being applicable at room temperature (20°C/68°F):

Electrolyte Specific Gravity	Battery State-of-Charge
1.260	100%
1.230	75%
1.200	50%
1.170	25%
1.140	almost none
1.110	dead

2. The battery should be recharged if the specific gravity of one or more cells shows that the battery is charged only 50% of its capacity or less (specific gravity 1.200 or less).

3. Batteries should not be charged on the motorcycle. This risks damage due to splashing electrolyte on painted or plated surfaces. It also makes it difficult to clean the case thoroughly, which should be accomplished after the battery is charged. In addition, some systems can be damaged unless the battery terminals are disconnected during charging.

4. When removing the battery, disconnect the ground side *first*. This will be the negative terminal on most motorcycles, although the positive terminal is the ground on British machines. Disconnect the battery overflow tube before removing the battery.

5. Before charging, remove the cell caps. During charging, keep a check on the electrolyte level, topping it up from time to time if necessary.

If the battery draws a lot of current from the charger, or if it gets very hot during the charging period, replacement of the battery will be necessary. Electrolyte temperatures should never exceed 110°F.

6. It is recommended that batteries be trickle-charged only at no more than 10% of their amp-hour rating. Therefore, the continuous charging rate for a 6 amp battery should be 0.6 amps. The amp-hour rating of a battery is stamped on the battery case for most batteries. Example: Yuasa battery No. 12N12A-4A indicates that the battery is a 12-volt, 12-amp-hour unit.

7. After charging, shake the battery gently to allow any trapped air bubbles to escape. Allow the battery to cool to normal temperature before checking state-of-charge.

8. After charging is completed, top up the electrolyte level if necessary, and install the cell caps. Clean off the top and sides of the battery case with a solution of warm water and baking soda. Be extremely careful that this solution does not enter the cells, since it will neutralize the acid.

9. Dirty or corroded battery terminals should be cleaned with a wire brush to ensure good contact. After the battery is installed and the terminal connections are secured, coat the terminals with petroleum jelly to reduce future corrosion.

10. When installing the battery, be sure that the overflow tube is connected and properly routed. Be sure that the battery is properly fitted. The polarity of each terminal will be clearly stamped or painted on the battery case. Even a momentary reversal of connections can destroy some electrical components.

11. Before connecting the battery, check that the cable connections are free of corrosion or oxidation. If possible, clean up the cable connectors with sandpaper.

Connect the power side of the battery first. This will be the positive terminal except on positive-ground (British) systems.

12. Ensure that the connections are tight. Check that the ground cable is securely fas-

tened to the frame or engine. A poor ground may not prevent the motorcycle from running, but it may eventually damage electrical components on some types of systems.

STORAGE

1. If the motorcycle is to be out of service for any length of time, the battery should be removed and stored in a cool, dry location.

2. Trickle-charge stored batteries every month.

TROUBLESHOOTING

1. If the electrical system goes completely dead suddenly, chances are that the trouble is either a fuse or a bad electrical connection somewhere in the circuit.

Most motorcycles are fitted with an in-line fuse on the battery positive lead usually right in the neighborhood of the battery itself. Check this fuse first.

Next, check that the battery terminal connections are clean and tight. It is possible for a bad connection to show up here for seemingly no reason all of a sudden. Even if the connections seem okay, disconnect the wires at the terminals and clean them off. Sometimes you will find that the electrical system suddenly has power again while you are in the process of disconnecting the battery. In this event you can be sure that a poor electrical connection was causing the trouble.

Other electrical connections should also be checked before suspecting the battery itself in case of a sudden failure such as we are discussing here. Most motorcycles have a large number of male-female connectors either in the headlight, under the gas tank, or under one of the side covers. These connectors can come apart, corrode, or fill with water.

2. If the battery self-discharges, check that the battery case has not become impregnated with sulphuric acid. This can be done by checking the resistance of the case with an ohmmeter. Hold one probe against the case near the positive terminal, the other to the case near the negative terminal. Resistance must be infinite. Sometimes acid on the top of the battery will form a current path between the terminals, causing the battery to discharge itself. If this is the case, it may be possible to save the battery for a while by sprinkling baking soda over the top, letting it sit for several minutes, and then washing it off with warm water. Take care not to let any of this get into the cells.

3. If one cell seems to loose more electrolyte than the others, check its charge with an hydrometer. It is probably shorted. Replace the battery if any cell is shorted or will not hold a charge.

4. Whitish sulfate deposits on the battery plates is a usual sign of battery age indicating that replacement will be in order soon. It may be possible to prolong the life of a sulfated battery by charging it at half the usual rate for twice the normal time.

Testing state-of-charge with an hydrometer

Electrical Troubleshooting

Problem	Possible Causes	Inspection/Remedy
Battery does not charge	Defective battery	Test each cell. Replace if shorted cell(s) are evident.
	Battery electrolyte level low	Top up.
	Broken or shorting wires in charging circuit	Check continuity and condition of insulation off all wires.
	Loose or dirty battery terminals	Clean terminals and secure connections.
	Defective voltage regulator	Test and replace if necessary.
	Defective alternator	Replace.
	Defective silicon diode	Replace.
Excessive battery charging	Defective battery (shorted plates)	Replace battery.
	Voltage regulator not properly grounded	Secure.
	Regulator defective	Replace.
Unstable charging voltage	Intermittent short	Check wiring for frayed insulation.
	Defective key switch	Replace.
	Intermittent coil in alternator	Replace.
Electric starter spins, but engine does not	Broken starter clutch	Replace.
Starter does not turn over, but warning lights dim when starter button is pushed; or engine turns over slowly	Low battery, or battery connections loose or corroded	Charge or replace battery; clean and tighten terminals.
	Starter armature bushings worn	Replace starter.
Clicking sound when starter button is pushed; engine does not turn over	Battery low or terminals loose or corroded	Charge or replace battery; clean and tighten connections.
	Defective starter solenoid	Replace.
Nothing happens when starter button is pushed	Loose or broken connections in the starter switch or battery leads	Check switch connections; check battery terminals; clean and tighten battery leads.
Engine turns over slowly when starter button is pushed (cold weather)	Low or dead battery	Recharge or replace battery.
	Engine oil too heavy	Use correct viscosity oil.
Turn signal will not light	Burned out bulb	Replace.
Turn signal will not flash	One bulb burned out	Replace.
	Low battery	Charge or replace battery.
Speed of flasher varies with engine rpm	Low battery	Charge or replace battery.
	Defective flasher unit	Replace.

Electrical Troubleshooting (cont.)

Problem	Possible Causes	Inspection/Remedy
No spark or weak spark	Defective ignition coil(s)	Replace.
	Defective spark plug(s)	Replace.
	Plug lead(s) or wires damaged or disconnected	Check condition of leads and wires; check all connections.
Breaker points pitted or burned	Defective condenser	Replace points and condenser.
Carbon-fouled spark plugs	Mixture too rich	Adjust carburetors; check air cleaner.
	Plugs too cold for conditions	Use hotter plugs.
	Idle speed set too high	Adjust carburetors.
Oil-fouled spark plugs	Worn rings, cylinders, or valve guides (four-stroke)	Rebuild.
	Badly adjusted oil pump cable (two-stroke)	Adjust.
Spark plug electrodes burned or overheated	Spark plugs too hot for conditions	Use colder plugs.
	Engine overheating	See above.
	Ignition timing incorrect	Adjust.
	Mixture too lean	See above.

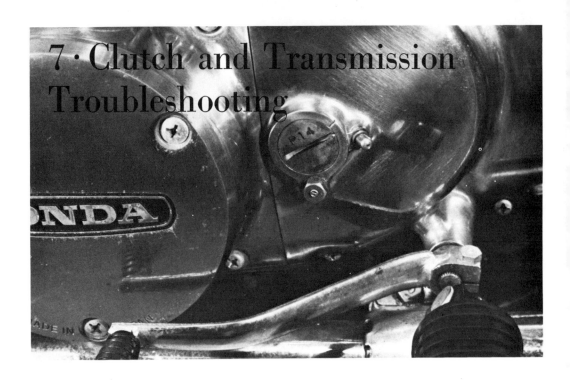

7 · Clutch and Transmission Troubleshooting

Automatic Centrifugal Clutch

Many of the small capacity Japanese bikes, such as the famous Honda 50, utilize an automatic centrifugal clutch. We'll use this Honda clutch, illustrated here, as an example to describe their operation.

The clutch functions according to engine speed, so you can sit at a light with the transmission in first gear without moving, and then as the engine picks up speed the clutch engages and away you go. The clutch is tied in with the shifter mechanism so it disengages when the shifter pedal is depressed, thereby allowing gear changes to be smooth and quiet.

The clutch is mounted, in this case, directly to the crankshaft, and the transmission is then gear driven from the primary drive gear. As engine speed increases the small rollers are forced outward by centrifugal force. They press against the clutch plates and cause them to engage; this in turn allows the power produced at the crankshaft to be transmitted through the clutch to the transmission, and then to the rear wheel. As engine speed decreases, the rollers move back in toward the clutch center, and the force they were exerting on the clutch plates is relieved and the clutch disengages.

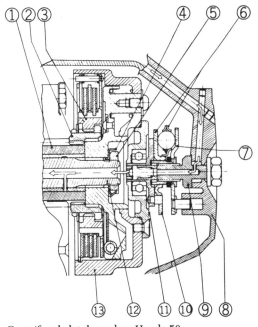

Centrifugal clutch used on Honda 50s

1. Primary drive gear
2. Drive outer
3. Clutch center
4. Lock washer
5. Lock nut
6. Ball retainer complete
7. Clutch lifter plate
8. Right crankcase cover
9. Clutch adjusting bolt
10. Clutch complete
11. Clutch outer cover
12. Crankshaft
13. Clutch outer

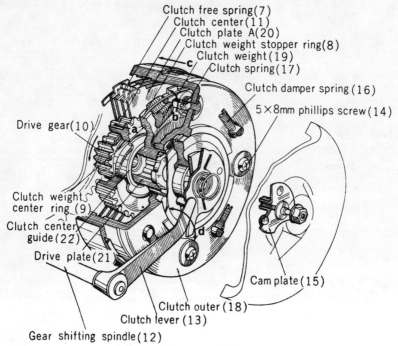

Clutch free spring(7)
Clutch center(11)
Clutch plate A(20)
Clutch weight stopper ring(8)
Clutch weight(19)
Clutch spring(17)
Clutch damper spring(16)
5×8mm phillips screw(14)
Drive gear(10)
Clutch weight center ring(9)
Clutch center guide(22)
Drive plate(21)
Cam plate(15)
Clutch outer(18)
Clutch lever(13)
Gear shifting spindle(12)

Centrifugal clutch used on Honda CT-200s. Instead of the rollers used on many models, this clutch uses four weights to operate the unit

Manual Clutch

There are several clutch variations used on motorcycles. Most of them are multi-disc wet or dry clutches known as the countershaft type because they are mounted on the transmission countershaft which runs at somewhere between one half and one third engine speed. In most cases the clutch is chain or gear driven from the crankshaft. The advantage offered by this configuration is that its low operating speed is conducive to smooth high speed shifting. Its greatest disadvantage is its relatively large mass and frictional area which necessitates the use of stiff springs which demand a lot of lever pressure.

A few machines, notably BMW, use an automotive type single plate clutch known as a flywheel clutch. These clutches are mounted on the crankshaft and spin at engine speed. This, in some cases, makes high rpm shifting a little rougher than on the countershaft type, but the single plate construction makes the lever light to the touch.

All manual clutches operate in pretty much the same manner, be they wet or dry, single or multi-plated. When the clutch lever is actuated the release worm moves in toward the clutch hub and presses the clutch push rod against the pressure (spring) plate. The force exerted by the push rod(s) compresses the clutch springs while moving the pressure plate away from the clutch plates, thereby allowing the plates to disengage and spin freely. When the hand lever is released, a

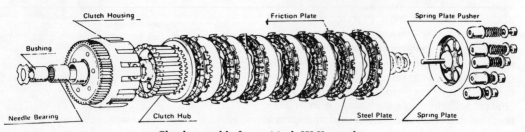

Clutch Housing
Friction Plate
Spring Plate Pusher
Bushing
Needle Bearing
Clutch Hub
Steel Plate
Spring Plate

Clutch assembly from a Mach III Kawasaki

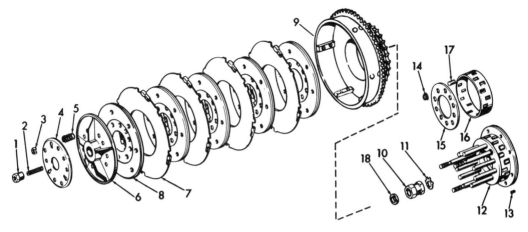

Clutch assembly from a H-D Glide model. Note that the plates on this clutch ride on studs rather than on a splined hub as on the Kawasaki

1. Push rod adjusting screw lock nut
2. Adjusting screw
3. Spring tension adjusting nut (3)
4. Spring collar
5. Springs (10)
6. Outer disc (pressure plate)

7. Steel disc (4)
8. Friction disc (5)
9. Clutch shell
10. Clutch hub nut
11. Hub nut lock washer
12. Clutch hub

13. Clutch hub key
14. Bearing plate spring (3)
15. Bearing plate
16. Bearing retainer
17. Bearing roller
18. Hub nut seal

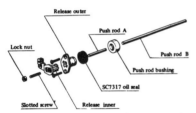

Release mechanism used on the Kawasaki H series model

Release mechanism used on 650 Triumphs

return spring moves the release worm back into its original position and the push rod(s) is pushed back against its seat by the pressure plate which again presses against the clutch plates causing the clutch to engage.

Constant Mesh Transmissions

Constant mesh transmissions enjoy a distinct advantage over their predecessors, the sliding gear type of gearbox.

Instead of having the gear teeth come into mesh as the gears slide along a shaft, the gears of the constant mesh transmission always stay smoothly meshed and are engaged by sliding dog gears. What you have are a bunch of idler gears that spin freely on their shaft while being meshed with driven gears which are affixed to their shaft—usually the main shaft. On the countershaft, called the layshaft on British bikes, with the idler gears are sliding dog gears, which are splined to the countershaft, with dogs designed to neatly fit into the holes provided in the idler gears. When you shift, the shifter fork moves the appropriate dog gear into mesh with the appropriate idler gear, and this causes the countershaft to spin because the idler gear

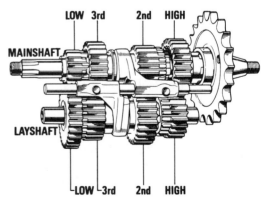

Transmission cluster from a Triumph Trident

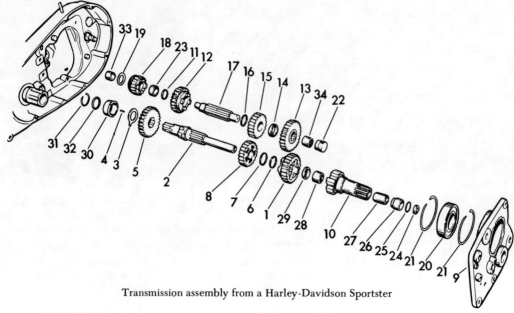

Transmission assembly from a Harley-Davidson Sportster

1. Mainshaft second gear
2. Transmission mainshaft
3. Mainshaft thrust washer (variable thickness)
4. Transmission mainshaft roller (23)
5. Mainshaft low gear
6. Mainshaft third gear retainer ring
7. Mainshaft third gear washer
8. Mainshaft third gear
9. Access cover
10. Clutch gear
11. Countershaft low gear washer
12. Countershaft third gear
13. Countershaft drive gear
14. Countershaft gear spacer
15. Countershaft second gear
16. Countershaft second gear thrust washer
17. Transmission countershaft
18. Countershaft low gear
19. Countershaft low gear washer (variable thickness)
20. Mainshaft ball bearing
21. Mainshaft ball bearing snap ring (2)
22. Countershaft oiler plug
23. Countershaft low gear bushing
24. Clutch gear oil seal (1970 only)
25. Clutch hub nut O-ring (1970 only)
26. Clutch gear oil seal extension (1970 only)
27. Clutch gear bushing
28. Clutch gear needle roller bearing
29. Mainshaft thrust washer
30. Mainshaft roller bearing race
31. Mainshaft roller bearing retainer ring
32. Mainshaft roller bearing washer
33. Countershaft bearing—closed end
34. Countershaft bearing—open end

is in mesh with a driven gear which is splined to the mainshaft. On most machines, such as Hondas, the clutch is affixed to the countershaft at one end, and the countershaft sprocket is at the other end. The clutch serves to disengage the countershaft, so when you pull in the clutch the countershaft spins but doesn't put out any torque to the rear wheel. There have been, and are, numerous variations in the construction of constant mesh boxes, but the basic principle remains the same.

SHIFTER MECHANISM

There are two basic shifter mechanism configurations in popular use today. The type found on most Japanese machines uses a shifter drum to guide the selector forks; the type in use on most British bikes, and some Harley-Davidsons, uses a camplate and a shift quadrant.

To better understand the workings of a shifter mechanism consider the following

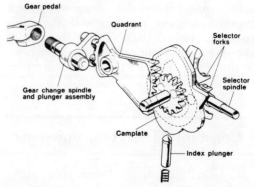

Camplate type shifter mechanism from a Triumph Trident

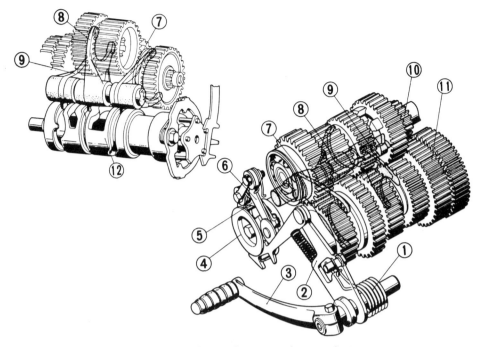

Drum type shifter mechanism used on Honda 750

1. Shift return spring	7. Left shift fork
2. Shift arm	8. Center shift fork
3. Shift lever	9. Right shift fork
4. Shift drum side plate	10. Transmission mainshaft
5. Shift arm stopper	11. Transmission countershaft
6. Shift drum stopper	12. Shift drum

diagrams (the gearbox is from a 650 cc BSA):

Neutral—Neutral is the only position in which the engine may be started on this particular model. The large (index) plunger, which operates at the large end of the camplate to select the gear position, is in the camplate's neutral position, and the selector quadrant plungers are compressed and ready to be moved into either First or Second gear.

First—As the shifter pedal is moved down to select First gear, the large plunger enters the camplate and moves it into the First gear position. This causes the countershaft (layshaft) First gear selector fork to slide the countershaft First gear dog gear into engagement with the countershaft First gear. At the same time the selector (quadrant) plunger moves into the second window of the camplate, ready to move it to Second gear.

Second—The shift to Second gear is performed in the same manner, only this time in the opposite direction. When the shift is completed, two selector plungers will be in the camplate windows making the transmission ready to shift into either Neutral or First and back again.

Third—Shifting into Third brings both selector forks into play; one fork slides the countershaft dog gear out of mesh, and the other brings the mainshaft dog gear into mesh with the mainshaft Third gear. Once again the selector plungers are ready to shift in either direction.

Fourth—Fourth is the top gear on this particular box, so when the shift is completed, the large and selector plungers are so positioned that they can only shift down to a lower gear. Shifting causes the mainshaft selector fork to slide the mainshaft dog gear into mesh with the mainshaft Fourth gear.

The principle is the same on the drum type of shifter except instead of moving the camplate the drum is rotated. The shifter forks ride in the drum at one end, and on the sliding dog gears at the other end. As the drum rotates, the forks ride in their grooves, and the shape of the grooves causes the forks to move the dog gears.

NEUTRAL

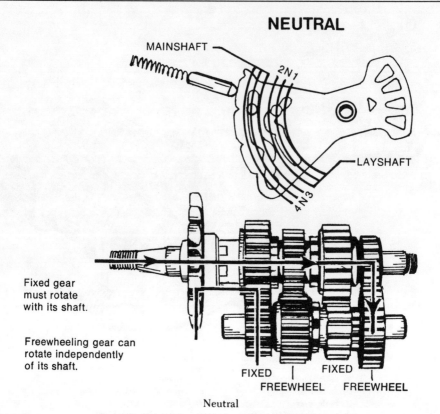

Fixed gear
must rotate
with its shaft.

Freewheeling gear can
rotate independently
of its shaft.

Neutral

FIRST

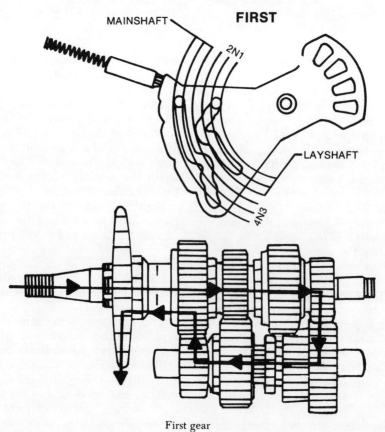

First gear

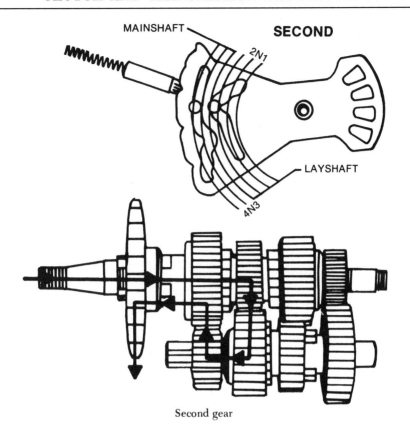

Second gear

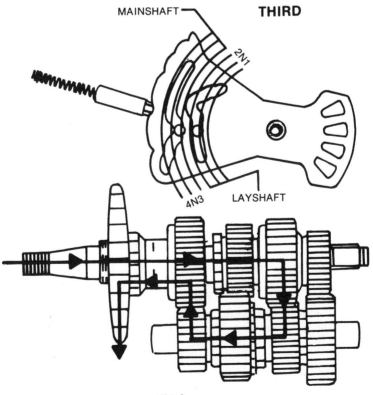

Third gear

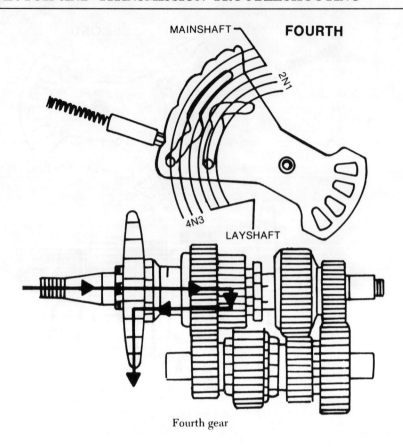

Fourth gear

KICKSTARTERS

Kickstarters, like all of the component systems in this chapter, vary in construction from marque to marque, and even from model to model within the same company. Some, such as the starter found on the big British twins, are only operable when in Neutral with the clutch engaged, and others, such as the starter used on the Yamaha Enduro models can be used in any gear as long as the clutch is disengaged.

To give you an idea of how a kickstarter with a kick gear system functions, let's examine the operation of a Kawasaki Mach III starter system.

When the kick lever is depressed the kick shaft is rotated, and therefore the worm gear which is part of the shaft is also rotated. This rotation sets up a centrifugal force which moves the kick gear along the worm until it meshes with the countershaft First gear. The force of the kick is transmitted through the kick shaft to the kick gear and from the kick gear to the countershaft First gear. Then it goes to the mainshaft First gear which causes the

mainshaft to spin; then through the clutch to the crankshaft primary gear (which is in mesh with the clutch hub gear) which causes the crankshaft to spin.

As soon as the engine starts, the motion of the countershaft First gear in conjunction with the pressure provided by the gear holder, causes the kick gear to slide back along its worm gear to its original position. When the kick lever is released the return spring brings the lever back to its rest position which is determined by the location of the kick stopper on the crankcase.

The other type of kickstarter system in general use, and this is the type which most British machines come with, is the ratchet method. As an example of this let's take a look at the kickstarter used on Harley-Davidson Sportsters.

The ratchet mechanism is in two parts and will only mesh in one direction. One half is on the starter clutch (18), and the other half is on the side of the starter clutch gear (6). The starter clutch is riveted to the clutch hub, and the clutch gear

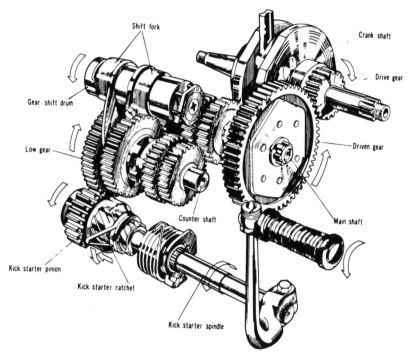

A Honda kickstarter assembly

is spring loaded (8) and free wheeling on the clutch sprocket spacer (7). The ratchet teeth are designed so that when the gears are turned in one direction they will mesh, and when they turn in the other direction they will ratchet or slide over each other without meshing.

The starter shaft has a crank gear, which is in mesh with the clutch gear (12), splined to it and a camplate (20) riveted to the gear. There is also a return spring (3)

which brings the pedal assembly (2) back to its original position, and a stop pin (21) which limits how far the shaft can spin by stopping the camplate.

When you step on the pedal the crank gear rotates with the shaft until the camplate is stopped by the stop pin. The crank gear turns the starter clutch gear which is held in mesh with the starter clutch by the pressure exerted by the clutch spring; this causes the clutch to spin and turn the en-

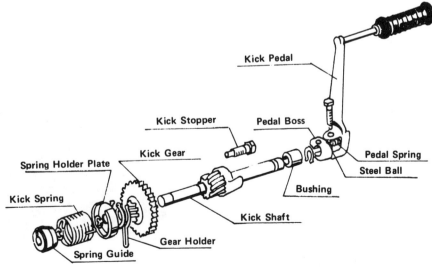

A Kawasaki kickstarter assembly

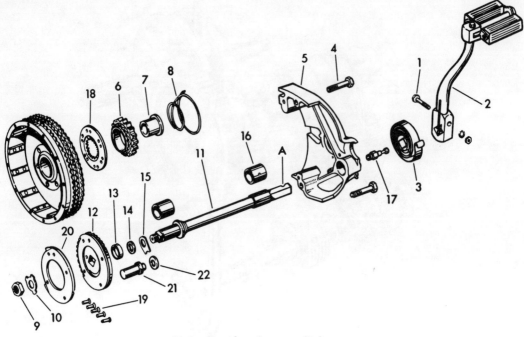

Harley-Davidson Sportster Kickstarter

1. Crank clamp bolt, lock washer and nut	8. Clutch spring	16. Shaft bushing (2)
2. Crank and pedal assembly	9. Shaft nut	17. Spring stud
3. Crank spring	10. Crank gear lock washer	18. Starter clutch
4. Sprocket cover bolt (2)	11. Crankshaft	19. Crank gear cam plate rivet (5)
5. Sprocket cover	12. Crank gear	20. Crank gear cam plate
6. Starter clutch gear	13. Crank oil seal	21. Crank gear stop pin
7. Clutch sprocket spacer	14. Crankshaft shim	22. Crank gear stop pin washer
	15. Shaft thrust plate	

gine over. When the engine starts, the clutch begins to spin faster and the return spring causes the pedal to return to its original position where the stop pin acts against the opposite end of the camplate. This is made possible by the ratcheting action of the ratchet teeth, and because the spring allows the clutch gear to move back against the lip of the sprocket spacer.

Troubleshooting the Clutch

ROUGH LEVER ACTION

Unsatisfactorily rough action of the clutch hand lever is almost always due to improper lubrication of the hand lever, clutch cable, or release mechanism.

Like all control cables, the clutch cable must be free of sharp bends or kinks along its route. If lever pull is hard, check this first.

Always keep the cable well lubricated by dribbling oil or a special cable lubricant between cable and sheath. Be sure that the lever itself has a well-lubricated pivot. Also, check

Clutch cable should have a bit of free-play allowing the hand lever to be moved as shown before the plates begin to separate

the fit of the cable end in the lever. The cable end must turn slightly when the lever is pulled toward the handgrip, and if it cannot do so, lever action will be stiff and cable life short. An uneven or snatching feeling when the lever is pullsed towards the handgrip is often due to the cable end fitting binding in the lever. This can usually be remedied by thoroughly lubricating the cable end fitting. If this does not work, the lever cut-out can be enlarged slightly with a file so that the cable end fitting is free to rotate in it.

The release mechanism on some machines requires occasional service. On some Hondas, the mechanism is fitted with a grease fitting easily accessible on the engine case. One or two shots of chassis grease every year or so should suffice here.

On some other makes no grease nipple is fitted, and the release mechanism must be removed for service. This is especially true of those makes in which the release mechanism is installed in the engine sprocket cover. In this location the mechanism can get very dirty due to its exposure, and rough clutch action will be the result.

CLUTCH DRAGS

A dragging clutch will cause your bike to creep or stall at stop lights when in gear, shift hard, and overheat. The reason is that the clutch plates never fully release when the hand lever is pulled in, and the end result is a burned out clutch or a wasted gearbox.

First, excessive heat is generated because the clutch plates and discs are unable to separate enough which creates a situation similar to running an engine without enough oil. All this friction will quickly glaze and then wear out the clutch friction disc material, and the heat will scorch and distort the discs and plates, weaken the clutch springs, and may fry the clutch hub bearings (if applicable). One good overheating is enough to sufficiently weaken the springs so the clutch will begin to slip; this will end your dragging problems but will bring on a whole new set of troubles.

The next thing that will happen is the pressure plate will become distorted, and the push rods may be damaged due to the inordinate amount of pressure placed on them. In some cases when people have installed oversize springs in order to get a more positive grab during high speed shifts, or when the spring pressure has been too great due to improper adjustment, push rods have been known to be poked right through the pressure plate causing extensive damage to the entire assembly.

Finally, after the clutch has been dragging for a while, the dogs on the dog gears will be rounded off so much that the gears no longer will engage smoothly. Chances are that you'll damage the gearbox before the clutch becomes completely burned out, but in any case all that rough shifting is going to do some damage to at least the dogs, and maybe even the shifter mechanism.

The most common cause of clutch drag is incorrect adjustment. Insufficient clearance at the hand lever, an incorrect adjustment of the pushrod at the release mechanism, a worn throwout bearing or release worm or an uneven or too tight adjustment of the clutch springs will cause a clutch to drag. The first thing to check is the adjustment at the lever, and then at the release mechanism. Make sure nothing is obstruct-

Checking the clutch spring adjustment on a 500 cc Triumph

Make sure the correct clutch springs are in use

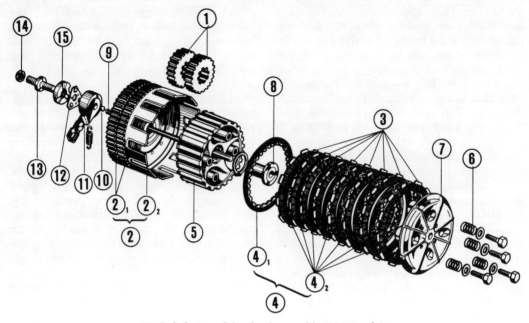

Exploded view of the clutch assembly (350 Honda)

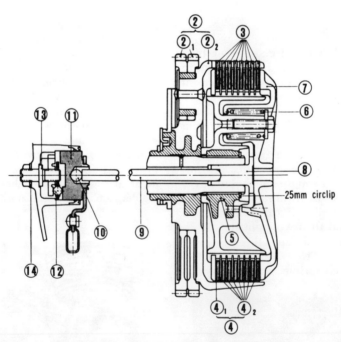

Sectional view of the clutch assembly (350 Honda)

1. Primary drive gear
2. Clutch housing complete
2_1. Primary driven gear
2_2. Clutch housing
3. Clutch friction disc (8 ea.)
4. Clutch plate
4_1. Clutch plate A

4_2. Clutch plate B
5. Clutch center
6. Clutch spring
7. Clutch pressure plate
8. Clutch lifter joint piece
9. Clutch lifter rod
10. No. 10 steel ball

11. Clutch lever
12. Steel ball (clutch ball retainer)
13. Clutch adjuster
14. Clutch adjuster locknut
15. Clutch adjusting cam

ing the motion of the release lever and preventing full disengagement. If this isn't the problem check the springs. On many British machines the springs are adjusted by screws which may come out of adjustment if the locking hubs are worn away. This would cause the pressure plate to move unevenly, resulting in only a partial release and eventual distortion of the plate. This may also be caused by one or more collapsed springs or by an already distorted pressure plate or clutch plate. If upon inspection you find that some damage has occured, the damaged parts should be replaced as necessary, preferably as a set in the case of plates, discs, and springs. It is possible that a piece of friction material or some other foreign object has gotten between the plates and taken up the necessary clearance. When securing the clutch springs do so in opposite pairs, making sure than an equal pressure is maintained, as tightening down the springs unevenly may cause an immediate distortion of the pressure plate.

CLUTCH SLIPS

A slipping clutch will prevent the power being fed into the clutch from ever reaching the rear wheel. The earliest symptoms are usually slippage during high speed shifts, or under power in the lower gears. It will sound like the clutch is being feathered, and the engine will continue to wind without accelerating. When it begins to slip in the higher gears the time for a clutch job is very near.

The causes of slippage are improper adjustment, weak springs, warped or distorted plates, discs, or pressure plate, oil impregnated, glazed, or worn friction material, a kinked or rusted cable, or anything that could interfere with the motion of the release lever.

The first thing to check is the adjustment at the hand lever and release mechanism. Too little play will cause slippage, and if the motion of the release mechanism is impaired by a hung up cable or something like that, the clutch may not be able to engage fully. Make sure the springs are adjusted correctly (if applicable), as insufficient tension can be responsible also.

If the problem is mechanical it should become immediately evident as soon as the clutch is taken down. The first thing to check here is the springs as they may be weakened even though they aren't obviously collapsed or damaged. Your dealer may have a device for measuring spring tension, or perhaps he will be able to determine their value by comparing them with new springs. Springs must be replaced as a set in order to assure equal tension.

A distorted pressure plate or warped discs and plates should be pretty obvious, and must be replaced if the warpage is greater than the limits specified by the manufacturer. Plates and discs, like the springs, should be replaced as full sets to ensure efficient operation. If you are hard up at the time and the friction discs are oil impregnated they may be cleaned up by soaking them in gasoline and then blowing them dry. Glazed discs may be roughed up

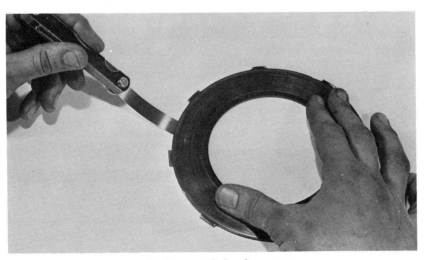

Checking a steel plate for warpage

Measuring clutch spring free length

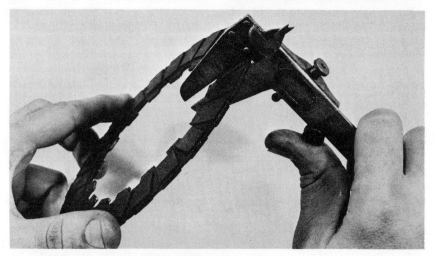

Checking friction disc thickness

Check for damage to the engaging dogs and corresponding wear to the clutch housing

in a tight spot, but this is definitely not the best setup and should only be considered a temporary measure. A quick way of determining whether or not the friction material has any life left in it, other than by measuring it with a micrometer or caliper, is to press a thumbnail into the material. If this leaves an impression the disc is OK to reuse. When you reassemble the clutch, make sure you install the plates and discs in the correct order. Try to keep everything as clean as possible, and go easy on it for about a hundred miles; if you do this you can be pretty sure the clutch will last a while.

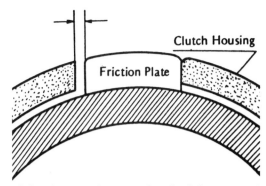

If the clearance between the clutch housing and the friction plates is excessive, the defective parts will have to be replaced

CLUTCH CHATTERS

A talkative clutch may or may not be a problem, but in any case it's annoying. If the problem is excessive play in the gears or chain that drives the clutch it won't sound too cool, but it probably won't hurt anything and isn't worth repairing if that's all that's wrong. A lot of 750 Hondas, for

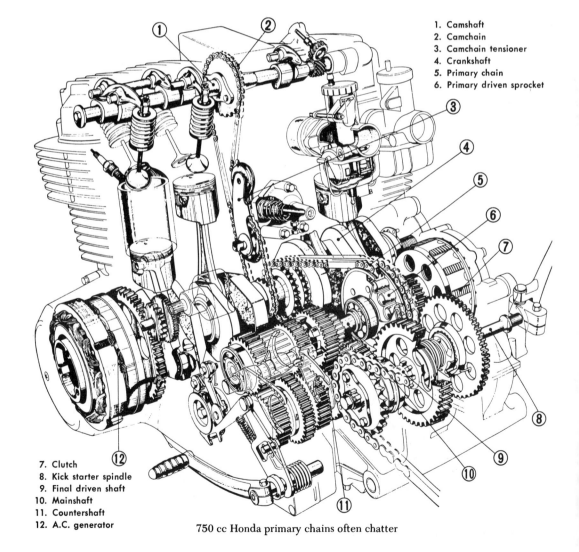

1. Camshaft
2. Camchain
3. Camchain tensioner
4. Crankshaft
5. Primary chain
6. Primary driven sprocket
7. Clutch
8. Kick starter spindle
9. Final driven shaft
10. Mainshaft
11. Countershaft
12. A.C. generator

750 cc Honda primary chains often chatter

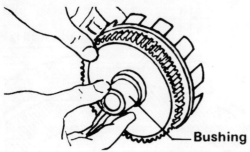

Noise can stem from a wornout clutch hub bushing

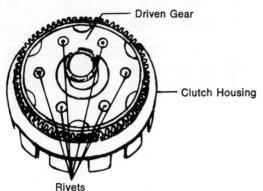

Driven Gear

Clutch Housing

Rivets

Loose rivets make a lot of noise until they give out. Then they make a mess

instance, make a lot of noise when the clutch is out, but as soon as you pull it in and put it in gear, the noise stops. This occurs because the chain(s) from the crankshaft to the clutch hub stretches a little and gets loud. Don't worry, that chain will probably last longer than the bottom end; it will just always be noisy.

If the chatter is caused by a flattened pressure plate, a bad bearing, loose or damaged clutch hub rivets, or wornout hub dampers you may have problems. A flattened pressure plate won't cause any serious damage that a clutch job won't

cure, but if the bearing or the rivets go, it'll get messy for sure. Take a look and show it to a mechanic if you can't figure it out. A bad bearing won't rotate smoothly and may even make perceptible noise when spun by hand. Loose or damaged rivets should be obvious. Also check for excessive play of the clutch hub on its shaft.

Troubleshooting the Gearbox

Determining what's wrong inside a gearbox can be pretty tricky if you aren't familiar with the way things are when they're right. If you have the opportunity to examine a new shifter mechanism and gear cluster do so because it sometimes is difficult to determine if a contour has been worn that way or if it was designed like that. Look for the little things like worn gear dogs, worn or warped shifter forks, worn grooves in the shifter drum or camplate, fatigued springs, bad bearings, etc. In effect, check out everything as thoroughly as possible, and measure all tolerances carefully as directed by the manufacturer.

When it comes to replacing components keep long-range economy in mind. Replace gear systems rather than just the gears that are obviously worn, or the new parts will soon be damaged by their contact with other used parts. This means that if you have a dog gear with a chipped dog you should replace at least the gears it meshes with, the gear that gear meshes with, and maybe the shifter fork which en-

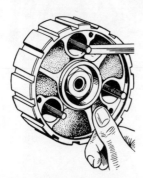

Check the hub dampers for a wornout condition that could cause noisy operation

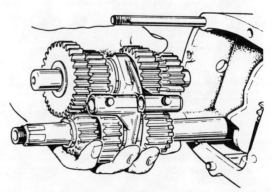

You can't tell anything until it's taken down. The cluster shown is from a BSA Rocket 3

Check gears for pitting or wear close to the base of the teeth

gages it. Worn parts cause accelerated wear to new parts; the best way is to use all new stuff so it will have a chance to wear in smoothly together. Also, if you replace just the obviously damaged parts, it probably won't be long before it becomes necessary to take down the engine again, and you already know what a hassle that is.

Most motorcycles use straight-cut spur gears in their transmissions, although a few, such as Moto Guzzi, use helical gears. "Helical" gears are so-called because the individual gear teeth describe a curve of "helix" across the gear. While straight-cut gears are somewhat stronger, helical gears are quieter in operation.

Check for wear to the gear splines and engaging dogs

Transmission gears are hardened, and the gear teeth, being constantly in contact, will usually not show significant wear for many miles unless foreign matter has been circulating in the gearbox, or the oil level has been allowed to get very low. Contrary to popular opinion, clumsy shifting or "grinding" the gears does not damage the gear teeth, since the gears are always meshed, but the engaging dogs are subject to damage from these causes.

Gears should be checked for wear to the teeth, which will most often be visible as pitting near the bottom of the tooth. Gears should be considered in pairs. If one of the pair is worn the other should be replaced as well.

Some manufacturers specify limits of gear "backlash" which is the amount of play between the engaged teeth of two meshing gears. Backlash is checked with a dial gauge by locking one gear in place and measuring the rotational movement of the other. If backlash is excessive, both gears of the set must be replaced.

Gears are of two types: splined and "wheel." Often other terms are used, but splined gears are fixed onto their shafts and must turn with them. Sometimes they are pressed onto the shaft, more often they are simply a sliding fit. Splined gears should be checked for abnormal wear to the splines both on the gear itself on the shaft. Fit of the gear on the shaft must be reasonably firm without rotational play.

Wheel gears are those with plain bushes which can turn freely on their shaft. The bush should be checked for scoring or wear. Fit of the gear onto its shaft must be close, without appreciable radial play, but the gear must spin freely. On some wheel gears the bushing can be removed by hand if replacement is needed, while on others the bushing must be pressed out. On the

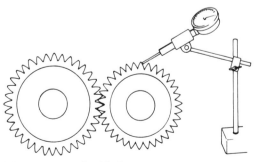

Measuring gear backlash

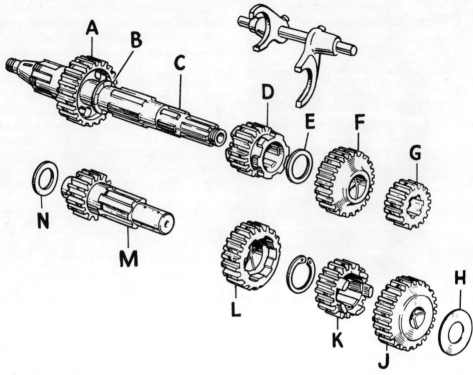

The weakest part of this BSA gearbox are the mainshaft fourth gear and the countershaft gear, neither of which can be replaced without their shaft

A. Mainshaft fourth gear
B. Thrust washer
C. Mainshaft
D. Mainshaft second gear
E. Thrust washer

F. Mainshaft third gear
G. Mainshaft first gear
H. Countershaft first gear shim
J. Countershaft first gear
K. Countershaft third gear

L. Countershaft second gear
M. Countershaft
N. Thrust washer

later type, the new bushing must often be reamed to size after installation, a point to be kept in mind.

While gearbox designs vary widely, most in use today use a fair number of shims to adjust gear side clearance, and circlips on the shafts to locate the gears. In this case, disassembly of the gear clusters should be avoided unless something is obviously wrong with the components. The shaft circlips are never reusable, and must always be replaced with new ones if they are removed from their shafts. Shim number and location should be noted before removal. If new gears are fitted, side clearance will probably have to be checked and shims added or subtracted as necessary. Procedures for operations of this nature are usually found in the shop manual, but are sometimes not within the ability of the average owner.

One last thing: change the oil in a new or rebuilt gearbox every 500 miles for at least the first 1,500 miles, and go easy for a couple hundred miles. New parts wear and this causes a certain amount of metal dust to be picked up and circulated in the oil. This isn't the best of situations so it is important to flush out the system often in the beginning.

GEARS GRIND WHEN SHIFTING

If the gears grind most notably when putting the bike in First the reason is probably a dragging clutch. On some models there will always be an audible clunk when it goes into First, but the rest of the gears should shift relatively smoothly. Very few boxes are butter smooth, but loud aggravated grinding is definitely not normal.

Grinding can also be caused by worn or damaged gear dogs that aren't engaging smoothly. This will result in the eventual failure of at least that particular gear system, and maybe in the whole transmission if a dog breaks off and is eaten. If this is the case, carefully examining the grit left in the bottom of the drip pan after an oil change will let you know. A little bit of metal is not altogether uncommon, but a lot of metal shreds is a bad sign.

A wornout shifter mechanism can cause grinding because it may prevent the gears from meshing as intended. Distorted shifter forks, worn camplate or drum contours, bad linkage, etc. can cause the gears to mesh only partially or intermittently. Check the alignment of the shifter forks (if applicable) as this is critical in most cases,

and take your time during reassembly to make sure everything is just right.

Bad transmission shaft bearings can cause some really horrendous grinding

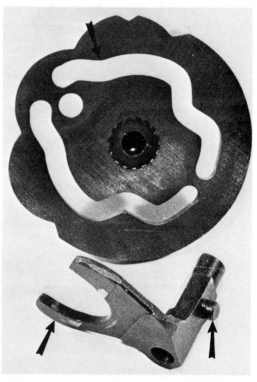

Shifter wear points: camplate grooves, shift fork fingers, and fork pin

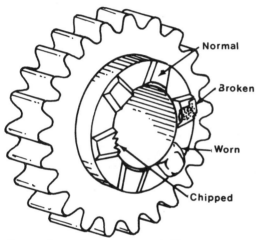

Damaged gear dogs can cause grinding

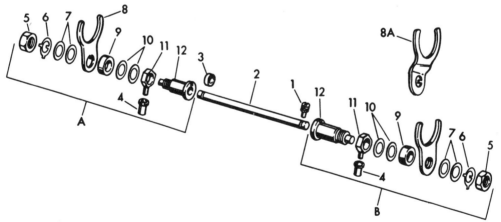

The shifter forks on this Harley-Davidson 74 shifter mechanism are adjusted through the use of variable thickness spacer shims

1. Lock screw
2. Shifter fork shaft
3. Rubber oil seal
4. Shifter finger rollers (2)
5. Nut (2)
6. Lock washer (2)
7. Spacing shim (variable number) (0.007 in.) (0.014 in.)
8. Shifter fork (1 or 2)
8A. Shifter fork (3-speed, reverse only)
9. Standard spacing shim (2)
10. Spacing shim (variable number) (0.007 in.) (0.014 in.)
11. Shifting finger (2)
12. Shifter fork bushing (2)

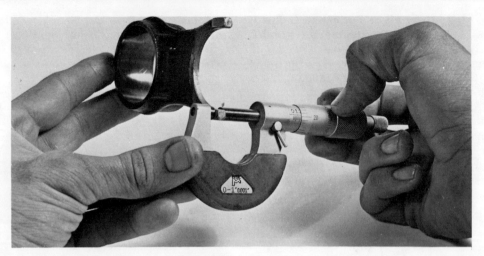

Checking shift fork fingers for wear

Check shift drum grooves for wear

since it causes eccentric rotation of the shafts. This in turn prevents the gears from meshing smoothly as they may be mis-aligned. Chances are that if this occurs, the damage to the gearbox will be extensive.

Worn or warped shafts can also cause grinding for the same reasons that bad bearings can. If this is the case it is best to pull out the whole assembly and start over with new parts.

SHIFTER POPS OUT OF GEAR

By this we mean the bike pops out of gear under power and of its own volition . . . not because there's an inherent defect in the machine such as on some of the early 500 cc Hondas that simply couldn't stay in Third gear, and not because you're feeling lazy and shifting sloppily.

Probably the most common cause of this situation is worn dogs and shifters caused by stomping on the shift lever, speed shift-ing without the clutch, and just general abuse of a relatively delicate mechanism. If this is the case it will probably be quite obvious once you've taken the gearbox down and the situation can be remedied by replacing the necessary components.

Once again the possibility of bad trans-mission shaft bearings or worn shafts comes up. This might only allow a partial engagement of the gears which could cause the gears to disengage when stressed or when in a certain position. Again, re-placement is the only solution.

A final possibility which shouldn't be overlooked is the shift linkage which may be improperly adjusted, inherently poor, or which may have been damaged in an accident. Some bikes, such as early CB/ CL 350 cc Hondas, just have linkage that

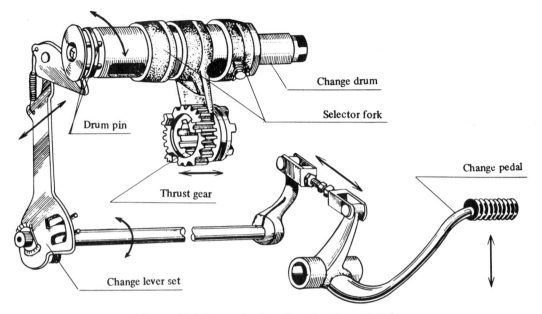

A Kawasaki shifter mechanism. Note the adjustable linkage

is difficult to set up right. If this is the case, it is sometimes possible to modify the existing system and get good results.

SHIFTER DOES NOT RETURN

In this case the shifter remains in the position you last moved it to, but does not return to the ready position. You still can shift the gears but you'll have to do it by hand, probably because the return spring has broken or is really worn out. Unless the spring gets involved with some other mechanism there won't be any noise, the shifter just won't work.

Another possibility is a bent shifter shaft, especially with bikes like Yamaha

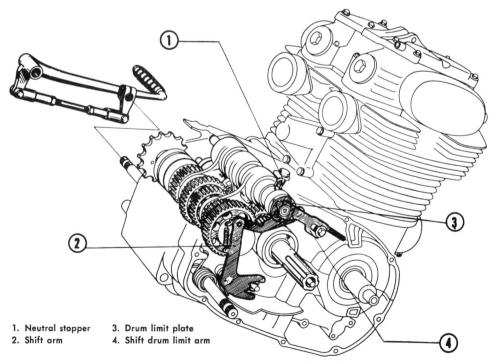

1. Neutral stopper
2. Shift arm
3. Drum limit plate
4. Shift drum limit arm

Location of the shifter mechanism on 350 cc Hondas

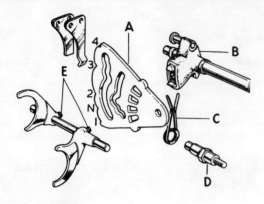

A. Camplate
B. Plunger quadrant
C. Return spring
D. Pivot
E. Shift forks, showing the camplate engagem
   rollers

BSA shifter mechanism

Enduros where the shifter shaft runs all the way through the crankcases. If this shaft is damaged or becomes warped it can easily become jammed and fail to return. The solution is replacement of course, but don't overlook the rest of the shifter mechanism as this too may have been damaged.

Check the bearing surfaces of the shifting mechanism for a galled, pitted, gritty, worn, or damaged condition and replace them as necessary. A situation such as this could conceivably cause the mechanism to hang up and therefore not return as it should. Don't overlook the possibility of grit in other places also, such as in the drum slots, joints, etc.

Finally there's the matter of the shifter itself. If the linkage is out of adjustment, or if the pedal has been bent by a chance meeting with the asphalt, it may rub against the cases or in some way be prevented from returning properly. This should be pretty obvious but don't write it off without taking a close look.

KICKSTARTER JAMS

If a kickstarter lever becomes jammed, not just temporarily stuck at the bottom of the stroke as some do pretty often without causing any damage, something's bound to be broken inside, and since these mechanisms are so simple you'll probably see what it is right away.

The most common failure is a broken worm, kick gear, or ratchet mechanism. As with the gearbox, the same rules apply about replacing broken parts. If the kick gear is damaged you should also consider replacing the gear it meshes with. If the worm splines on the starter shaft are dam-

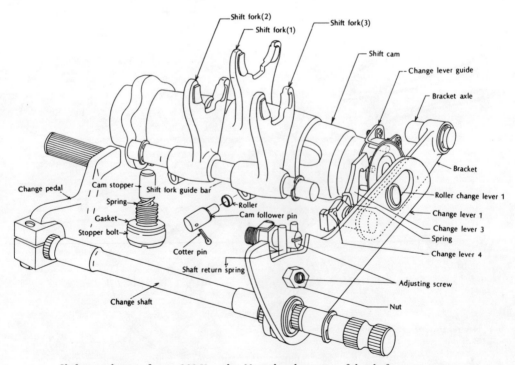

Shifter mechanism from a 360 Yamaha. Note the placement of the shaft return spring

Kickstarter return spring from a 650 Triumph. The arrow indicates where the spring is to be seated

aged it would be unwise to reuse the kick gear.

The second most common failure is a broken return spring. Consult an appropriate manual for instructions on pre-loading the spring if necessary, but you probably won't hurt anything if you figure it out by trial and error.

Other possibilities are improperly meshing gear teeth caused by damaged teeth, a weak or damaged clutch spring, warped shafts, grit in the ratchet mechanism or in the kick gear worm, damage to the kick gear worm, or damage to the kick lever which could cause it to jam against the side of the engine case.

KICKSTARTER SLIPS

A slipping kickstarter may indicate broken or worn gear teeth or a damaged ratchet mechanism that causes the starter lever to slip the length of the damage. If there are still teeth remaining, the starter may grab and operate normally after the point at which the slipping stops. If this is the case, you can get some more life out of the unit by depressing the lever until the slipping stops and then kick the engine over. Although this may work as a temporary measure, the kickstarter should be looked into before one of those broken gear teeth jam something.

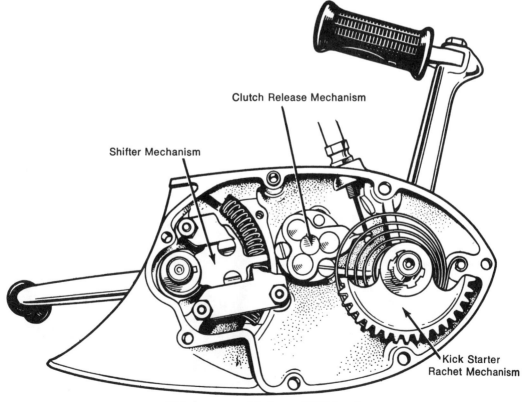

Clutch Release Mechanism

Shifter Mechanism

Kick Starter Rachet Mechanism

Kickstarter assembly from a 650 Triumph

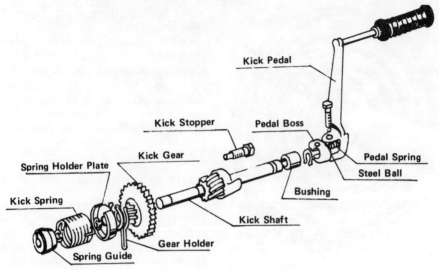

A Kawasaki kickstarter assembly

Stripped splines between the gear pedal and the kickstarter shaft, or a bent starter shaft, could also cause slipping. This probably won't wreck too much that isn't already damaged but should be attended to as soon as possible. Like any of the other kickstarter problems you won't really know what's going on unless you take it apart and have a look.

Finally, it should be mentioned that a badly slipping clutch or insufficient cranking compression can cause a kickstarter to slip. You'd probably be aware of such situations long before they'd become so bad that the starter would slip, but if the machine hasn't been run lately these may be the reasons. Also, if your machine has a compression release, check its operation carefully as this may be the source of a no compression problem.

Frequency of lubrication is dependent upon the type of lubricant used, riding habits, average speeds, weather conditions, and so on.

The rider should check chain condition frequently until he finds the maintenance interval compatible with his riding style. As in the case of engine oil (see preceeding), maintenance will be necessary at shorter intervals if the chain is subjected to severe use: high speeds, off-road riding, jack-rabbit acceleration, etc.

Many riders find that an application of chain lube every 300 miles or so gives satisfactory chain life.

When applying a chain lube, be sure to follow the manufacturer's instructions for use. Many lubes are dispensed in a very fluid state. This facilitates their penetration into the chain. In a few minutes they become thick and sticky, enabling them

Final Drive

LUBRICATION

Some models now come with permanently lubricated drive chains, but most do not. Automatic oiling devices found on some models meter engine oil onto the chain, but this oil is not usually sufficient to keep the chain well-lubricated.

A good brand of lubricant designed specifically for motorcycle drive chains is recommended.

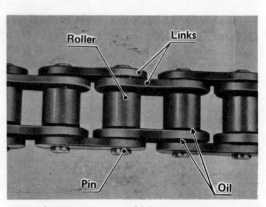

Drive chain components and lubrication points

to adhere to the chain as it spins around the sprockets while riding.

When applying the lubricant, direct it towards the edges of the chain plates so it will reach the pins beneath the rollers.

At extended intervals, about every 2000 miles, the chain should be removed from the motorcycle for cleaning.

NOTE: *Models with endless chains will require a special tool to break the chain. On all models, removal and installation of the masterlink spring clip should be done with a pliers—not a screwdriver—to avoid deforming the spring clip.*

Having an old chain on hand makes chain removal somewhat simplier, since the old chain can be attached to one end of the chain on the bike and pulled through over the engine sprocket, so that it is not necessary to remove the sprocket cover or other components.

Remove heavy deposits of dirt and grease with a stiff brush and solvent. Then soak the chain for several hours in a light motor oil. Hang it up to drain.

Check that each chain link can pivot freely. If there are any kinked or binding links which cannot be freed, or if the chain is rusted or has suffered damage from corrosion (such as might happen if it is touched by acid from an incorrectly routed battery overflow tube), replace it.

Methods of measuring chain wear are discussed in a following section.

After cleaning the chain, refit it to the

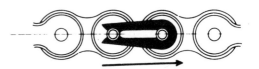

DIRECTION OF TRAVEL

Be sure to install the chain masterlink with the closed end facing the direction of chain rotation

machine, lubricate it in the usual way, and adjust the tension.

When joining the chain, note the following points: models which use an endless type chain will require a new masterlink. On other models, the masterlink may be reused if in good condition. Also, check the condition of the masterlink spring clip. Be sure to install the spring clip with the closed end facing the direction of chain rotation. Also, if the clip is "sprung," the concave side must face the chain.

ADJUSTMENT AND INSPECTION

1. The drive chain slack is the total up and down movement of the chain measured at a point midway between the sprockets. The specifications may differ for various machines, but is usually about 20mm (¾ in.).

2. Conditions under which the chain slack is measured differ from make to make. Some manufacturer's specify that the machine be on the center stand with the rear wheel off the ground, while others state that the slack is measured with the weight of a rider on the bike. Refer to your owner's manual for the correct method.

3. On all machines, however, it is imperative that the chain be clean and well lubricated before checking slack.

4. The chain must be checked for tight spots before making this adjustment. Rotate the wheel slowly and note any variances in chain tension. If the tension varies greatly, it is probable that the chain or the sprockets are worn to the point of replacement.

5. If a tight spot is found, make a mark on the rear sprocket relative to some fixed point. Continue to rotate the wheel. If the chain becomes tight each time the sprocket mark passes the point you chose, the sprocket is warped and should be replaced. If there is no relation be-

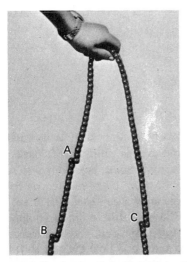

Chains with stiff or binding links (A,B,C) should be replaced if lubrication does not ease movement

Measure the drive chain free-play between the two sprockets on the lower chain run

tween the periods of chain tightness and the rotation of the sprocket, chances are that the chain itself is the problem.

6. Although a chain with a tight spot must soon be replaced, if it must remain in service for a period of time be sure to adjust the chain tension to the given specification at the tight spot. This will probably mean that the chain will have some very loose spots at which it may slap and hit the chainguard, but the potential of breaking the chain will be somewhat reduced.

7. After adjusting the chain to the manufacturer's specification, check for wear by attempting to pull the chain off the rear wheel sprocket. If you can see more than $\frac{1}{2}$ of the sprocket tooth at the point this is done, the chain is worn and should be replaced as soon as possible.

8. Other methods of checking the chain for wear involve first removing it from the machine. Stretch the chain out

to its full length and measure it. Then compress the links so that the chain is as short as possible, but not bent. Measure the chain again. If the difference between the two measurements amounts to more than $\frac{1}{4}$ in. per foot of chain, or more than 3% of its total length, the chain should be replaced.

9. In the event of a worn chain, the sprockets should be inspected closely. A worn chain can ruin sprockets, and conversely, worn sprockets will quickly wear out a new chain.

Check that the sprocket teeth are not hooked. This is the most common sign of a damaged sprocket. Also check for wear on the edges and sides of the teeth. If possible, remove the sprockets, place them on a flat surface and check for warpage. The sprockets must be perfectly flat.

If one of the sprockets is worn, it is recommended that both of them be replaced.

If a properly adjusted chain can be pulled off the sprocket so that more than ½ of a sprocket tooth is visible, the chain should be replaced

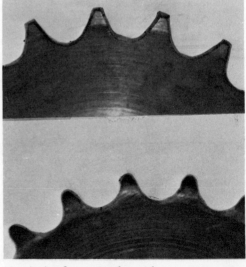

New (top) and worn sprocket teeth

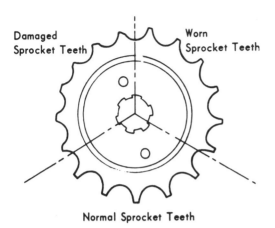

Sprocket wear patterns

Be sure that the adjuster index mark (arrow) is aligned with the same swing arm mark on both sides of the wheel

10. Proper alignment of the rear wheel is very important for handling and for chain and sprocket life. Most motorcycles have axle alignment marks on the swing arm, and care should be taken when adjusting the chain that the index on the adjuster are lined up with the same mark on both sides of the wheel.

If such alignment marks are not fitted, it is possible to align the wheel by "eyeballing" it using the front wheel as a reference. Alternately, if there is not too much in the way, you can measure the distance from the swing arm pivot to the center of the axle and make sure it is the same on both sides.

Clutch and Transmission Troubleshooting

CLUTCH SLIPS

Possible Causes	Remedy
Release mechanism improperly adjusted	Readjust
Release worm and lever sticking	Check cable for binding, and lever spring for damage
Clutch spring tension too loose	Readjust progressively, and evenly, until proper operation is achieved
Worn or damaged clutch spring(s)	Replace as necessary
Friction discs or steel plates worn, warped, or oil impregnated	Replace as necessary
Distorted pressure plate	Replace as necessary

CLUTCH DRAGS

Possible Causes	Remedy
Release mechanism incorrectly adjusted	Readjust
Release worm and lever, or throwout bearing, excessively worn or damaged	Replace as necessary
Clutch spring tension too tight	Readjust
Friction discs gummy and sticking	Replace as necessary

Clutch and Transmission Troubleshooting (cont.)

CLUTCH DRAGS

Possible Causes	Remedy
Steel plates or pressure plate warped or damaged	Replace as necessary
Clutch sprocket keys excessively worn or damaged	Replace as necessary

CLUTCH CHATTERS

Possible Causes	Remedy
Clutch disc rivets loose	Replace as necessary
Pressure plate excessively flattened	Replace as necessary
Excessive play in the clutch drive chain	None.
Bad clutch hub bearing	Replace as necessary

GRINDING WHEN SHIFTING (ESPECIALLY FIRST GEAR)

Possible Causes	Remedy
Clutch drags	Consult the Clutch Drags section
Worn gear dogs	Replace as necessary
Worn shifter mechanism (ie. distorted selector forks or worn shift drum or cam)	Replace as necessary
Bad transmission shaft bearings	Replace as necessary
Worn transmission shafts	Replace as necessary
Foreign objects in the gearbox	Flush out gearbox
Idle speed too high	Adjust
Excessive oil level in the primary case	Drain and refill according to specifications
Transmission oil too heavy for conditions	Drain and refill with lighter oil
Insufficient or diluted gearbox oil	Drain and refill

TRANSMISSION POPS OUT OF GEAR

Possible Causes	Remedy
Shifter rods improperly adjusted or damaged	Readjust or replace as necessary
Shifter forks improperly adjusted or damaged	Readjust or replace as necessary
Insufficient shifter spring tension	Replace as necessary
Worn or damaged gear dogs	Replace as necessary
Worn transmission shaft splines	Replace the shafts as necessary
Worn, damaged, or improperly adjusted shifter mechanism	Replace or adjust as necessary
Improperly adjusted or damaged shift linkage	Readjust or replace as necessary

Clutch and Transmission Troubleshooting (cont.)

TRANSMISSION SHIFTS HARD

Possible Causes	Remedy
Clutch drags	Consult the Clutch Drags section
Worn, damaged, or misadjusted shifter mechanism	Readjust or replace as necessary
Worn or damaged gear dogs	Replace as necessary
Worn return spring	Replace as necessary
Improper mainshaft and countershaft alignment	Replace as necessary
Transmission oil too heavy for conditions	Drain and refill with a lighter oil

EXCESSIVE GEAR NOISE

Possible Causes	Remedy
Excessive gear backlash	Replace the worn components as necessary
Worn or damaged transmission shaft bearings	Replace as necessary
Worn or damaged gears	Replace as necessary

FOOT SHIFTER OPERATES POORLY

Possible Causes	Remedy
Worn, damaged, or misadjusted shifter mechanism	Replace or readjust as necessary
Worn or damaged shift lever return spring	Replace as necessary
Galled, gritty, or damaged shifter bearing surface	Repair or replace as necessary
Gritty shifter mechanism	Thoroughly clean out mechanism
Bent or distorted shifter shaft	Replace as necessary
Bent shifter lever which contacts engine case	Repair or replace as necessary

KICKSTARTER JAMS

Possible Causes	Remedy
First tooth on kick gear badly worn	Replace as necessary
Damaged ratchet pinion teeth	Replace as necessary
Broken, worn, or improperly meshed gear teeth	Replace as necessary
Broken return spring	Replace as necessary
Grit on kick gear worm or in ratchet mechanism	Thoroughly clean out mechanism
Kick lever hung up	Repair or replace as necessary

KICKSTARTER SLIPS

Possible Causes	Remedy
Worn or damaged kick gear or ratchet mechanism	Replace as necessary
Clutch slips	Consult Clutch Slips section

Clutch and Transmission Troubleshooting (cont.)

KICKSTARTER SLIPS

Possible Causes	Remedy
Stripped splines between gear pedal and kick-starter shaft	Replace the shafts as necessary
Bent starter shaft	Replace as necessary
Lack of engine compression	Determine cause

CHAIN WHINE

Possible Causes	Remedy
Chain too tight	Adjust chain correctly
Chain rusted or kinking	Lubricate or replace chain

CHAIN SLAP

Possible Causes	Remedy
Chain too loose	Adjust chain correctly
Bent chain guard	Repair chain guard so chain rotates freely

ACCELERATED CHAIN AND SPROCKET WEAR

Possible Causes	Remedy
Sprockets improperly aligned	Align sprockets
Rear wheel out of alignment	Align wheels
One or both sprockets slightly damaged	Replace sprockets and chain
Chain worn or damaged	Replace chain and sprockets
Chain insufficiently lubricated	Keep chain lubricated thoroughly

8 · Chassis Troubleshooting

Most chassis components do not require constant attention once they are properly set up, but some attention should be paid to them since handling and braking are so very important from the safety point of view.

This chapter deals with tires, wheels, brakes, and the various suspension components and the checks and adjustments you should make from time to time to ensure safety on the road.

Tires

TIRE PRESSURES

1. Tire pressures are recommended by the manufacturer and you should abide by the recommended pressure unless the motorcycle is being put to some special use, such as competition.

These pressures are determined by considering the design of the motorcycle, tire sizes, the weight of an average rider, and several other factors. The resultant pressure should give a comfortable ride, reasonable tire life, and, most importantly, safe handling. It is therefore not wise to deviate from the recommended pressures unless you really know what you are doing.

2. On most late-model motorcycles, the tire pressure is given somewhere on the mo-

torcycle. If it isn't here, check your owner's handbook or a shop manual.

You will note that pressure may be different for the front and rear wheels. Also, pressure variations may be necessary if you carry luggage, ride two-up, or will ride at high speeds for extended intervals (no longer very wise). In general, you might add 4–6 psi to the rear wheel and 2–3 psi to the front over normal pressure to compensate for these conditions.

3. Tire pressure should be checked every two weeks or so. A hand-held gauge is recommended, since it is a fact that the pressure meters on the air hoses found in service stations are not particularly accurate in many instances.

Check pressures when the tires are *cold*. Tire pressure will build up as you ride. The tire gets hot, and the air inside tries to expand. A ride of a mile or so probably will not affect pressure significantly, however, so you can ride to the local gas station before checking the tires.

4. Overinflated tires will wear rapidly, give a harsh ride, and may decrease braking ability. Underinflated tires may cause "squirrely" handling.

TIRE INSPECTION

1. Tire tread depth is one of the most critical items you can check. The minimum safe tread depth for your machine should be given by the manufacturer either in the owner's

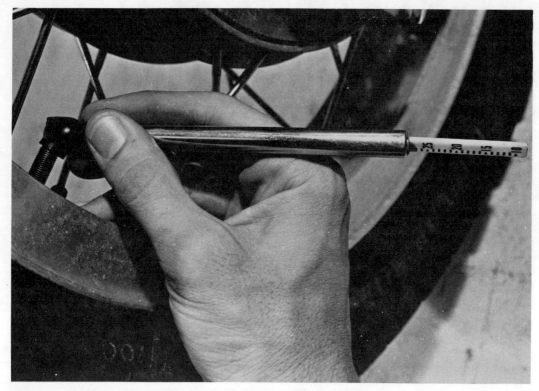

Checking tire pressure

handbook or a shop manual. Since many states have their own laws in this regard, however, it is not possible to generalize with a great degree of accuracy as to what depth constitutes the "safe" limit. The following is provided only as a rough guide based on a survey of various manufacturers' recommendations:

For road machines: 1.5 mm (0.06 in.) front
                    2.0 mm (0.08 in.) rear

For light-weight off-road bikes: 1.0 mm (0.04 in.)

For Superbike-class machines used at high speeds: 2.0 mm (0.08 in.) front
                    3.0 mm (0.12 in.) rear

This measurement is taken at the center of the tire tread, and at the point of minimum depth if the tire is unevenly worn.

2. Occasionally spin each tire and remove any pebbles, nails, etc., which may have become stuck in the tread grooves.

3. Check for uneven or unusual tire wear or feathering of the tread. Any number of things may cause uneven tire wear: a misaligned wheel due to clumsy rear chain adjustment or bent forks; a rim out of true; an unbalanced wheel; or worn or damaged bearings.

4. Occasionally, loosen the valve stem lock-

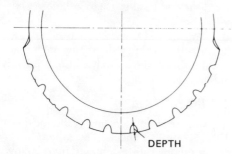

DEPTH

Tire tread depth

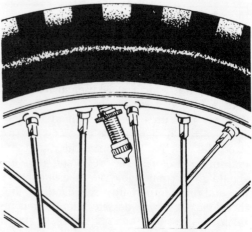

Loosen the locknut on the valve stem; if the stem tilts as shown, the tire has slipped around the rim and must be repositioned

nut. If the valve stem tilts to one side when this is done, it indicates that the tire has slipped around the rim during use.

This condition must be corrected, or the tire may slip enough to pull the stem out of the inner tube causing a blow-out. Deflate the tire and move it back so that the stem protrudes at right angles to the rim. If a rim lock is fitted, do not forget to loosen this first and push it off the tire bead. If it isn't possible to move the tire by hand, you should remove the wheel and break the tire off the rim by walking around on the sidewall.

TIRE CHANGING

To change a tire you will need two motorcycle tire irons, a lubricant such as soapy water or dishwashing liquid, and a plastic mallet which, while not entirely necessary, is certainly helpful.

You can purchase suitable tire irons at any motorcycle shop, or it is possible that they may have been included in your bike's toolkit. Tire irons are specifically designed for the job. They are angled to provide good leverage and have smooth, rounded spoons to prevent pinching the tube. Although some irons may seem small, if you are using the right method they should provide sufficient leverage to get the tire off the rim. There is no acceptable substitute for good tire irons. Attempting to use screwdrivers or other levers for this job is only asking for trouble.

If you have cast alloy wheels, tire irons should be used with care to avoid damaging the wheel. The same is true to a lesser extent with alloy spoked rims which can be scratched. It may be possible to cover the shaft of the irons with a piece of an old inner tube or the like to obviate the chances of damage.

A large sheet of cardboard can also decrease chances of damage to the wheel or brake disc (if fitted). Changing the tire on a concrete surface can easily chip chrome or scratch the rim or brake disc, while changing it on the lawn will certainly get dirt or grass into the wheel bearings unless a rag is placed under the hub.

1. After removing the wheel from the motorcycle, take out the valve core. Remove the valve stem nut(s). If a rimlock is fitted, remove its nut and push the rimlock down off the tire bead. If the same tire is to be refitted, mark the location of the valve stem and the direction of rotation on the tire sidewall.

2. Place the wheel on the ground and walk around the tire to break the bead off the

Mark the location of the valve stem on the sidewall before removing the tire

rim. This may be necessary if the tire has been on the rim for some time.

3. Smear some soapy water or dishwashing liquid around the beads on both sides of the tire.

4. Beginning at the valve stem, use the tire irons to lever one bead off the rim. The tire bead opposite the valve stem should be pressed well down into the rim well. Kneel on the tire, if necessary to hold the bead down. Start by inserting both tire irons under the bead a few inches apart. Do not insert them too deeply or you may catch the tube. Pull back on both irons simultaneously until a portion of the bead is over the rim. Then remove one of the irons and use it again sev-

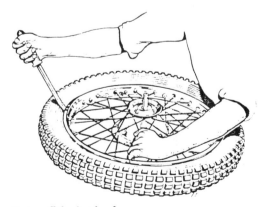

Prying off the first bead

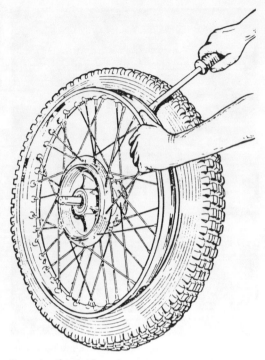

Removing the tire from the rim

eral inches away from its first position. Continue around the tire until one side is completely free of the rim.

5. Pull out the tube. If the tire is to be replaced, remove the rimlock and lever the remaining bead off the rim.

6. Check the tube for leaks. Patching the tube is not recommended except in emergency situations. The patch may leak or may upset tire balance. Get a new tube if a puncture is evident.

7. Carefully remove the rim band and, using a wire brush, remove any rust deposits from the rim. Excessive use of tire lubricant can cause rust on steel rims. Check the bead of the tire as well. Remove any deposits here with the wire brush.

8. Check the spokes for looseness and tighten if necessary. If this is done, check that no spoke end protrudes from its nipple. Grind down any protruding spoke ends to obviate the chances of a puncture. Carefully refit the rim band so that it covers all the nipples.

9. The tire must be mounted so that the mark on the sidewall aligns with the valve stem. New tires will have this alignment mark painted near the bead. Also note direction of rotation, if applicable. On some tires the direction of rotation will be different depending on whether the tire is mounted on the front or the rear of the motorcycle. If a rimlock is fitted, be sure to install it before the tube, but do not fit its locknut.

10. If you have only replaced the tube, and the tire is still on the rim, care must be exercised when stuffing the tube into the tire since it is possible to twist it. If the tire has been completely removed, the easiest method is to

Note direction of rotation on the sidewall

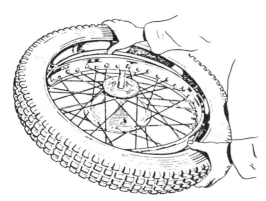

Fitting tire and tube together

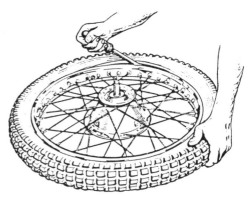

Levering on the second bead

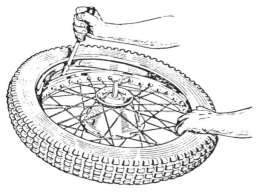

Levering on the first bead

mount tire and tube together. Install the valve core into the stem and put just a few lbs of air in the tube. You should inflate the tube just enough so that it holds its shape, but not so much that the tube expands. Place the inflated tube into the tire. Approximately aligning the valve stem and the hole in the rim, lever tire and tube together over the rim. Be sure to lubricate the tire beads as on removal.

11. If it is very difficult to lever the tire bead on, use a plastic mallet to strike the bead, thus forcing it over the edge of the rim as you move around the tire with the tire irons.

12. After the tire and tube are installed, temporarily overinflate the tube to seat the tire. The tire will have an aligning mark which is a thin line molded into the sidewall and which will appear just above the edge of the rim. This line should be equidistant from the rim edge all the way around the tire. If it is not concentric, the tire is not properly seated. This is sometimes caused by rust on the rim

Check that the alignment mark is equidistant from the edge of the rim all the way around

and can often be remedied by thoroughly lubricating the beads and temporarily overinflating the tube.

13. After the tube has been inflated to the correct pressuren tighten the valve stem locknut(s) and the nut on the rimlock if one is fitted.

14. The wheel should be balanced after completing this operation.

Wheels

SPOKES

1. Spokes should be checked periodically for proper tension. Spin the wheel slowly while striking each spoke lightly with a screwdriver. Each one should emit a "ping" of approximately the same pitch.

2. A loose spoke will emit a dull sound. Such spokes should be tightened. The nipple, however, should not be turned more than two revolutions. To exceed this risks puncturing the tube with the end of the spoke. If two turns will not tighten the spoke, remove the tire and tube before continuing.

Spoke nipples should be turned only with a genuine spoke nipple wrench which you should be able to purchase from your dealer.

3. If more than two adjacent spokes are found to be loose, the rim should be checked for run-out, and trued if necessary. On-bike tightening of loose spokes is intended only to secure spokes which may have loosened from vibration or settling. It is not intended to true up rims which have been knocked out of kilter. Continuous loosening of spokes should be remedied by removing the wheel and having it properly trued.

WHEEL BALANCING

Wheels should be balanced each time the tire is removed or replaced. A badly balanced tire may make itself evident by vibration (especially if the front tire is out-of-balance) or by unusual tire wear.

1. Wheels should be balanced on a wheel stand. Balancing on the machine is not recommended due to drag imposed by chains, brake pads, and even wheel bearing grease seals. If a stand is not available, it is permissible to hang the wheel by the axle between two benches or chairs. Only make sure that both surfaces are of equal height. To obtain the most accurate balance it is necessary to remove as much ro-

Each spoke should emit a tone of about the same pitch

Securing a spoke with the special wrench

tational friction as possible. On some designs, wheel bearing grease seals contribute to friction, and really should be removed if possible. It may also be helpful to oil the axle as the wheel is turned. If the wheel will not rotate freely, determine the cause (i.e. bad bearings) before balancing.

2. The tire and tube must be in place and properly installed during balancing. If the wheel has a disc brake, leave it in place. Drum brake hubs should be removed.

3. If there are tire balancing weights already on the spokes, leave them there. Remove or reposition these weights once you are into the procedure.

4. Spin the wheel slowly several times in

Installing a balance weight

succession, marking the tire with a grease pencil or the like at the lowest part of the wheel each time it stops. If the same mark rotates to the lowest position several times in succession, this is the heaviest part of the assembly. Ideally, the wheel would stop rotating at random locations. If a heavy point is noted, attach a tire balance weight to a spoke directly opposite the heavy point. Repeat the procedure, adding or repositioning weights so that the wheel will not stop at any one point in particular when it is spun.

5. Balance weights are available in several forms, the most popular being the type which fits over the spoke nipple and is secured with pliers. Another kind is an almost-flat piece of lead which attaches to steel rims by means of adhesive. Cast alloy wheels may require special kinds of balance weights. On this kind of wheel, always install the balance weight on the outer part of the rim, not on the sides of the spokes.

Balance weights may be available in different weights. Use the lightest ones to start. If you have to add more than three or four weights to correct balance, there is probably something amiss.

As an alternative to balance weights, there are several brands of balancing *fluid* currently on the market. This is added to the tube and automatically balances the tire when the machine is ridden. It will also change as changes are made to the system, so that fitting a new tire will bring about an automatic compensation on the part of the fluid.

RIM RUN-OUT

1. Rim run-out can be checked with a dial gauge or a simple pointer. This check can be made with the wheels on the motorcycle. Before this is done, however, be sure that the wheel bearings are in good condition (see "Wheel Bearings") or misleading results may be obtained. All spokes must be secure.

2. Rims should be checked for lateral (side-to-side) run-out, and for concentricity (up-and-down movement). In both cases, the maximum acceptable variance is 2.0 mm (0.08 in.). If either lateral or vertical run-out exceeds this amount, the rim should be trued. To true a rim, the tire and tube must be removed, and a wheel stand should be used.

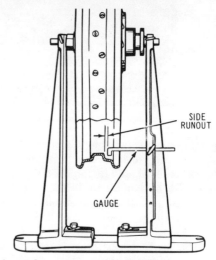

Checking side run-out on a wheel stand

Measuring rim run-out with a dial gauge

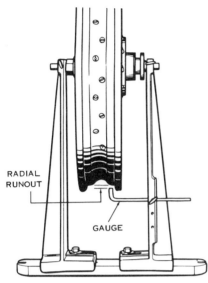

Checking radial run-out

3. It is not possible to true rims which are bent, even if the damage is slight, since the spokes cannot exert enough force to bend the rim back into shape. Such rims must be replaced.

4. If the rim shows both lateral and vertical run-out, the vertical run-out should be corrected first. This can be done by first loosening those spokes opposite the high-spot, and then tightening the spokes at the high-spot. Spokes should be loosened or tightened in small, even increments since lateral run-out will be affected while correcting vertical run-out.

5. If a new rim is being fitted, it is necessary to have the rim at least approximately centered on the hub before attempting to true it. This can be accomplished in most cases by tightening the spoke nipples by approximately the same amount: that is, so that about the same number of spoke threads show at each nipple. File off the ends of any protruding spokes.

6. The fitting of a new rim can be facilitated by securing each set of two spokes loosely with lengths of wire or tape before removing the old rim.

WHEEL BEARINGS

Most motorcycle wheels are fitted with ball bearings, although a few use roller or tapered roller bearings.

Each wheel has two bearings which in most cases are press-fit into the hub and are separated by a spacer tube. Some wheels use threaded retainers or perhaps circlips to se-

Checking wheel bearings for play

cure one or both bearings. Grease seals are usually fitted to both sides of the hub to keep the bearing grease in and dirt and moisture out.

Some larger bikes also have a "wheel bearing" in the rear wheel sprocket assembly for added rigidity.

Wheel bearings can usually be inspected on the bike simply by grasping either side of the tire and checking for play. There should be none.

If play is evident, the bearings may be worn and replacement will be in order. Bearings are always replaced in pairs.

Removal and Installation

Removal of the bearings is obviously necessary for replacement and also for repacking which should be carried out in accordance with the periodic maintenance schedule for your motorcycle.

You should note that the removal process frequently ruins bearings because they are press-fit in the hub and must be driven out. This is especially true on high-mileage machines. In addition, grease seals should always be replaced with new ones if removed.

1. Remove the wheel from the motorcycle.

Prying out a grease seal

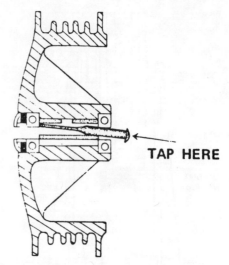

Wheel bearing removal

2. Remove any dust covers, spacers, etc. from either side of the hub.

3. Pry out the grease seals, if accessible. Machines with tapered-roller bearings use the seals to hold the bearings, and once the seals are removed, the bearings will come out.

4. Remove any retainers or circlips from the hub. Note that some threaded retainers are *left-hand thread.* An example is the retainer on the right side of Norton rear wheels. This retainer doubles as the speedometer drive, and a standard right-hand threaded retainer might loosen up because of this. Be cognizant of situations such as this, and check your shop manual to be sure.

5. Wheel bearings are driven out with a drift in most cases. It is sometimes helpful to heat the hub very gently to facilitate removal. Heating the hub with a rag soaked in boiling water is one way to due this. Some manufacturers specify that the hub should not be heated to more than 212°F (100°C).

6. The best way to remove wheel bearings is to tap around the *outer* race with a punch and hammer. This is not possible in most cases, however. If the axle is suitable, it can be inserted into the bearings. A sharp blow on one side of the axle may then be used to dislodge the bearing on the opposite side. It is possible that the bearing will not even look like it moved, but check anyway. In some in-

stances a slight movement is all that is necessary, and the bearings will be free.

If this is not possible, the bearing can be removed by reaching through the hub with a long punch. Try to move the spacer tube to one side so that ample purchase can be obtained. Tap the bearing out evenly, alternating your blows around the circumference of the race.

Driving out a wheel bearing

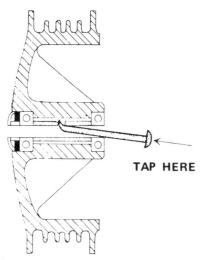

Removing a wheel bearing with a hooked tool (Yamaha)

Packing a wheel bearing

Yamaha motorcycles are equipped with a hole in the spacer tube which allows the bearing to be removed without striking the bearing directly. If a properly hardened hooked tool is available, it can be used as illustrated to remove the bearings.

7. Once one bearing is removed, you can take out the spacer tube. If this is only a routine repacking, leave the other bearing in place if possible. As noted, removal risks ruining the bearings, and repacking is possible with one removed.

8. Remove old grease from the hub and the bearings with a solvent. After the bearing is clean, lubricate it with oil and check for smooth rotation. Any roughness, binding or clicking sounds which appear indicate that both bearings should be replaced. Place each

Play or movement of the inner race indicates a worn bearing

bearing on a flat surface and hold the outer race firmly in place. Attempt to move the inner race back and forth. Little or no movement should be noted, or a worn bearing is indicated.

9. Repack bearings with a good grade of wheel bearing grease of the type recommended for your motorcycle. Grease should be pressed into the bearing until it is full. Place a quantity of grease into the hub as well.

10. Bearings should be installed by tapping them into place. Drive the bearing in squarely and evenly. Do not allow the bearing to become cocked while entering the hub. Tap on the *outer* bearing race only.

Bearings which have one side sealed are always installed with the sealed side facing *out*.

If a retainer or circlip is fitted to one side of the hub, the bearing on that side should be installed first. After the bearing is installed, fit the retainer or circlip. This will ensure proper location of the bearing to ease fitting the other one.

11. Install new grease seals.

Brakes

DRUM BRAKES

Drum brakes are either *single leading shoe* or *double leading shoe* types. *Four leading shoe* brakes as found on machines such as early Moto Guzzi Sports or early Suzuki GT750s are actually two twin leading shoe

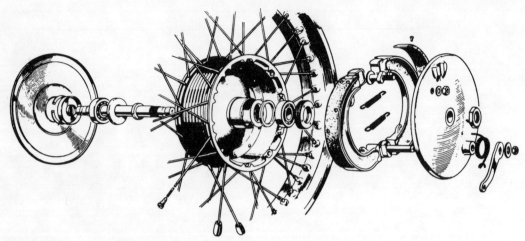

Single leading shoe brake assembly from BSA

brake assemblies one mounted on each side of the wheel.

A single leading shoe brake consists of two brake shoes mounted on a plate. On one side, the shoe rests on a stud or pivot, while the other end of the shoes bear against a cam. The shoes are held in place by coil springs. When the brake lever or pedal is activated, the cam is turned, pressing the brake lining against the drum. Since there is only one cam, only one end of the brake shoe is pressed against the drum. The other end is a fixed pivot. No matter how the brake plate is arranged on the motorcycle, the *leading side* of one shoe and the *trailing* side of the other will be resting on the cam.

Drum brakes are self-energizing. That is, once the leading shoe has been brought into contact with the drum, the drum's rotational movement tends to draw it against it. The trailing shoe, on the other hand, tends to be forced away from the drum.

Twin-leading shoe brakes are different in the following way. Instead of a single fixed pivot and single cam, each shoe is mounted on its own pivot and has its own cam. The shoes are mounted so that the leading end of both shoes are those activated by the cam.

Adjustment

1. Drum brakes are operated by either cable or rod. In most cases, front brakes have cable adjusters at the brake plate and at the hand lever. Rear brakes usually have an adjuster at the brake plate.

Generally, brake adjustment should be maintained so that the brake hand lever or brake pedal has about 1 in. of movement before the linings contact the drum.

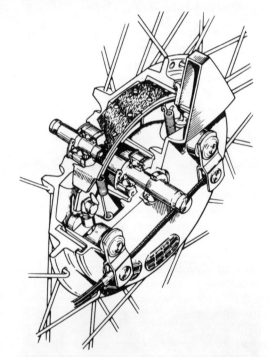

Self-adjusting twin-leading shoe brake (Triumph/BSA)

The brake lever should have about 1 in. of freeplay before the linings contact the drum

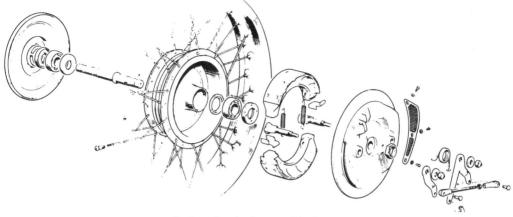

Twin leading shoe brake assembly from BSA

In the case of rod-operated rear brakes, this adjustment should be made with the machine off the stands and with a rider sitting on it. The reason for this is that the movement of the swing arm may vary the distance between the brake cam and the pedal pivot, thereby changing the brake adjustment as the machine is operated.

2. On front brakes, the adjustment is usually made at the brake plate, with fine adjustments made at the hand lever.

3. Twin-leading shoe brakes are fitted with a linkage connecting the two cams, and the linkage may not need routine adjustment unless the brake plate has been disassembled or new shoes have been fitted. One type of the linkage has both brake levers connected with a cable and the levers are pulled together when the brake is applied. This type is self-adjusting.

A more common method is to have the brake cable connected to one brake level, the remaining lever being connected to the first by means of a rod and clevises. The rod is usually threaded and means of varying the length of the rod to make an adjustment is possible.

This is done in one of two ways, depending upon how the rod is attached.

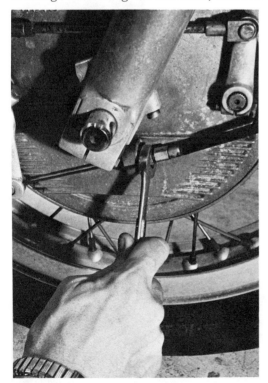

Adjusting the brake at the brake plate

When the brake hand lever is applied so that one brake shoe fully contacts the drum, pushing the other shoe's lever until it too is in contact should result in the alignment of the lever and clevis holes. If not, the brake linkage is improperly adjusted

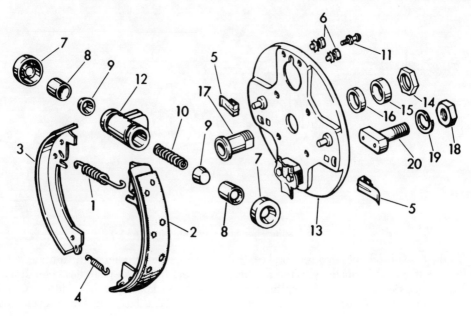

1. Shoe return spring	7. Boot (2)	14. Nut
2. Front brake shoe	8. Piston (2)	15. Spacer
3. Rear brake shoe	9. Cup (2)	16. Collar
4. Brake shoe spring	10. Spring	17. Brake sleeve
5. Hold-down spring (2)	11. Bleeder nipple	18. Nut
6. Cylinder screw and lock washer	12. Wheel cylinder	19. Lockwasher
(2 each)	13. Brake side cover	20. Anchor stud

Hydraulically assisted drum brake used on Harley-Davidson Glide models

To check the adjustment, disconnect the rod at the main brake lever. There is usually a retaining clip or cotter pin at the clevis pin. Apply the brake hand lever until the shoe contacts the drum. Holding this position, apply the secondary brake lever with your hand until that shoe contacts the drum. The clevis holes should line up at this point. If they do not, lengthen or shorten the brake rod so that the holes align.

Checking for Wear

1. Late model drum brakes have wear indicators fitted to the brake cam. In most cases these consist of arrows. If the arrows align when the brake is applied, the brake linings are worn to the point of replacement.

2. Brakes not fitted with indicators can be checked with the wheel in place. When the brake is applied, the angle formed by the brake rod or cable and the brake lever should not exceed 90°. After this point, braking effectiveness will be reduced.

3. On brakes without wear indicators, an occasional check of lining thickness is recommended. Minimum allowable lining thickness is usually given by the manufacturer, and may

The brake rod can be lengthened or shortened to achieve proper adjustment

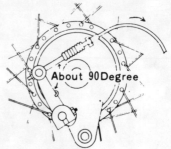

The angle between the brake lever and the cable end should not exceed 90° when the brake is applied. If it does, check the linings for wear

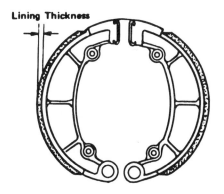

Lining Thickness

be given in your state's motor vehicle code. It is approximately 0.08 in. (2.0 mm) measured at the lining's thinnest point, but this value is only a generalization, and the exact figure must be obtained from your owner's handbook or shop manual, as it differs from bike to bike.

On machines with riveted brake shoes, the thickness of the lining must be measured from the top of the rivets. On bonded shoes, it is measured from the surface of the shoe casting.

Brake Troubleshooting

INEFFECTIVE BRAKES

1. If the brakes become ineffective even if adjustment is correct, check lining thickness first. If thickness is within acceptable limits, the loss of braking power may be caused by an excessive angle between the brake rod or cable and the brake lever. *If* enough material is left on the linings, this can be remedied by moving the brake lever back one spline on the brake cam. It must be noted that this can be done only if the linings are not excessively worn, for if they are, a dangerous situation may develop.

2. A common cause of poor operation of cable-operated drum brakes is caused by the build-up of dirt or corrosion between the inner brake cable and the cable sheath. Ensure proper cable lubrication by periodically disconnecting the brake cable from the hand lever and pouring motor oil or one of the molybdenum disulphide or graphite-based lubricants between the inner and outer cables. Apply sufficient amounts. The lubricant should appear at the lower end of the cable to show that the entire length is lubricated. An alternate method involves removing the cable from the motorcycle completely and immersing it in a pan of light oil. Leave one end of the cable above the oil in the pan so the lubricant can seep through.

Try to get some light grease into either end

of the cable after lubrication to keep out dirt and moisture.

You should note that cables which have gone without periodic lubrication for an extended length of time can usually not be repaired by lubrication. If the sticking or binding persists, the cable must be replaced.

3. Glazed linings can also cause poor braking. This can be fixed by removing the wheel and inspecting the surfaces of the brake linings and the brake drum.

Use sandpaper to rough up the linings. Sandpaper can also be used to clean up rust or corrosion on the brake drum. The drum should be shiney.

Also, check the drum for wear. On most late-model motorcycles, brake drum maximum allowable diameter is stamped somewhere on the hub. If not, it is contained in the shop manual. Worn drums must be replaced.

4. Although not common, ineffective brakes can be the result of oil or grease on the linings. It is almost impossible to remove lubricant from the porous linings surfaces, and brakes in this condition should be replaced.

5. On some motorcycles, it is necessary to "center the brakes" in the drum any time the wheel has been removed. Failure to do so will cause a decrease in braking power.

To perform this operation, and assuming that the axle nut is loose, simply apply that brakes hard, and, holding them on, tighten the axle nut to its proper torque.

6. On twin leading shoe brake, improper adjustment of the brake connecting rod will cause a lack of performance. Adjust this according to the manufacturers instructions, or refer to the "Adjustment" section above for a general guide.

Another cause, often overlooked, is worn or damaged clevis pins. Once these pins wear a good deal of slop may develop in the brake linkage. The remedy is replacement of the pins.

BRAKES DRAG

1. Dragging brakes may be caused by an improperly lubricated cable as discussed above. Other causes include worn or damaged return springs. Most manufacturers give a maximum allowable length for brake springs, and those which exceed this limit should be replaced.

2. Binding of the brake cam(s) in the brake plate is another cause of dragging brakes. This may happen either because the cams have not

been properly lubricated or because they are bent.

BRAKES SQUEAL

This problem is most often caused by dirt on the brake linings. Clean linings and drum thoroughly.

Brake Service

The following procedure is to be considered a general guide to inspecting and servicing a drum brake assembly. The procedure may vary in detail depending upon the design of the brake assembly in question.

1. Remove the wheel from the motorcycle and separate the hub from the brake plate assembly.

2. Wear of brake linings can be checked with the linings in place. Be sure to measure brake lining thickness at the linings' thinnest points. On riveted brakes, measure the distance from the top of the rivets to the lining surface.

3. Check the linings for grooves, scoring, or other signs of unusual wear. Most damage of this sort is caused by particles of dirt, which have entered the brake drum. If badly scored, the shoes must be replaced. If the shoes are scored, the drum should be checked for the same type of damage.

Be sure that there is no oil or grease present of the linings. Oil-impregnated linings must be replaced. If the linings show this condition, determine the source of the lubricant: defective wheel bearing grease seals, excessive chain lube, etc.

4. If the linings are usable, rough up their

Sand brake shoes to remove glazing

surface with sandpaper. Then clean them with alcohol or lacquer thinner. Polish the brake drum surface removing any rust or dirt and clean the drum thoroughly.

5. To disassemble the brake plate, remove the shoes. On some models, this is possible simply by grasping both shoes and folding them towards the center of the brake plate. Other models, however, are fitted with retainers or guards. Remove any cotter pins and washers from the brake cam(s), then remove the shoes.

NOTE: *The plurals refer to the twin-leading shoe brakes.*

6. To remove the cam(s) from the brake plate, remove the brake lever pinch bolt(s). Most brake levers are fitted on splines and will have to be pried off carefully. After the lever is removed, the brake cam can be tapped or pushed out of the brake plate. Note any dust seals or washers on the brake cam.

7. Check that the brake lever pinchbolts are not bent. This can easily happen if they are overtightened. Replace any bolts in this con-

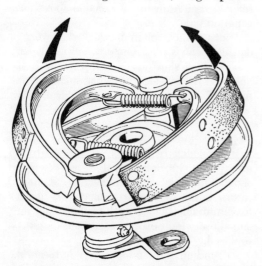
Most brake shoes can be removed by bending them off the cam(s) and pivot(s)

Prying off a brake cam lever

dition. Inspect the brake lever splines and replace the lever(s) if these are worn or stripped.

8. Inspect the splines on the brake cam(s). These should be in good condition. Check that the brake cam(s) are not bent and that they can rotate freely in the brake plate passage. If it will not, use a fine grade of sandpaper on the camshafts and the surface of the brake plate passage.

9. Clean the cam(s) thoroughly in a solvent to remove any old grease, rust, or corrosion. Use sandpaper or emery cloth to polish the cams. Clean off any residue; before reassembly, smear the cams with chassis grease.

10. Inspect the brake plate for cracks or fractures, and replace it if necessary.

11. On twin-leading shoe brakes, the brake plate linkage should be checked. The connecting rod is secured to each brake lever by a clevis pin and cotter pin or clip. They should be checked for wear, especially on high mileage machines, and replaced if necessary.

12. Check the condition of the brake springs, noting any twisted or fatigued hooks. Replace any broken, rusted, or old springs with new ones. Check spring free length if specified for your bike.

13. Clean all metal parts thoroughly with a suitable solvent, making a special effort to remove the dust and built-up dirt from the backing plate.

14. When reassembling the brake plate, note the following points:

a. Ensure that the brake cams are lubricated with chassis grease;

b. The use of new dust seals is recommended;

c. Lubricate the brake shoe pivot points with a little grease;

d. Install the shoes as on removal. Hook them together with the springs, and fold them down over the brake cam(s) and pivot(s). Install new cotter pins to the pivot points;

e. When installing the brake lever on the brake cam, be sure that the punch marks on the lever and cam align, if applicable.

15. The drum should be checked for concentricity. An out-of-bound condition is usually noticeable as an on-off-on feeling when the brake is applied while riding. With the wheel assembly mounted on the machine, spin the wheel while applying the brake very lightly. The rubbing noise of the brakes

against the drum should be heard for the entire revolution of the wheel.

16. An out-of-round condition and most scoring can be removed by having the drum turned on a lathe. This operation should be entrusted to a qualified specialist with the proper equipment. Usually, the tire and wheel bearings will have to be removed so that the wheel can be checked to the lathe. If the rim needs to be trued, have this done before any work on the drum is performed, as the action of the spokes while truing the rim may further aggravate the drum warpage.

Before beginning a project of this sort, it is advisable to consult your dealer.

HYDRAULIC DISC BRAKES

Disc brakes are all quite similar in operation. The main components of a disc brake system are the master cylinder, the caliper, and the disc or rotor.

The *mastery cylinder* is mounted on the handlebar for front disc brakes or on the chassis for rear wheel discs. The master cylinder contains a fluid reservoir, a piston assembly for applying hydraulic pressure to the system, and a lever for moving the piston assembly.

The *caliper* is mounted on the forks for front discs, or the swing arm for rear disc brakes. The caliper houses the brake pads which bear against the disc when pressure is applied.

There are several types of caliper. One kind, which is used on machines such as Norton, Triumph, Yamaha, and Honda (for rear brakes), consists of a rigidly mounted caliper with two moveable pistons, one on each side of the disc. Fluid pressure is applied to both pistons, they, in turn, pressing their respective pads against the disc.

Another type of caliper is used on Suzuki and many Kawasaki motorcycles. This is the "sliding caliper" type. As opposed to the fixed caliper described above, this assembly mounts the caliper to a bracket by means of sliding shafts.

There is only one piston, and when pressure is applied to this piston, it presses its pad against the disc, and the caliper shifts slightly in the opposite direction bringing the opposing pad into contact as well.

Along the same lines as the "sliding caliper" is the "swinging caliper" used by Honda for front brakes. This is also a single-piston unit, and the caliper is mounted on a bracket which is pivoted at the fork slider. When the brake is applied, the one piston moves its pad into con-

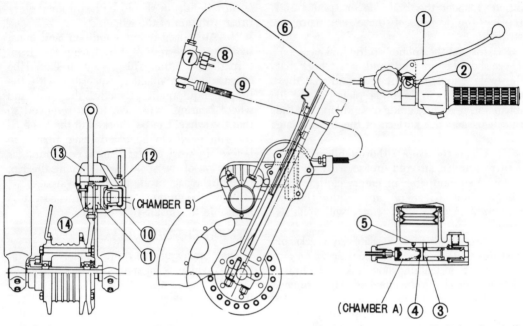

1. Brake lever
2. Lever cam
3. Master cylinder
4. Primary cup

5. Fluid passage
6. Brake hose
7. Brake line junction
8. Brake light switch

9. Brake hose
10. Caliper piston
11. Left brake pad
12. Left caliper half

13. Right caliper half
14. Right brake pad

The Honda disc brake system. Chamber A is in the master cylinder and chamber B is in the brake caliper

tact with the disc, and the caliper moves slightly to bring the other pad against the disc.

Maintenance

1. Disc brake systems need little routine maintenance other than an occasional check on pad wear and fluid level.

2. Pads should be replaced when they are worn to the limit lines. These are fitted to most types of disc brakes. Other types will have tab-type wear indicators. On others, the manufacturer will specify minimum pad thickness.

3. The master cylinder fluid level is usually inscribed on the master cylinder. The fluid level may drop slightly over a period of time as the pads wear, but this drop will be slight. Do not top up a master cylinder reservoir whose level has dropped slightly due to pad wear, since the level will return to the normal level when new pads are fitted. An exception, of course, will be made if braking effectiveness is reduced due to a low level.

4. Brake pedal or hand lever travel should be about 1 in. measured at the end of the pedal or lever—the same as for drum brakes. On some systems, there is an adjustment for lever travel. Once properly set, no readjust-

Brake fluid level line. Late model bikes have transparent master cylinder reservoirs removing the need to remove the cap

ment should be necessary. If lever travel becomes excessive, the system should be checked over.

5. Periodically check condition of hoses and lines. Be sure that all hoses are arranged as

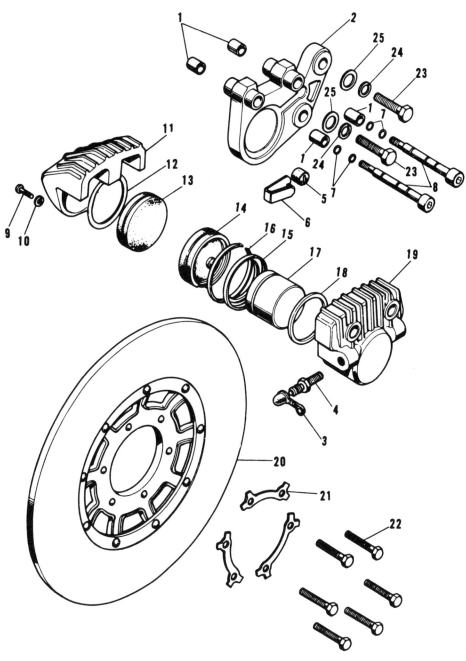

Typical sliding caliper brake assembly

1. Dust seal	14. Pad A
2. Caliper mounting	15. Dust seal
3. Bleeder valve cap	16. Band
4. Bleeder valve	17. Piston
5. Bushing	18. Ring
6. Stopper	19. Caliper A
7. O ring	20. Disc
8. Shaft	21. Lock washer
9. Screw	22. Bolt
10. Lock washer	23. Bolt
11. Caliper B	24. Lock washer
12. Ring	25. Washer
13. Pad B	

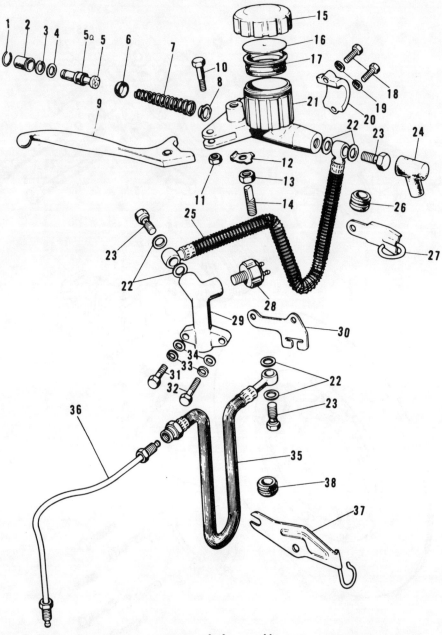

Master cylinder assembly

1.	Stopper, dust seal	13.	Nut
2.	Dust seal	14.	Bolt
3.	Circlip	15.	Cap
4.	Stopper, piston	16.	Plat
5.	Piston assembly	17.	Cap seal
5.a	Secondary cup	18.	Bolt
6.	Primary cup	19.	Washer
7.	Spring assembly	20.	Master cylinder mounting
8.	Check valve assembly	21.	Master cylinder body
9.	Brake lever	22.	Washer
10.	Bolt	23.	Banjo bolt
11.	Nut	24.	Dust cover
12.	Lock washer	25.	Hose

26.	Grommet
27.	Bracket
28.	Pressure switch
29.	3-way fitting
30.	Guide
31.	Bolt
32.	Bolt
33.	Lock washer
34.	Washer
35.	Hose
36.	Pipe
37.	Bracket
38.	Grommet

the manufacturer intended, and are properly mounted. Check for abrasion damage. Check banjo fittings for signs of seepage.

Bleeding

A mushy feeling at the brake lever or pedal is most often due to air in the lines. This can happen if the fluid level drops too low, or if any line or hose is disconnected for any reason. This requires bleeding of the brake to remove the air.

PRECAUTIONS

Certain precautions should be taken when working with disc brake fluid.

a. Brake fluid absorbs moisture very quickly, and then becomes useless. Therefore, never use fluid from an old or unsealed container.

b. Do not mix brake fluids of different types. If the fluid in the system is the original factory fluid, it may be incompatible with what you can purchase. In this case, the entire system should be flushed and refilled with the new fluid.

c. DOT #3 hydraulic disc brake fluid is recommended for almost all motorcycles at this time. However, you should check your owner's manual to be sure.

d. Brake fluid will quickly remove paint. Avoid damage to the gas tank by placing a protective cover over it.

To bleed the brake system, obtain a length of transparent plastic hose, the inside diameter of which is such that the hose will fit tightly over the bleed nipple of the brake caliper.

Also needed is a small cup.

Fit the plastic hose to the bleed nipple, and put the other end in the cup which should have an inch or so of new brake fluid in it. Be sure that the end of the hose is below the surface of the fluid in the cup.

The hose should not have any sharp bends or kinks in it. It should loop up from the bleed nipple, and then down towards the cup.

The motorcycle should be on the center stand with the forks centered.

Remove the master cylinder cap and diaphragm and check that the fluid level is topped up to the indicated line.

Apply the brake lever slowly several times, then hold it on.

While holding the brake lever on, loosen the caliper bleed nipple. The brake lever will be pulled towards the handgrip (or if a rear brake, will bottom out), and fluid will be

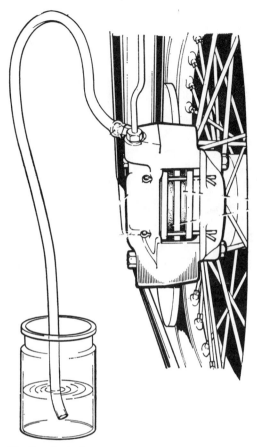

Bleeding the brake

forced through the plastic hose. Try to tighten the bleed nipple before the lever bottoms out.

Note the brake fluid being forced out of the plastic hose. If there was air in the lines, air bubbles will be noted coming out of the hose.

Pump up the lever again, and loosen the nipple as before, once again checking the fluid being forced out. When air bubbles no longer issue from the plastic hose, the system is bled.

Be sure that the master cylinder reservoir is kept topped up during the bleeding procedure.

Flushing

The procedure for flushing a brake system is identical to that for bleeding, except that the process should be continued until new brake fluid begins to issue from the plastic hose. You will begin by pumping out the old fluid with the lever while adding the new fluid in its place. After the new fluid starts coming out, begin checking for air bubbles as outlined above.

Honda swinging calipers need occasional adjustment

Fitting Brake Pads

This procedure will vary according to the make and model of the motorcycle, but all have certain points in common.

a. When new pads are fitted, avoid hard braking if possible for at least 50 miles to give the new pads a chance to seat themselves.

b. Brake fluid and solvents must be kept off the brake pads. Some manufacturers recommend that the back and sides of the pad(s) be lubricated with special PBC grease. If this is necessary for your motorcycle, it should be available from your dealer.

c. Some calipers (i.e. Honda) must be adjusted periodically. This procedure should be outlined in your shop manual or owner's manual.

Front Forks

OPERATIONAL DESCRIPTION

Front forks may be of several different types, but the overwhelming majority of motorcycles in production today use the "telescopic" type. Other kinds of forks include the "Earle's type" which was used on BMWs several years ago, and the "leading-link" suspension which was found on NSU machines and others such as the Honda "Dream" of years gone by and a large number of step-through "50s" of the last decade.

Telescopic Forks

Telescopic forks consist of two fork tubes or stanchions which are attached to the frame by a pair of triple clamps. At the lower end of the tubes are fork sliders which, as the name implies, move up and down on the tubes in response to road irregularities. Cushioning is provided by fork springs, which may be internal or external, that is, either inside the fork tube or outside it. Of the two types, the former is now more popular. Rebound damping is accomplished by means of a damper unit in the fork tube. On some forks, this damper unit provides both compression *and* rebound damping, while on others the fork springs themselves are responsible for all compression damping.

Damper units vary infinitely in design, but basically they carry out the function of slowing the fork slider's movement when the fork spring attempts to force it to the fully extended position.

When the front forks strike a bump in the road, the fork sliders are forced up along the fork tubes, compressing the springs, and, at the same time, forcing oil through a number of orifices in the damper mechanism.

When this force on the sliders is released, the compressed springs attempt to return to their normal length. Rather than allow the sliders to be bounced back to the extended position all at once, the damper mechanism resists sudden movement of the slider, the resistance being provided by the oil which the slider must suck through the orifices as it moves back down the fork tube.

Fork sliders are usually alloy castings which are a close fit on the fork tubes. On some forks, this fit is obtained through the use of a replaceable bushing, while on others the slider itself is machined to fit the fork tube. One or two oil seals are incorporated into the top of the slider to hold the damping oil.

The fork slider may be secured to the fork by means of a bolt at the bottom of the slider which threads into the damper or the fork tube itself, or a large circular nut may be fitted to the top of the slider. Sometimes, both are found.

Fork springs may be one of two types: straight or progressively wound. The difference between the two types is evident

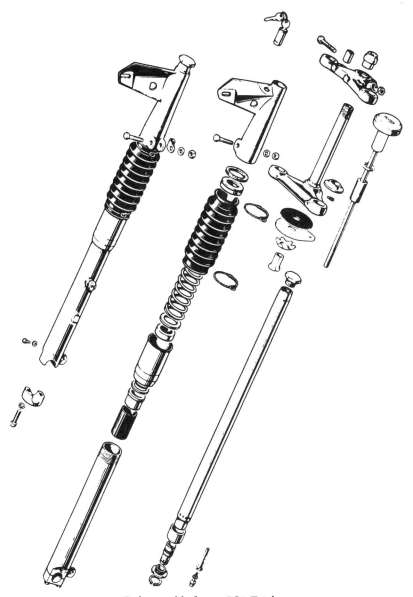

Fork assembly from a BSA Triple

upon inspection. A straight-wound spring will compress a given distance by the application of a certain force. Doubling the force will double the compressed distance, and so on. The relationship between the applied force and the compressed distance is therefore linear. Progressively-wound springs, however, have no such linear relationship. After the initial force is applied, multiples of that force will provide increasingly less compression.

Fork tubes are commonly hard-chromed, and are always provided in this way on forks without rubber gaiters or covers below the lower triple clamp. Fork tubes are secured by pinchbolts at the triple clamps.

Leading-Link and Earle's Forks

Earle's forks function in exactly the same way as the rear swing arm and shock absorber assembly, consisting of a pivoted arm and two sealed damper units which incorporate the springs.

Leading-link forks are similar in principle, but use two pivoted links, which are mounted independently, each of which has its own spring-and-damper assembly.

ROUTINE MAINTENANCE

Earle's type and leading-link front forks require little or no maintenance, except for those few which may have grease fittings on the link pivots. For the most part, inspection is confined to noting whether operation is satisfactory. If it is not, check the condition of the shock absorbers; leakage would tend to be the most common problem. The shock units are sealed, and replacement is the remedy if problems are in evidence.

Link bushings should also be checked for excessive play.

Telescopic fork components are usually long-lived, the most common problem being slider seal leakage. Other components wear much less slowly, and deterioration of fork operation may come on so gradually as to be unnoticeable. Other potential troublespots include permanent spring compression, slider bushing wear, damage to fork tube plating, and damper wear.

Telescopic front forks all require routine oil changes at intervals which will be specified by the manufacturer of the motorcycle. This is necessary to extend seal life, and to drain off dirt or water which may have gotten into the oil supply to cause accelerated wear to the damper components.

A wide range of fork oils is available including specially-designed motorcycle fork oil, several viscosities of plain motor oil, and Automatic Transmission Fluid or hydraulic fluid. The type of oil recommended by the manufacturer should be used, and this will be specified in the owner's manual.

The viscosity of the oil used in the forks will to some extent determine the fork's damping characteristics, a heavier oil giving stiffer damping, and vice-versa. This is not always true, however, some forks such as those used on late-model Moto Guzzis having sealed damper units, the fork oil being used only to lubricate the moving parts.

Therefore, oils of varying viscosities may be experimented with, until you find one which suits your needs. It is wise, however, not to vary the recommended oil type or viscosity without due cause.

As important as choosing the correct oil vis-

Labels on fork diagram:
Top Bolt
Fork Cover
Spring
Inner Tube
Oil Seal
O Ring
Metal Slide
Dust Shield
Outer Tube Nut
Spring Holder
Outer Tube

Fork assembly from a Mach III Kawasaki

Earle's forks used on BMWs

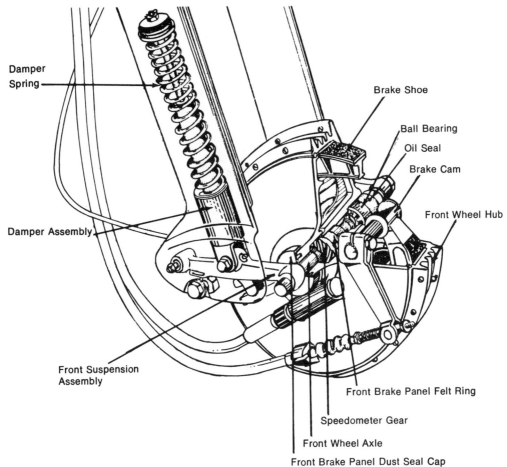

Damper Spring

Brake Shoe

Ball Bearing

Oil Seal

Brake Cam

Front Wheel Hub

Damper Assembly

Front Suspension Assembly

Front Brake Panel Felt Ring

Speedometer Gear

Front Wheel Axle

Front Brake Panel Dust Seal Cap

Leading link assembly used on small Hondas

cosity is choosing an oil which is compatible with the oil already in the forks. Of course, if the forks are disassembled and cleaned, there is no problem here. But routine oil changes always leave some of the old oil in the sliders, and refilling them with an incompatible brand will probably have an adverse effect on damping.

Fork capacities are given by the manufacturer and can be found in the owner's manual or shop manual. The amount is always given for each fork leg. It is important to realize, however, that some of the old fork oil will remain in the slider as we noted above, and this will naturally affect the amount you add. Some bike makers will give two fork capacities: one for routine changes, the other for a completely dry fork. In general, the amount added to a dry fork will be about 10% greater than that for routine oil changes. That is, if

Leading link forks pivot over obstacles

you are to add 200 cc of fluid to each leg for a routine change, about 220 cc should be added if the fork has been disassembled.

OIL CHANGES

1. Drain plugs are fitted near the bottom of each fork slider. To remove the old oil, take out the drain plug once you have placed a reasonably sized container beneath the plug.

2. On some models, removal of the drain plug will allow the oil to come out. On others, however, it will be necessary to pump the slider up and down to force out the oil. The easiest way to do this is by applying the front brake and pushing the bike forward (off the stands). Pressure may force the oil stream out several inches, so position the container accordingly. Pump the forks until oil stops coming out. Turn the forks all the way to the right to completely drain the right fork leg, and to the left for the left leg. Check the condition of the drain plug gasket, if applicable, then refit the plug and tighten securely.

3. Check the condition of the drained oil. If oil changes have been carried out reasonably close to the recommended schedule, the oil should be free of dirt, water, etc. If water has been present for some time, the oil may have a foamy consistency and may be tinged green in color for some kinds of oil. Water or dirt in the fork oil may indicate defective fork gaiters or dust covers which have allowed such matter to get to the slider seals and from there into the oil supply. Any gaiters with tears or other damage should be replaced. Dust seals are found on many forks with internal springs. These are attached to the slider just above the oil seals. These dust seals are necessary to keep dirt and water away from the slider oil seals, and they should be replaced if they are cracked, ripped, or dry-rotted. Impurities in the oil can also be due to bad fork slider oil seals.

4. To add oil to the forks, first put the machine on the center stand or otherwise support the front wheel off the ground. This is a safety measure since removing the filler caps on some forks will release the fork spring, causing the forks to collapse and possibly toppling the machine. This is not true of all forks, and on some it may be necessary to compress the forks to free the filler cap from the damper rod. This is true of Nortons, early 350 and 500 Honda Fours, late Honda 450s, and some other bikes.

If you are not sure of the exact procedure, have the front wheel off the ground when the

If defective, dust covers may allow dirt and water to pass through to the oil seal

filler cap is removed. Remove one cap, fill the fork leg with the correct amount of oil, and reinstall the cap before removing the other one. If you have the kind of fork which may collapse in the way explained previously, leaving one filler cap in place at all times will serve to keep the forks extended during the oil change procedure.

5. Fork oil should be measured out carefully, and one way to do this is with a plastic baby bottle which is calibrated in "cc" or ounces. It will be necessary to cut off the end of the nipple to allow the oil to flow freely. On some machines, you can get away with a simple measuring cup, while on others, the close proximity of handlebars, instruments, etc., will make spillage likely.

6. After adding oil, be sure to tighten the filler caps very securely. Check for seepage around the slider oil seals after several miles of operation. Oil leakage indicates that the seals should be replaced.

SEAL REPLACEMENT

1. Fork slider oil seals may simply wear out over a period of time and then begin to leak. Some causes of *rapid* wear of the seal lips include damage during installation, dirty, con-

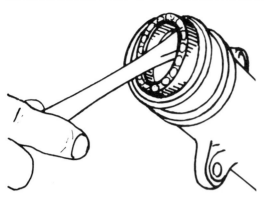

Care must be taken when removing seals to avoid damaging the fork leg as this may result in leaking

taminated fork oil, damaged dust seals or fork gaiters, rust, corrosion, or scratches on the fork tube, a bent fork tube, or rubber-damaging oil in the forks.

Seals may also leak if the forks are over-filled.

2. On most motorcycles, the seals can be replaced simply by removing the fork sliders. It is necessary to remove the front wheel, fender, brake caliper (if applicable), etc. Refer to a shop manual for removal procedures. These will of course vary depending on the make and model of the machine.

3. The slider seals are pressed into the top of the fork slider on most bikes, although on a few, the seals may be in the circular nut threaded onto the top of the slider.

Seals must be pried out with a suitable lever. Seals should always be replaced once the slider is removed from the fork tube. Condition of the seals cannot be determined from examination of the lips.

When prying out the seals, be sure to protect the upper lip of the fork slider. This can be accomplished by placing a soft metal pad beneath your lever. Also take care that the

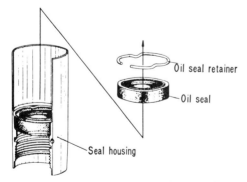

Seals should be installed straight in the housing. If necessary, check the alignment of the top of the seal relative to the retainer clip groove

end of the lever does not score the inner wall of the slider.

Install new seals by pressing them straight into the slider. Often, one of the old seals can be used, placing it on top of the new seal and tapping around the edges to force the new seal into place. Alternately, a suitably sized socket can be placed over the seal to use as a drift.

4. Always coat the lips of seals with the type of oil you are going to put in the forks.

COMPONENT INSPECTION

1. As previously noted, fork disassembly procedures vary from model to model. There are, however, two popular methods of holding the forks together, and these are by means of a large circular nut at the top of the slider, and by means of a bolt at the bottom of the slider which will be accessible after removing the axle. Some forks have both.

2. Drain fork oil before disassembly is attempted. Be sure the motorcycle is firmly supported with the front wheel off the ground.

3. Some forks require special tools for disassembly. On models with a bolt under the slider, you should note that often this bolt is threaded into the fork damper, which may turn with the bolt when you attempt to remove it. A special tool is used, inserted through the top of the fork, to hold the damper while the slider bolt is removed. It is often possible to work around this tool by leaving the filler cap and inner fork spring in place, the spring tension being used to hold the damper.

4. Forks with sliders secured by circular nuts may be somewhat easier to disassemble. The slider must be secured when attempting to remove the nut, and this can be accomplished by inserting the axle through the fork legs. Removal of the nut itself is done with a special strap wrench or pin wrench in most cases. It is possible to remove the nut by wrapping a piece of inner tube around the nut, securing a large heater-hose clamp over it, and using a vise-grip pliers on the clamp screw to turn off the nut.

5. In the event that the fork tubes are to be removed from the triple clamps, be sure that all applicable pinchbolts are loosened. If the fork tubes are stuck, try spreading the lower triple clamp slot with a wedge, if such a slot is provided. Alternately, install the filler cap, turning it in several turns, then strike it sharply with a plastic mallet. This should serve to free the tube. This treatment should

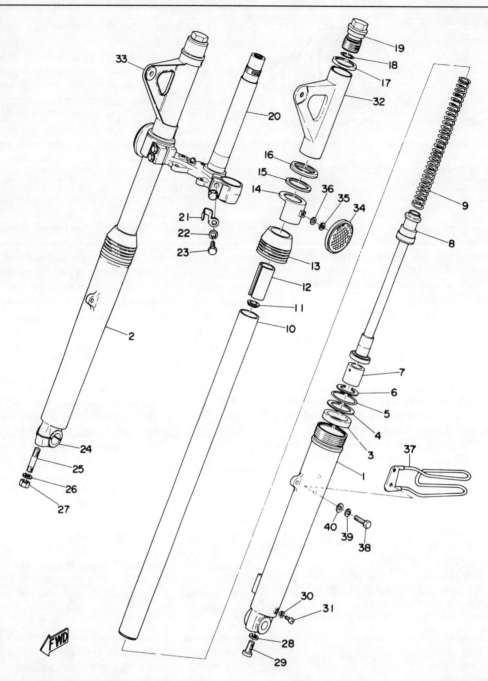

1. Fork slider
2. Fork leg, complete
3. Slider oil seal
4. Washer
5. Circlip, oil seal
6. Circlip
7. Piston
8. Damper tube
9. Fork spring
10. Fork tube
11. Upper spring seat
12. Spacer

13. Dust seal
14. Cover
15. Gasket
16. Cover guide
17. Cover guide
18. O-ring
19. Filler cap
20. Steering stem and lower triple clamp
21. Cable clamp
22. Lockwasher
23. Bolt
24. Axle cap

25. Stud
26. Lockwasher
27. Axle capnut
28. Gasket
29. Allen bolt
30. Gasket
31. Drain plug
32. Left headlight bracket
33. Right headlight bracket
34. Reflector
35. Lockwasher
36. Washer

37. Cable holder
38. Bolt
39. Lockwasher
40. Washer

Yamaha Enduros fork assembly

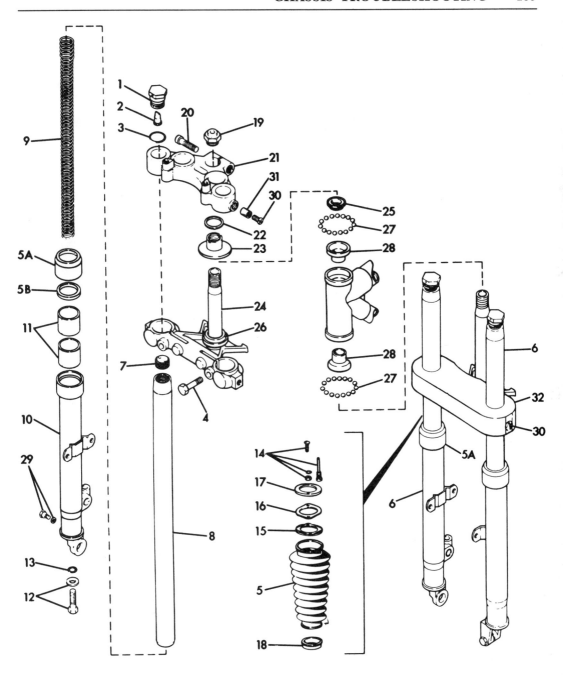

1. Tube cap
2. Tube breather valve
3. Tube cap seal
4. Pinch bolt
5. Fork boot (1970)
5A. Fork boot (1971)
5B. Seal (1971)
6. Fork side
7. Spring retainer
8. Fork tube and shock absorber assembly
9. Fork spring

10. Fork slider
11. Fork slider bushing (2)
12. Tube end bolt and washer
13. O-ring
14. Vent screw and plain screw (1970)
15. Boot retainer (upper) (1970)
16. Boot gasket (1970)
17. Boot retaining disc (1970)
18. Boot retainer (lower) (1970)
19. Stem sleeve end nut
20. Upper bracket pinch bolt

21. Upper bracket
22. Upper bracket spacer
23. Stem sleeve
24. Stem and bracket assembly
25. Upper bearing cone
26. Lower bearing cone
27. Ball bearings (28)
28. Steering head cups (2)
29. Drain plug and washer
30. Cover screw (2)
31. Insert
32. Cover

Fork assembly from a Harley-Davidson Sportster

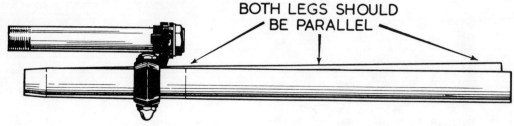

Check fork tube alignment

not be carried to extremes, however, since it is possible to crush the filler cap threads.

6. Fork tubes should be checked for condition. If chromed, all plating in the area on which the slider or slider oil seals ride must be in good condition. If the plating is scratched, flaking, or worn, the tube must be replaced.

On fork tubes which are not plated, check for rust or corrosion on the surface of the tubes on which the slider seals ride. Any roughness or build-up must be removed with a low-abrasive method. Pitting or extreme rust would necessitate replacement of the fork tubes.

7. Check the fork tubes for a bent condition. Minor bends may not be visible to the eye, and run-out should be checked with a dial gauge. If a tube is only slightly bent, it may be possible to return it to its original condition with a large press, but it is usually necessary to replace tubes which are bent.

8. Check the fork springs for a compressed condition by comparing their measured free length with the standard free length if given in the shop manual specifications.

9. Check the condition of the fork slider and its fit on the fork tubes. Some forks use a replaceable bronze slider bushing. Check this bushing for scoring or wear on the inner surface. Check its fit on the fork tube. The bushing should move freely, but any wobbling or play from side-to-side would indicate that replacement is necessary.

10. Clean all damper components, blowing clear any oil passages.

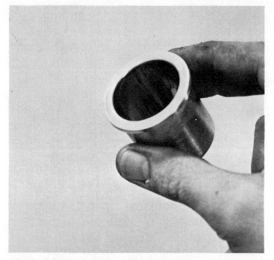

Check slider bushing for wear or scoring

Steering Stem

The steering stem assembly consists of the upper and lower triple clamps, their connecting shaft, and the bearings on which the assembly rides in the frame lug.

Checking steering head bearing adjustment

1. Speedometer cable clip
2. Upper frame race
3. Lower frame race
4. Dust seal
5. Steering stem/lower triple clamp
6. Top cone race
7. Lower cone race
8. Steering lock cover
9. Washer
10. Adjuster nut
11. Steering lock
12. Spring
13. Steering stem nut
14. Washer
15. Lower triple clamp pinch-bolt
16. Screw
17. Washer
18. Washer
19. Steering stem bearings

Steering stem assembly

The bearings in most cases are uncaged balls which ride on bearing races, the inner halves of which are pressed into the frame lug. Some models use tapered roller bearings (Moto Guzzi), or caged ball bearings (late Norton), or a combination of the two.

The condition of the steering stem bearings should be checked periodically in the following manner:

a. Support the front wheel of the motorcycle off the ground.

b. Grasp the fork sliders, and attempt to move them back and forth in line with the motorcycle. No play should be noted here. An alternate method, applicable to machines with a sturdy front fender is to grasp the tip of the fender and pull upwards, plac-

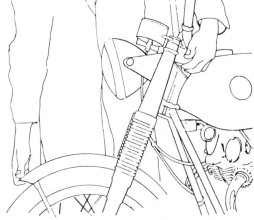

Checking steering head bearing adjustment, alternative method

ing your other hand at the junction of the triple clamp and frame to feel for play.

Ordinarily, play indicated by either of these two methods can be remedied by simply adjusting the bearings. There is, in most cases, a nut or nuts beneath the upper triple clamp which are used to make this adjustment.

c. With the front wheel free of the ground, and any steering damper loosened or disconnected, turn the forks slowly from lock to lock. Movement should be smooth, effortless, and without noise. If fork movement is rough, or if there seems to be a detent spot somewhere during the movement of the forks, the bearings or races may be worn.

d. Position the forks about 5–10° off the centered position and release them. The forks should fall to either side of their own weight. If they do not, the bearings may be too tightly adjusted.

In general, bearings which cannot be properly adjusted, or will not hold an adjustment for any length of time, can be said to be worn to the point of replacement.

For uncaged ball bearings, all of the balls and all races must be replaced at the same time.

Removal procedures vary for different types of assemblies. In all cases, however, the frame races must be driven out with a drift, and installed with a block of wood until firmly seated in the frame lug.

The outer race of the lower bearing is

Adjusting the steering head bearings

usually a tight fit on the steering stem and will have to be chiseled off.

If you have disassembled the steering stem for routine lubrication, you can check the condition of the balls and races after cleaning them thoroughly in solvent to remove all the old grease.

Any balls which are pitted, rusted, or dented will necessitate replacement of the entire bearing and race assembly.

Races themselves should be checked for a rippled surface, indentations, and other imperfections. Frame races should not be removed unless defective, since they will probably be rendered useless by the removal procedure. The same is true of the steering stem lower race.

When installing a steering stem assembly, always be sure that the proper number of balls are fitted to each race. Imbed the balls in a high grade bearing grease.

Adjust the bearings so that fork action conforms to those standards outlined above. If new frame races have been installed, make frequent checks of adjustment during the first several hundred miles, since the frame races will probably settle over a period of time.

STEERING DAMPER

A steering damper is a device whose purpose is to provide some resistance to the lateral (side to side) movement of the forks. This is especially useful for travel over rough terrain or corrugated road surfaces as the damper will resist rapid deflection of the front wheel and will protect

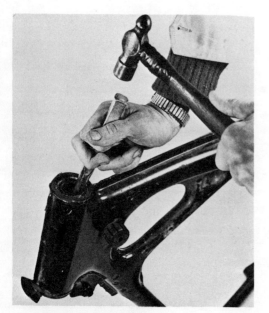

Removing a steering head bearing race

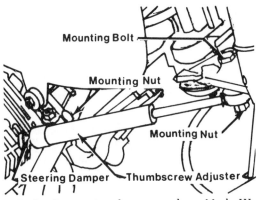

A hydraulic steering damper used on Mach III Kawasakis

to some extent against lock-to-lock oscillations of the fork.

Dampers are of two types: friction type and hydraulic. Friction type dampers rely upon spring loaded "friction plates" to provide resistance to fork turning. These plates are found on the steering stem (or immediately beneath the stem) and are activated by tightening the damper knob which forces them against the steering stem. The knob can be tightened until the desired degree of damping is reached.

A second type of damper is the hydraulic type. This damper is usually fitted between the fork triple clamp and the frame. It functions in much the same manner as the damper unit found on household storm doors, but is, of course, much smaller. Unlike the friction damper, which provides a uniform resistance, the hydraulic unit automatically varies the degree of damping in proportion to the speed at which the forks are turned. For example, if the forks are moved slowly from side to side, little damping will be noticed. But if an attempt is made to yank the forks over quickly, a strong damping action will slow the movement.

Swing Arm

Except on shaft-drive motorcycle, swing arms are very simple components and usually free of trouble.

Swing arms are usually attached to the

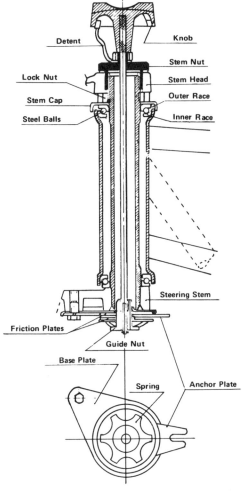

A mechanical steering damper

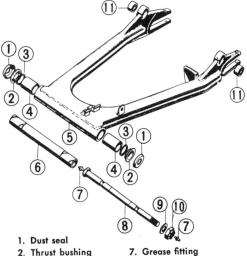

1. Dust seal
2. Thrust bushing
3. Felt ring
4. Pivot bushing
5. Swing arm
6. Pivot tube
7. Grease fitting
8. Pivot shaft
9. Washer
10. Locknut
11. Shock absorber bushing

Bushed swing arm assembly, with grease fitting, from a 750 Honda

frame by means of a heavy shaft which may ride in bushings or needle bearings. Wear to these bushings is the prime trouble spot of the swing arm.

To check your swing arm, proceed as follows:

a. Remove the rear wheel, shock absorbers, and chain guard.

b. Measure the distance between the top and bottom shock absorber mounts on both sides. The two measurements must be identical, or the swing arm will have to be replaced.

c. Check that the rear wheel mounting plates are parallel.

d. Grasp the legs of the swing arm and attempt to move it from side-to-side. Any noticeable side-play will indicate that the swing arm bushings need replacement.

The swing arm is most likely to be damaged if the machine is operated for any length of time with a broken or otherwise defective shock absorber.

Bushings are usually press-fit in swing arms, and, if worn, they should be driven out and replaced with new ones. Do not remove pressed-in bushings unless you intend to replace them, since they will be ruined by the removal process.

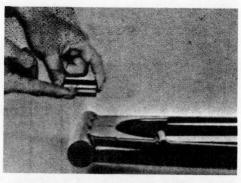

If your swing arm doesn't have a grease nipple this is the way to lubricate the bushings

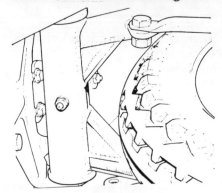

Sometimes, as with this Trident, it takes a little searching to find the grease fitting

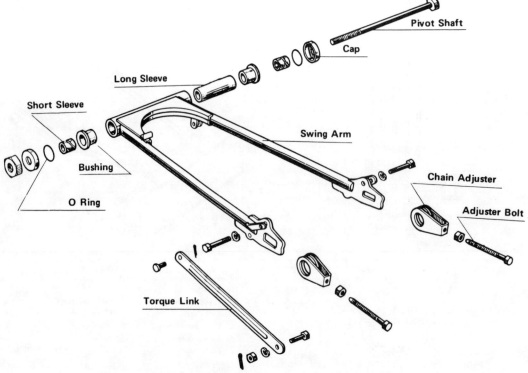

Bushed swing arm assembly from a Mach III Kawasaki

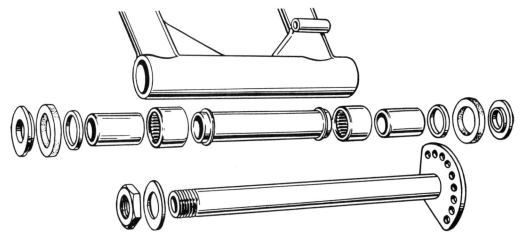

Swing arm assembly with needle bearings used on BSA 250s

When disassembling a swing arm bushing, make careful note of how each component is installed as placement of shims, bushings, sleeves, etc., is critical.

Bushings should be lubricated according to manufacturer's instructions. Most have a grease fitting on the swing arm shaft to facilitate the operation, while others must be lubricated by hand.

After a rebuilt swing arm is installed, tighten the shaft nut (if fitted) to the proper

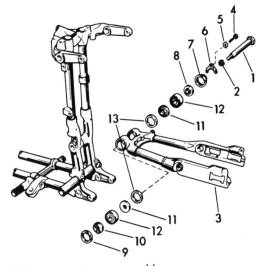

A Sportster swing arm assembly

1. Pivot bolt	8. Outer spacer
2. Bearing lock washer	9. Bearing lock nut—left
3. Rear fork	10. Pivot bolt nut
4. Bearing screw	11. Bearing inner spacer (2)
5. Shakeproof washer	12. Bearing (2)
6. Lockwasher	13. Bearing shield (2)
7. Bearing lock nut—right	

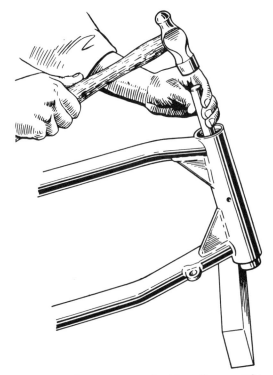

Removing the swing arm bushings from a BSA frame

torque, and check for free movement of the swing arm. Movement should be relatively free (not loose) and noiseless.

New bushings should be checked carefully before installation. Be sure they are the correct ones for your machine, and that any lubrication holes or grooves which are supposed to be there are there.

REAR SHOCK ABSORBERS

Rear shocks are similar in operation to telescopic forks with external springs. The

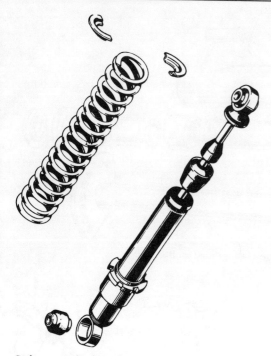

Girling rear shock used on most British twins

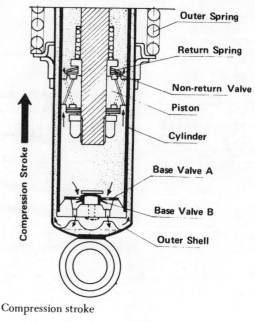

Compression stroke

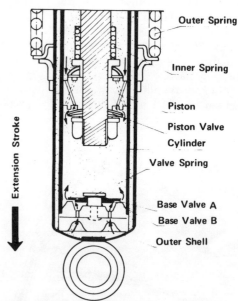

Extension stroke

spring provides controlled restriction for the downward pressure of the bike or the upward pressure of the wheel, and the shock unit itself controls the rebound rate of the spring, most of which are progressively wound, and serves to keep the wheel on the ground while the rest of the bike is bouncing around.

The operation of a typical shock absorber can be described as follows:

The compression stroke of the rear shock absorber begins when it receives a load compressing both the outer spring and the shock hydraulic unit itself. The cylinder, which contains fluid, rises along the piston rod, causing pressure on the oil beneath the piston. This slows or "damps" the rate of compression. The oil flows through the piston orifice and enters the space above the piston after pushing up the non-return valve held down by valve spring C. At the same time, a small amount of the oil is forced through base valve A, and then base valve B, and enters the chamber between the cylinder and the shock outer shell. When the cylinder, rising along the piston rod, meets the rubber bumper at the top of the rod, the compression ends.

The spring tension caused by compression eventually forces the shock absorber

to extend to its normal or static length. The cylinder moves down along the piston rod; the oil which had been forced above the piston returns through the piston orifice and through the piston valve to the space beneath the piston. The oil which had been forced between the cylinder and the outer shell also returns to the reservoir beneath the piston after passing through base valve A. The oil resists the attempt of the outer spring to return suddenly to its normal length. This is known as rebound damping.

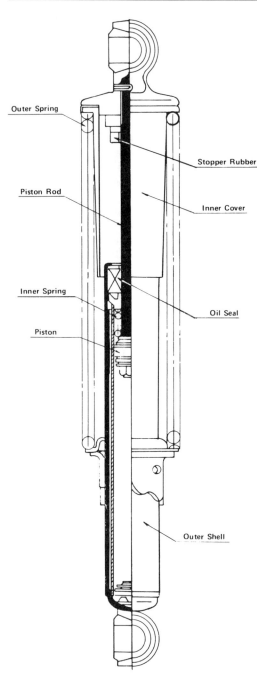

Outer Spring

Piston Rod

Inner Spring

Piston

Stopper Rubber

Inner Cover

Oil Seal

Outer Shell

Cross section of Kawasaki shocks

Some motorcycles use a combination gas/oil shock instead of the oil type just described.

Almost all production motorcycle rear shock absorbers are sealed, and cannot be disassembled. In fact, on some models, it is dangerous to attempt to do so.

If the shock leaks oil, looses its damping ability, is damaged through collision or extreme use, both units should be replaced. The springs, however, should have an unlimited life.

To check a shock absorber, remove it from the motorcycle, and compress the spring so that the spring keepers or collars can be removed. Take off the spring and dust cover, if fitted.

Push the damper rod into the damper body and pull it out. There should be considerable resistance when attempting to pull out the rod. If movement is easy, or if the two shocks show different characteristics, both should be replaced.

Adjusting Shock Absorbers

Most rear shock absorbers are equipped with a spring adjuster which can preload the spring in order to maintain the proper riding position when the bike is carrying two-up or is heavily laden.

As noted above, most rear shocks have sealed damping units, and therefore damping rate is not adjustable. One exception is Koni® shock absorbers. This procedure is as follows:

1. The shock allows a range of damping adjustment to improve performance when the damping rate is matched to the motorcycle and the springs.

2. The shocks are usually set on the mini-

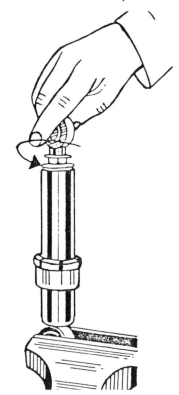

Koni shock adjustment

mum damping position as purchased, and this position should be tried first, as it is adequate for most motorcycles.

3. If a change in damping rate is desired, remove the shocks from the motorcycle. Compress the spring, remove the collar, and remove the spring.

4. The rubber stopper should be moved down the damper shaft. Use a screwdriver or the like to pry it down off the top eyelet, if necessary, but take care not to damage or knick the damper shaft's chrome surface. Moving the rubber stopper down will expose a locknut against the top eyelet.

5. Use the right size wrench to hold the locknut, then insert a rod into the eyelet and break it loose, then remove it. Remove the locknut. If the locknut resists removal, secure the damper shaft in a soft-faced vise by the threaded portion, then loosen the locknut as far as possible. Remove the damper shaft from the vise, and remove the locknut.

CAUTION: *Do not attempt to secure any part of the damper shaft which must enter the damper during adjustment or operation.*

The shaft is very easily knicked and the damper oil seal will be ruined.

6. Remove the rubber stopper from the damper shaft. Refit the eyelet, and locknut, but do not tighten them excessively.

7. The adjuster mechanism is at the very bottom of the damper unit. Push the damper shaft in as far as possible without using excess pressure, then turn it a few degrees in either direction while maintaining a light pressure. The bottom of the shaft will engage the adjustment mechanism which can be felt when it happens.

8. Turn the damper shaft to the left until it stops. This is the minimum damping position. Turn the damper shaft to the right until the desired damping position is reached. Adjustments are made in increments on ¼ turn. Maximum damping position is 2¼ turns.

9. After adjustment, pull the damper shaft out an inch or so to disengage it from the adjustment mechanism. Refit the rubber stopper. Secure the eyelet and locknut.

10. Both shocks must have the same adjustment to provide satisfactory operation.

Chassis Troubleshooting

EXCESSIVE VIBRATION

Possible Causes	Remedy
Loose, broken, or worn motor mounts	Secure, replace, or repair motor mounts
Loose axle nuts	Secure axle nuts
Excessive hub bearing play	Adjust or replace hub bearings
Loose spokes	Secure spokes and true wheel if necessary
Rear wheel out of alignment	Align wheels
Wheel rims out of true or damaged	True or repair wheel rims
Irregular or peaked tire wear	Replace tire and check wheel alignment and trueness
Tires overinflated	Check air pressure with tires cold
Tire and wheel unevenly balanced	Balance wheels
Worn steering head bearings	Adjust or replace bearings as necessary
Worn rear shock bushings or shocks	Replace shocks or bushings as necessary
Swing arm bushings too tight or too loose	Adjust bushings as directed by manufacturer
Excessive front end loading	Remove excessive weight from front end

Chassis Troubleshooting (cont.)

EXCESSIVE VIBRATION

Possible Causes	Remedy
Cylinder head bracket loose or broken (models on which head and frame are attached)	Secure or repair cylinder head bracket
Broken or bent frame, forks, or swing arm	Repair or replace damaged components
Primary chain badly worn, insufficiently lubricated, or too tight	Replace, lubricate, and/or adjust chain
Incorrectly adjusted ignition timing	Adjust timing to specifications
Incorrectly assembled clutch mechanism	Inspect and repair clutch as necessary
Excessively worn crankshaft	Repair or replace crankshaft assembly

UNCERTAIN OR WOBBLY STEERING

Possible Causes	Remedy
Worn or bad steering head bearings	Adjust or replace bearings
Worn or bad hub bearings	Adjust or replace bearings
Bent forks or swing arm	Repair or replace damaged components
Worn swing arm bushings	Adjust or replace bushings
Bent steering stem or frame neck	Repair or replace damaged components
Wheels improperly aligned	Align wheels
Tires improperly seated on rim	Seat tire so bead is even all around
Tires unevenly worn	Replace tires as necessary
Defective steering damper	Replace as necessary
Loose front wheel	Secure wheel

PULLS TO ONE SIDE

Possible Causes	Remedy
Faulty right or left shock	Replace shocks as a set
Incorrectly adjusted drive chain	Adjust as necessary
Wheels improperly aligned	Align wheels as necessary
Wheels out of true	True wheels as necessary
Incorrectly balanced tires and wheels	Balance wheels as necessary
Defective steering head bearings	Adjust or replace bearings as necessary
Faulty steering head damper	Replace as necessary
Bent or damaged forks, frame, or swing arm	Repair or replace damaged components

Chassis Troubleshooting (cont.)

HEAVY OR STIFF STEERING

Possible Causes	Remedy
Low front tire pressure	Check tire pressure with tires cold
Bent or damaged steering stem or frame neck	Repair or replace damaged components
Bad steering head bearings and/or races	Replace or adjust bearings as necessary
Defective steering damper	Replace as necessary
Incorrect damper adjustment	Adjust as necessary

POOR FORK OPERATION

Possible Causes	Remedy
Contaminated fork oil	Drain and replace fork oil
Worn or leaky seals evidenced by dirt or water in the fork oil or by oil on tubes	Replace seals
Weak or damaged fork springs	Replace springs as necessary, preferably as a set
Worn shock absorber assembly (leading link type forks)	Replace as a set as necessary
Worn breather valves	Replace as necessary
Excessive clearance in slider bushings as evidenced by excessive play between the slider and the tube	Replace worn components as necessary
Bent tubes, brackets, dampers, or sliders	Replace damaged components as necessary
Too little fork oil, oil is diluted, or oil is of wrong viscosity	Drain and replace fork oil
Wrong fork springs in use	Replace springs as necessary

STIFF FORK ACTION

Possible Causes	Remedy
Excessive amount of fork oil	Drain and replace fork oil according to specifications
Wrong fork oil viscosity	Drain and replace oil with a lighter grade
Wrong fork springs in use	Replace springs as necessary

WORN REAR SHOCK ABSORBERS

Possible Causes	Remedy
Weak or collapsed springs	Replace springs as a set
Faulty damper unit	Replace shocks as a set
Wrong spring in use	Replace springs as necessary
Shocks adjusted incorrectly	Adjust shocks as necessary

Chassis Troubleshooting (cont.)

STIFF REAR SHOCK ABSORBERS

Possible Causes	Remedy
Faulty damper valve	Replace shock absorbers as a set
Wrong spring in use	Replace springs as necessary
Shocks incorrectly adjusted	Adjust shocks as necessary

WHEEL ROTATES OUT OF TRUE

Possible Causes	Remedy
Wheel and tire out of balance	Balance wheel as necessary
Excessive hub bearing play	Adjust or replace bearings
Deformed wheel rims	Repair or replace rim as necessary
Loose spokes	Adjust spokes for even tension
Loose swing arm bushings	Adjust as necessary
Drive chain too tight	Adjust chain as necessary
Bent frame or swing arm	Repair or replace damaged components

BRAKES DO NOT HOLD (DRUM BRAKES)

Possible Causes	Remedy
Brake shoes glazed or worn	Repair or replace shoes
Brake shoes oil or grease impregnated	Replace shoes
Brake linings worn away	Replace linings
Brake drum worn or damaged	Replace or have drum turned down
Insufficient hydraulic fluid or air in brake lines	Drain system and refill with fresh fluid, then bleed system
Brake linkage incorrectly adjusted	Adjust linkage as necessary
Brake control cables insufficiently lubricated or binding	Lubricate or replace cable as necessary

BRAKES DRAG (DRUM BRAKES)

Possible Causes	Remedy
Lack of play in the linkage	Adjust linkage as necessary
Weak or damaged return springs	Replace springs as a set
Rusted cam and lever shaft	Replace as necessary

UNADJUSTABLE BRAKES (DRUM BRAKES)

Possible Causes	Remedy
Worn brake shoe linings	Replace shoes or rotate the actuating lever a few degrees on its splined shaft (if applicable)

Chassis Troubleshooting (cont.)

UNADJUSTABLE BRAKES (DRUM BRAKES)

Possible Causes	Remedy
Worn brake shoe cam	Replace the cam as necessary
Worn or damaged brake·drum	Replace the drum or have it turned down

BRAKES MAKE SCRAPING SOUNDS (DRUM BRAKES)

Possible Causes	Remedy
Linings worn down to the rivets	Replace the linings and have the drum turned or replaced as necessary
Broken brake shoe	Replace the shoes and repair or replace the drum as necessary
Dirt in the drum	Blow the assembly out with compressed air and replace or repair the drum as necessary
Scored or out of round brake drum	Repair or replace the drum as necessary
Broken pivot	Replace the pivot

BRAKES SHUDDER (DRUM BRAKES)

Possible Causes	Remedy
Unevenly worn shoes	Replace shoes
Out of round brake drum	Repair or replace drum

EXCESSIVE LEVER TRAVEL WITH A LOSS OF BRAKING POWER (DISC BRAKES)

Possible Causes	Remedy
Air in hydraulic system	Drain and replace fluid, then bleed system
Master cylinder low on fluid	Refill the cylinder and bleed system
Loose lever adjuster bolt	Secure and adjust lever and bolt
Leak in hydraulic system as evidenced by fluid loss	Rebuild system as necessary
Worn disc pads	Replace pads as necessary

BRAKE SQUEAL (DISC BRAKES)

Possible Causes	Remedy
Glazed pads	Clean up or replace pads
Improperly adjusted caliper (Honda)	Adjust caliper
Extremely dusty brake assembly	Thoroughly blow out assembly

BRAKE SHUDDER (DISC BRAKES)

Possible Causes	Remedy
Warped disc	Replace disc

Chassis Troubleshooting (cont.)

BRAKE SHUDDER (DISC BRAKES)

Possible Causes	Remedy
Distorted pads	Replace pads
Oil or brake fluid impregnated pads	Replace pads
Loose mounting bolts	Secure assembly

BRAKE PADS REMAIN ON DISC (DISC BRAKES)

Possible Causes	Remedy
Loose adjusting ring	Secure adjusting ring
Piston binding in bore	Rebuild caliper assembly
Relief port blocked by piston in master cylinder	Rebuild caliper assembly
Caliper out of adjustment (Honda)	Adjust. See owner's manual
Caliper pivot frozen (Honda)	Clean and lubricate pivot

Appendix

Conversion—Millimeters to Decimal Inches

mm	inches	mm	inches	mm	inches	mm	inches	mm	inches
1	.039 370	31	1.220 470	61	2.401 570	91	3.582 670	210	8.267 700
2	.078 740	32	1.259 840	62	2.440 940	92	3.622 040	220	8.661 400
3	.118 110	33	1.299 210	63	2.480 310	93	3.661 410	230	9.055 100
4	.157 480	34	1.338 580	64	2.519 680	94	3.700 780	240	9.448 800
5	.196 850	35	1.377 949	65	2.559 050	95	3.740 150	250	9.842 500
6	.236 220	36	1.417 319	66	2.598 420	96	3.779 520	260	10.236 200
7	.275 590	37	1.456 689	67	2.637 790	97	3.818 890	270	10.629 900
8	.314 960	38	1.496 050	68	2.677 160	98	3.858 260	280	11.032 600
9	.354 330	39	1.535 430	69	2.716 530	99	3.897 630	290	11.417 300
10	.393 700	40	1.574 800	70	2.755 900	100	3.937 000	300	11.811 000
11	.433 070	41	1.614 170	71	2.795 270	105	4.133 848	310	12.204 700
12	.472 440	42	1.653 540	72	2.834 640	110	4.330 700	320	12.598 400
13	.511 810	43	1.692 910	73	2.874 010	115	4.527 550	330	12.992 100
14	.551 180	44	1.732 280	74	2.913 380	120	4.724 400	340	13.385 800
15	.590 550	45	1.771 650	75	2.952 750	125	4.921 250	350	13.779 500
16	.629 920	46	1.811 020	76	2.992 120	130	5.118 100	360	14.173 200
17	.669 290	47	1.850 390	77	3.031 490	135	5.314 950	370	14.566 900
18	.708 660	48	1.889 760	78	3.070 860	140	5.511 800	380	14.960 600
19	.748 030	49	1.929 130	79	3.110 230	145	5.708 650	390	15.354 300
20	.787 400	50	1.968 500	80	3.149 600	150	5.905 500	400	15.748 000
21	.826 770	51	2.007 870	81	3.188 970	155	6.102 350	500	19.685 000
22	.866 140	52	2.047 240	82	3.228 340	160	6.299 200	600	23.622 000
23	.905 510	53	2.086 610	83	3.267 710	165	6.496 050	700	27.559 000
24	.944 880	54	2.125 980	84	3.307 080	170	6.692 900	800	31.496 000
25	.984 250	55	2.165 350	85	3.346 450	175	6.889 750	900	35.433 000
26	1.023 620	56	2.204 720	86	3.385 820	180	7.086 600	1000	39.370 000
27	1.062 990	57	2.244 090	87	3.425 190	185	7.283 450	2000	78.740 000
28	1.102 360	58	2.283 460	88	3.464 560	190	7.480 300	3000	118.110 000
29	1.141 730	59	2.322 830	89	3.503 903	195	7.677 150	4000	157.480 000
30	1.181 100	60	2.362 200	90	3.543 300	200	7.874 000	5000	196.850 000

To change decimal millimeters to decimal inches, position the decimal point where desired on either side of the millimeter measurement shown and reset the inches decimal by the same number of digits in the same direction. For example, to convert 0.001 mm into decimal inches, reset the decimal behind the 1 mm (shown on the chart) to 0.001; change the decimal inch equivalent (0.039″ shown) to 0.000039″.

Conversion Table

To change			Multiply		
cc → cu in.	cc	×	0.0610	=	cubic inches
cc → oz (Imp)	cc	×	0.02816	=	ounces (Imperial)
cc → oz (U.S.)	cc	×	0.03381	=	ounces (U.S.)
cu in → cc	cu in.	×	16.39	=	cubic centimeters
°C → °F	°C + 17.8	×	1.8	=	°F
ft-lb → in. lbs	ft-lb	×	12	=	inch pounds
ft-lb → kg-M	ft-lb	×	0.1383	=	kilogram-meters
gal (Imp) → liter	Imp gal	×	4.546	=	liters
gal (U.S.) → liter	U.S. gal	×	3.785	=	liters
in → mm	in	×	25.40	=	millimeters
kg → lbs	kg	×	2.205	=	pounds
kg-M → ft lbs	kg-M	×	7.233	=	foot-pounds
kg/sq cm → lbs/sq in	kg/sq cm	×	14.22	=	pounds/square inch
km → mi	km	×	0.6214	=	miles
lb → kg	lb	×	0.4536	=	kilograms
lb/sq in → kg/sq cm	lb/sq in.	×	0.0703	=	kilograms/square centimeter
liter → cc	liter	×	1,000	=	cc
liter → oz (U.S.)	liter	×	33.81	=	ounces (U.S.)
liter → qt (Imp)	liter	×	0.8799	=	quarts (Imperial)
liter → qt (U.S.)	liter	×	1.0567	=	quarts (U.S.)
mi → km	mi	×	1.6093	=	kilometers
mm → in	mm	×	0.03937	=	inches
qt (Imp) → liter	Imp qt	×	1.1365	=	liters
qt (U.S.) → liter	U.S. qt	×	0.9463	=	liters

Tap Drill Sizes

| National Fine or S.A.E. | | |
Screw & Tap Size	Threads Per Inch	Use Drill Number
No. 5	44	37
No. 6	40	33
No. 8	36	29
No. 10	32	21
No. 12	28	15
1/4	28	3
5/16	24	1
3/8	24	Q
7/16	20	W
1/2	20	29/64
9/16	18	33/64
5/8	18	37/64
3/4	16	11/16
7/8	14	13/16
1 1/8	12	1 3/64
1 1/4	12	1 11/64
1 1/2	12	1 27/64

| National Coarse or U.S.S. | | |
Screw & Tap Size	Threads Per Inch	Use Drill Number
No. 5	40	39
No. 6	32	36
No. 8	32	29
No. 10	24	25
No. 12	24	17
1/4	20	8
5/16	18	F
3/8	16	5/16
7/16	14	U
1/2	13	27/64
9/16	12	31/64
5/8	11	17/32
3/4	10	21/32
7/8	9	49/64
1	8	7/8
1 1/8	7	63/64
1 1/4	7	1 7/64
1 1/2	6	1 11/32

Conversion—Common Fractions to Decimals and Millimeters

| INCHES | | | INCHES | | | INCHES | | |
Common Fractions	Decimal Fractions	Millimeters (approx.)	Common Fractions	Decimal Fractions	Millimeters (approx.)	Common Fractions	Decimal Fractions	Millimeters (approx.)
1/128	.008	0.20	11/32	.344	8.73	43/64	.672	17.07
1/64	.016	0.40	23/64	.359	9.13	11/16	.688	17.46
1/32	.031	0.79	3/8	.375	9.53	45/64	.703	17.86
3/64	.047	1.19	25/64	.391	9.92	23/32	.719	18.26
1/16	.063	1.59	13/32	.406	10.32	47/64	.734	18.65
5/64	.078	1.98	27/64	.422	10.72	3/4	.750	19.05
3/32	.094	2.38	7/16	.438	11.11	49/64	.766	19.45
7/64	.109	2.78	29/64	.453	11.51	25/32	.781	19.84
1/8	.125	3.18	15/32	.469	11.91	51/64	.797	20.24
9/64	.141	3.57	31/64	.484	12.30	13/16	.813	20.64
5/32	.156	3.97	1/2	.500	12.70	53/64	.828	21.03
11/64	.172	4.37	33/64	.516	13.10	27/32	.844	21.43
3/16	.188	4.76	17/32	.531	13.49	55/64	.859	21.83
13/64	.203	5.16	35/64	.547	13.89	7/8	.875	22.23
7/32	.219	5.56	9/16	.563	14.29	57/64	.891	22.62
15/64	.234	5.95	37/64	.578	14.68	29/32	.906	23.02
1/4	.250	6.35	19/32	.594	15.08	59/64	.922	23.42
17/64	.266	6.75	39/64	.609	15.48	15/16	.938	23.81
9/32	.281	7.14	5/8	.625	15.88	61/64	.953	24.21
19/64	.297	7.54	41/64	.641	16.27	31/32	.969	24.61
5/16	.313	7.94	21/32	.656	16.67	63/64	.984	25.00
21/64	.328	8.33						

Decimal Equivalent Size of the Number Drills

Drill No.	Decimal Equivalent	Drill No.	Decimal Equivalent	Drill No.	Decimal Equivalent
80	.0135	53	.0595	26	.1470
79	.0145	52	.0635	25	.1495
78	.0160	51	.0670	24	.1520
77	.0180	50	.0700	23	.1540
76	.0200	49	.0730	22	.1570
75	.0210	48	.0760	21	.1590
74	.0225	47	.0785	20	.1610
73	.0240	46	.0810	19	.1660
72	.0250	45	.0820	18	.1695
71	.0260	44	.0860	17	.1730
70	.0280	43	.0890	16	.1770
69	.0292	42	.0935	15	.1800
68	.0310	41	.0960	14	.1820
67	.0320	40	.0980	13	.1850
66	.0330	39	.0995	12	.1890
65	.0350	38	.1015	11	.1910
64	.0360	37	.1040	10	.1935
63	.0370	36	.1065	9	.1960
62	.0380	35	.1100	8	.1990
61	.0390	34	.1110	7	.2010
60	.0400	33	.1130	6	.2040
59	.0410	32	.1160	5	.2055
58	.0420	31	.1200	4	.2090
57	.0430	30	.1285	3	.2130
56	.0465	29	.1360	2	.2210
55	.0520	28	.1405	1	.2280
54	.0550	27	.1440		

Decimal Equivalent Size of the Letter Drills

Letter Drill	Decimal Equivalent	Letter Drill	Decimal Equivalent	Letter Drill	Decimal Equivalent
A	.234	J	.277	S	.348
B	.238	K	.281	T	.358
C	.242	L	.290	U	.368
D	.246	M	.295	V	.377
E	.250	N	.302	W	.386
F	.257	O	.316	X	.397
G	.261	P	.323	Y	.404
H	.266	Q	.332	Z	.413
I	.272	R	.339		

Spark Plug Comparison Chart

Thread Size / Heat Range	NGK Standard Type	NGK Pro-jected Type	Champion Y—Projected Type / G—Gold Palladium Electrode	AC S—Projected Type	Denso (ND)	Bosch	KLG P—Pro-jected Type	Auto-Lite
14 mm, ⅜ in. Reach (hot → cold)	B—4	BP—4	J14J, J14Y, UJ18Y J12J, UJ12 J11, J11J	C49, 46S 48, C47, C47W, M47 46, C46, M46	W14	W45T3 W145T3	FS20 FS30, FS45P	A82 A11, AT10, AZ9, A9, AT8, A9XM
	B—6S	BP—6S	J13Y, UJ12Y, J11Y, J12Y J10Y, UJ10Y, J8, J8J J7, J7J, UJ8 J6, UJ6, J6J J5	45, C45, C45W, M45, 45S 44, C44, M44, M44B, 44S MC44	W17	W175T3	FS50, FS55P FS70	A7, AT6, A42 AT4
	B—7S			43, C42-4, C43, 43S, MC42 M44C, M43	W22	W225T3	FS75	A3, AT3
	B—7C ° B—77C °		J62R					A23 AT2
	B—8S		J4, J4J, J61Y, J60R	42, C42-1, M42	W24	W240T3	FS100	AT1
	B—9S B—10		J2J, J57R	41			FS100-2	A90I
14 mm, 7⁄16 in. Reach (hot → cold)	B—4L		H12 H11 H10, H10J, H18Y H8, H8J H14Y	47L 45L, C45L, TC45L		W125T4	FA50, FA50H FA70	AL11 AL9, ATL8 AL7, A7 ATL4, ATL3
	B—6L			43L, C43L, C43LY				
14 mm, ½ in. Reach (hot → cold)	B—4H	BP—4H	L14, UL15Y, L10 L90	46FF, 46FFS, 45FFS, 45FF 45F, M45FF	W9FP W14F	W95T1 W145T1	F20, F50 F55P	AE52, AE6
	B—5HS							
	B—6HS	BP—6HS	L86, L85, L95Y UL12Y, L88	44FFS, 44FF, M43FF 42F, 43F, 43FFS	W17F	W175T1, W175T7 W200T7, W200T35	F70, F65P F75	AE4, AE42 AE3, AE32
	B—7HS	BP—7HS	L7, L87Y, UL87 L81, L82Y, UL82Y L5	42F, 42FF, 42FS M42FF, MC42F	W22F	W225T1, W225T35 W225T7	F80	AE2, AE22
	B—7HC ° B—7HZ B—77HC °		L62R		W24F	W240T1, W240T16	F100	
	B—8HS B—8HC ° B—8HCS °		L4J, L64Y, L66Y			W260T1 W270T16		AE903
	B—9HS B—9HC ° B—9HCS ° BUHX °°		L60R, L3C L2G L57R			W280M1 W310T16		AE603
	B—10H		L54R					

14 mm

Heat	NGK (B)	NGK (BP)	Champion	AC	(W9EP)	(W95T2)	(FE)	(AG)
hot ↕	B—4E	BP—4E	N21, N16Y / N18	47XL	W9EP	W95T2, W125T2	FE20	AG9
	B—5ES	BP—5ES	N8, N14Y, N13Y	46XLS	W14E	W145T2	FE30	AG7, AG52
	B—6ES	BP—5ESL / BP—6ES	N84, N88 / N6, N12Y, UN12Y / N11Y, N10Y, N5	46—, 46XL, 45XLS	W14EP	W145T30, W160T2	FE50, FE45P	AG5
	B—7ES / B—7EC°	BP—7ES	N9Y, N8Y	45N, 45XL, C45XL	W17E	W175T2, W175T30	FE70, FE55P	AG4, AG42
	B—77EC°		N4	44N, 44XL, 44XLS	W20EP	W200T27, W200T30	FE75	AG3, AG32
	B—8ES	BP—8ES	N62R	44XLS, 43XLS, 43N, 43XL	W22E, W22ES	W225T2, W230T30	FE80, FE65P	AG2, AG23
			N6Y, N7Y	C42N	W24E, W24ES	W240T2, W240T28	FE100	
¾ in. Reach	B—9ES/EV		N3, N3G	42XL, 42XLS	W27E	W250P21, WC250T28	FE220	
↕ cold	B—10E		N60R, N2	41XLS	W31E	W260T28, W265P21	FE250	AC701
						W280M2, W300M2		

14 mm Taper Seat

Heat	NGK	Champion	AC	(WA125T40)	(AF)
hot ↕	BP—6FS	UBL13Y / BL11Y	46TS, 45TS / 44TS	WA125T40	AF52 / AF42
↕ cold	BP—7FS	BL7Y, BL9Y	43TS, 42TS, 40TS	WA200T40	AF32

12 mm

Heat	NGK	Champion	AC	(X17F)	(X175T1)	(TW)	(HE)
hot ↕	D—4H						
	D—5HS	P—8Y	S124FS	X17F	X175T1	TW270	HE3
	D—6HS	P—7	S122F	X20FS	X260T1	TW275	HE2
	D—8HS	P—6	S121F	X24FS	X300T1	TW280	HE1
½ in. Reach ↕ cold	D—10HS			X28FS	X320T1		

12 mm ¾ in. Reach

Heat	NGK	Champion	AC	(X20E)	(X240T17)
hot ↕	D—4E			X20E	X240T17
	D—6ES				
	D—7E	R—61			
	D—7ES	A—8Y—MC		X22E, X22ES	X270T17
	D—8E	R—6, R—6G	S123XL	X24E, X24ES	X300T2
	D—8ESL				
	D—8ES				
	D—10E		S121XL		
↕ cold	D—10ES				

10 mm

Heat	NGK	Champion	AC	(U20FS)	(U175T1)	(T)	(PE)
hot ↕	C—4H						
	C—6H	Z—10	S104F	U20FS	U175T1	T30	PE3
	C—7HS	Z—8		U22FS	U260T1	T70	
	C—9H						
½ in. Reach ↕ cold	C—10H	Z—6	S102F	U24F		T90	

° Competition type with short side electrode
•• Surface-gap type for CDI systems

Comparison of Wrench Sizes

U.S.	Metric	Whitworth	Decimal Inches
5/32			.156
	4 mm		.157
		7BA	.172
3/16			.187
		6BA	.193
	5 mm		.197
13/64			.203
7/32			.218
		5BA	.220
15/64			.234
	6 mm		.236
		4BA	.248
1/4			.250
17/64			.265
	7 mm		.276
9/32			.281
		3BA	.282
5/16			.312
	8 mm		.315
		2BA	.324
		1/8W	.338
11/32			.343
	9 mm		.354
		1BA	.365
3/8			.375
	10 mm		.393
		0BA	.413
	11 mm		.433
7/16			.437
		3/16W	.448
15/32			.468
	12 mm		.472
1/2			.500
	13 mm		.512
		1/4W	.525
17/32			.531
	14 mm		.551
9/16			.562
	15 mm		.591
19/32			.593
		5/16W	.600
5/8			.625
	16 mm		.630
21/32			.656
	17 mm		.669
11/16			.687
	18 mm		.709
		3/8W	.710
	19 mm		.748
3/4			.750
25/32			.781
	20 mm		.787
13/16			.812
		7/16W	.820
	21 mm		.827
	22 mm		.866
7/8			.875
	23 mm		.906
29/32			.906
		1/2W	.920

Comparison of Wrench Sizes

U.S.	Metric	Whitworth	Decimal Inches
15/16			.937
	24 mm		.945
31/32			.968
	25 mm		.984
1			1.000
		9/16W	1.010
	26 mm		1.024
1 1/16			1.062
	27 mm		1.063
		5/8W	1.100
	28 mm		1.102
1 1/8			1.125
	29 mm		1.142
	30 mm		1.181
1 3/16			1.187
		11/16W	1.200
	31 mm		1.220
1 1/4			1.250
	32 mm		1.260
	33 mm		1.299

Common Abbreviations

ABDC	after bottom dead center
ATDC	after top dead center
BBDC	before bottom dead center
BDC	bottom dead center
BTDC	before top dead center
cc	cubic centimeters
cu in.	cubic inches
ft	foot, feet
ft lbs	foot-pounds
gal	gallon
hp	horsepower
in.	inch
in. lbs	inch-pounds
kg	kilogram, kilograms
kg/cm²	kilograms per square centimeter
kg/m	kilogram meters
km	kilometer
kph	kilometers per hour
lbs	pounds
lbs/sq in.	pounds per square inch
l	liter
m	meter
mi	mile
mm	millimeters
mph	miles per hour
oz	ounce
psi	pounds per square inch
pt	pint
qt	quart
rpm	revolutions per minute
sec	second
TDC	top dead center

Degree Wheel

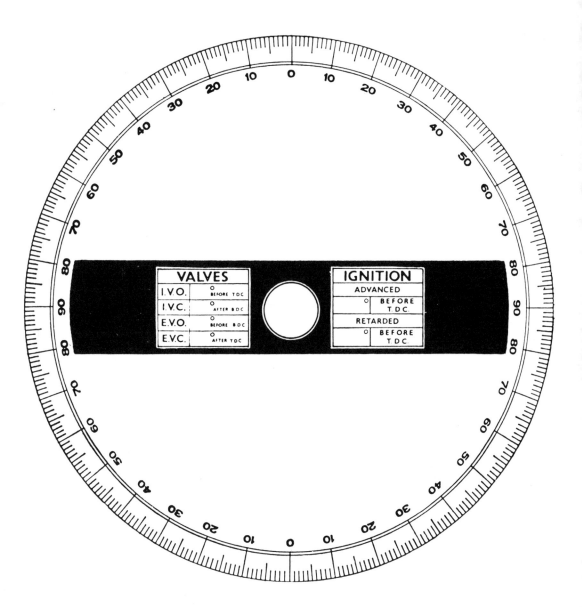

Service Record

Date/Mileage	Service	Next Due